Mixed up about Israel?

People have some strange ideas about Israel, ideas like these:

- Israel is a land of deserts, camel caravans, and Arab sheiks riding white horses.

- Israel is settled by brave pioneers who drain swamps all day and sing Hebrew songs and dance the hora (round dance) all night.

- Israel is the home of pious, bearded, Jews in black coats and hats who study Bible and pray all the time.

- Israel is a land of history, filled with ruins, holy places, and archaeologists.

All those strange ideas are true. Israel is all of those things—and much more.

This book will tell you about the land and the people who live in it. You can try some Israeli recipes, do some Israeli crafts, and play some Israeli games. And you can learn about Israeli customs and history and read Israeli stories.

Israel may still seem a little strange to you when you finish, but you'll also find ideas and interests that you share with Israelis and Israeli kids.

a kid's catalog

written and illustrated by

Chaya M. Burstein

The Jewish Publication Society

Philadelphia • New York • Jerusalem   5748 / 1988

# of Israel

Designed by Adrianne Onderdonk Dudden

Burstein, Chaya M.
      A kid's catalog of Israel.

         Bibliography: p. 240
         Summary: Examines the history, customs, language,
crafts, recipes, geography, and music of Israel.
         1. Israel—Juvenile literature.   [1. Israel]
I. Title.
DS102.95.B87 1988   956.94   85–24190
ISBN 0–8276–0263–4 (pbk.)

Acknowledgments

My thanks to all those who helped with ideas, suggestions and work in the preparation of this book: to Reuven Koppler, the patient custodian at the Central Zionist Archives in Jerusalem; to Ed Toben, Ehud Ryden, Nat Schwartz, Ranan Burstein, Teak Silberman, and Ben-Zion and Rivka Dorfman, who generously shared their photographs with me; and to Eddie Bady, who carefully reprinted difficult, old photos. Thanks also to Mickey ben Naftali, Yitzhak Shapira, and the kids of the Fifth and Eighth Grades in Karmiel and Kfar Saba, to the sabras and their grandparents, and to all the other Israelis who cheerfully let themselves be interviewed. For help with the music my thanks to Velvel Pasternak and ACUM, the Israel Composer's Association.

        I want to express warm appreciation to my editors, David Adler and Barbara Spector, who were able to work with me to solve problems though many miles separated us.

        The publisher gratefully acknowledges: World Over magazine, for permission to reprint "Pearl to Star"; the Board of Jewish Education, for "Pigeon to the Rescue" and "The Brothers"; Funk and Wagnalls Inc., for "Ahmed"; Harcourt Brace Jovanovich Inc., for "On Eagles' Wings"; Yediot Aharonot, for "Azit"; Dodd, Mead & Co., for "Little Guy"; The Jewish Publication Society, for "The Crowning Flower" and "The Girl, the Donkey, and the Dog"; The University of Chicago Press, for "The Two She-Goats from Shebreshin"; Hebrew Publishing Company, for recipes for pita sandwiches, felafel, and tehina sauce; Velvel Pasternak of Tara Publications for preparing the music in the "Hit Songs of One Hundred Years" section. Music and lyrics for "Finjan," "Kumah Echah," "Chai, Chai, Chai," and "Ha-Naavah ba-Banot" provided by ACUM, the Society of Authors, Composers, and Editors of Music in Israel.

To Mordy,
my best friend and partner
in a wonderful,
continuing adventure.

Contents

7 Holidays Are the Same . . . But Different 118

8 Crafts 142

9 Milk and Honey and More 154

more

1 All around Israel

You can explore a new country as though it were a new house, a house you had just moved into. First you go from the basement to the attic and snoop into all the corners. Then you check the yard, say hello to the neighbors, and wander through the neighborhood to find the playground, library, record store, and other important places.

This chapter will give you some facts about Israel and take you on a zigzag walk from the attic to the basement of the country, from north to south. Then you will look around Israel's neighborhood—the Middle East—and meet the countries that are next-door neighbors: Egypt, Jordan, Syria, and Lebanon.

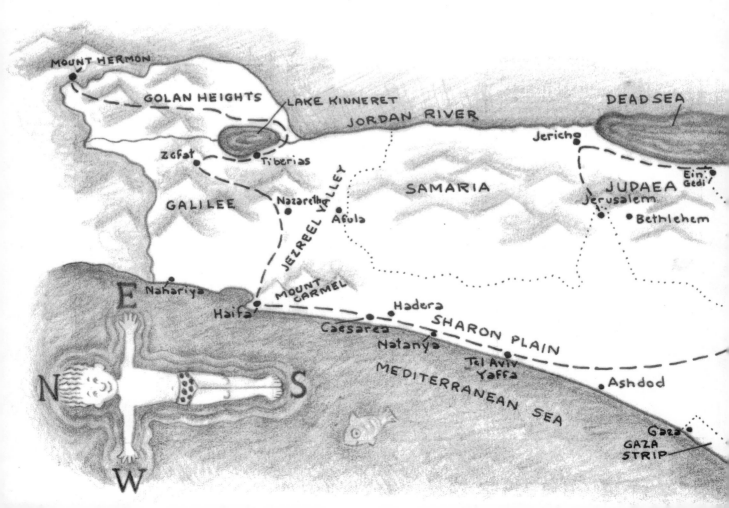

- Israel is 6,000 miles from New York City and 9,000 miles from Los Angeles.
- It sits in the middle of the Middle East, in southwest Asia.
- It has an area of about 8,000 square miles, as big as the state of Massachusetts.
- It contains one big river—the Jordan—and two big lakes—the Kinneret and the Dead Sea.
- The climate is warm and dry, like the climate of southern California. But the winters are often rainy and chilly.
- Over 4 million people live in Israel. Chapter 2 tells more about them.
- The government is a parliamentary republic, with a president, prime minister, one house of representatives (the Knesset), and at least twenty political parties.

FACTS

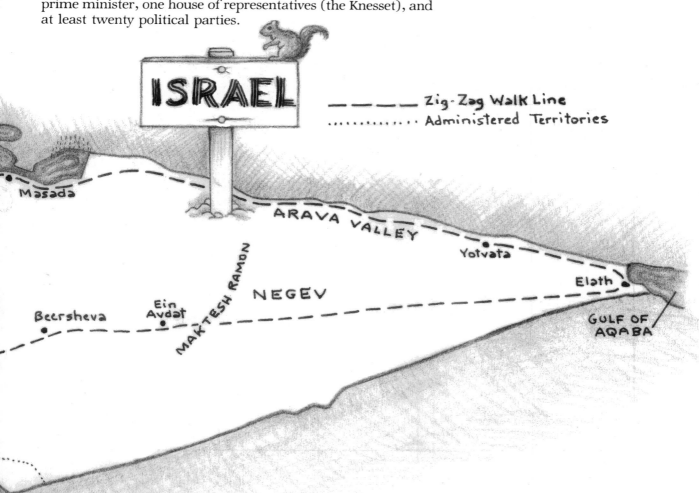

A ZIGZAG WALK THROUGH ISRAEL

Follow the zigzag trail on the map on pages 10 and 11 to see where you are going. It will take you up, down, and all around **Israel**.

You'll need good walking shoes, a hat, sunglasses, suntan lotion, and a full canteen of water. The sun is bright and hot. That's why movie makers like to film here. Tuck a Bible into your backpack. You'll be passing places where many Bible stories happened. And put your lunch in the backpack to leave your hands free for climbing mountains and for shooing away goats and sheep.

If it's March or April, you can even take skis or a sled because you're starting your walk high on snowy **Mt. Hermon** in the **Golan Heights**. It's cold and windy up here and very crowded. Israelis are so excited to see snow (because the rest of the country is warm) that they come up here with plastic bags, cookie sheets, and roasting pans to sit on and go sliding around the mountainside. Soldiers from the nearby army camp watch the fun. Sometimes they go sliding, too.

Turn up your hood, zip up your boots, and slide down to the Golan plateau. You'll be walking through rain and rushing streams. So much water comes down from the Golan that it's called the water tower of Israel. You pass huge piles of black volcanic rock and clusters of blue flowers sparkling out of the melting snow. If you suddenly hear a loud roar, don't run to climb the nearest tree because, first of all, you won't find any (only shrubs and dwarf trees grow on most of the Golan Heights today) and, second of all, there are no big, dangerous animals on the Golan Heights any more. The last bears were shot eighty years ago. Today the largest wild animals are shy boars (wild pigs), hares, and porcupines. You probably won't see them, but you may find their tracks in the soft earth. The roaring on the Golan Heights comes only from tractors or trucks working on the farming settlements.

This is an Arab saying about Mt. Hermon:

> *At its foot, summer; on its slopes, flowering spring; on its shoulders, chilly autumn; at its peak, eternal winter.*

Keep walking west until you reach the edge of a cliff. It's the end of the Golan plateau. Just past your toes, the mountain drops steeply into the green **Jordan valley**. Sparkling **Lake Kinneret** sits in the middle of the valley. You can see the **River Jordan** wiggling down from the north to feed the lake and then running out the southern end toward the **Dead Sea**. Abraham and Sarah, the first Jews, looked down into the green land of Israel, just as you are doing, at the end of their long trek from **Mesopotamia** 4,000 years ago.

As you scramble down the steep slope, hang on to the wiry little oak trees that grow out of the cracks between the rocks. It's hard going down but even harder going up. In 1967 Israeli soldiers had to drive tanks up these cliffs while their Syrian enemies fired down from the top.

The air gets warmer and warmer as you go down. When you reach the bottom, jump into the clear water of Lake Kinneret to cool off. Then have a sandwich under the shady eucalyptus trees. Behind you are the steep cliffs of the Golan Heights, and right across the lake are the round, purple mountains of the **Galilee**. Have another sandwich. You'll soon need the energy to climb up into the Galilee.

The Jordan valley is part of one of the deepest gashes on the earth's surface, the **Great Rift Valley**, which runs far south into **Africa**. Lions and hippos lived here in Biblical times. Every two hundred or three hundred years, the valley heaves and trembles with earthquakes. But right now it's peaceful and filled with gleaming fishponds, big-leafed banana trees, and other crops. Stop to get a drink at one of the flower-filled kibbutzim (collective farms) by the lake. A sunburned old-timer may sit you down and tell you about the good old days, seventy years ago, when this valley was all swamp, filled with hungry malaria-carrying mosquitoes. He and his comrades drained the soil, planted it, and made it fruitful.

There are still a few mosquitoes left to smack as you follow the shore up to the lakeside town of **Tiberias**. Watch the fishing boats crisscross the blue lake and pull into the town docks. And watch out for the big tourist buses. They're going to nearby ancient synagogues and churches, and to the burial places of historic leaders like Maimonides, the twelfth-century scholar.

Many parts of the Middle East are too rocky or too dry for farming. Even the once-fertile fields of the land of Israel were barren and empty for hundreds of years. But today the land is fruitful again, just as the Bible promised:

For the Lord your God is bringing you into a good land, a land with streams and springs and fountains issuing from plain and hill; a land of wheat and barley, of vines, figs, and pomegranates, a land of olive trees and honey.

—*Deuteronomy 8:7–8*

Now get your sweater out. The air is cooling off fast as you climb out of the green Jordan valley and head into the rolling hills of Galilee. If it's springtime, bright red, yellow, and purple wildflowers cover the hills. A short time later the earth will turn a thirsty yellow-brown, polka-dotted with gray rocks.

There are plenty of rocks in the Galilee—enough to build houses, roads, fences, and layers of terraces around the Arab villages. Groves of gray-green olive trees, vineyards, and broad fig trees surround the villages. Shady forests of pine trees planted by the Jewish National Fund climb the mountain slopes. Drop your pack, and rest on the soft pine needles. Once, many years ago, the mountains of the Galilee were covered with oak and cedar forests. But by 1900 only bushes, rocks, and deep gullies were left. Jews all over the world bought trees, and the Jewish National Fund foresters quickly got to work. By 1982 they had planted more than 150 million trees and made many of the hills green again. Maybe your family bought a tree in the Galilee forest where you are sitting.

Hilltop villages dot the Galilee. The farmers build stone terraces to keep the earth from washing down into the valley. Then they plant vegetables, olive and fig trees, and grapevines in the terraces below their homes.

Rivka Dorfman

Do you hear bells jingling round the bend in the road? Grab your lunch! A herd of nosy, ever-hungry goats and sheep led by a barefoot Arab shepherd girl is coming your way. Wave *"Shalom"* as the flock clatters past, sniffing at your pack. *"Salaam,"* the shepherd waves back.

A scorpion asked a camel to carry him across the Jordan River. "How do I know you won't sting me?" asked the camel. "Don't be silly," said the scorpion, "if I stung you we'd both drown." The camel agreed and started to swim across with the scorpion on his back. In midstream the scorpion stung the camel. "Why did you do such a stupid thing?" cried the drowning camel. "Because this is the Middle East, stupid!" answered the drowning scorpion.
—an Arab parable

The Bad Guys of the Middle East

Goats are smart, curious, cute—and very, very good eaters. They don't eat tin cans, but they do eat most other things. Over the years herds of goats have chewed the bushes and trees of the Middle East right down to the ground. They're the bad guys who have turned forests into badlands. The Jewish National Fund tries to keep goats out of its new young forests.

It gets windier as you climb higher. By the time you reach the narrow, winding main street of the mountaintop town of **Zefat**, you may feel as if you could be blown back into the valley. Duck into one of Zefat's ancient synagogues, and say a prayer for a safe journey. Three hundred years ago, when many of these synagogues were built, Zefat was a great center of Jewish religious study. The city is so high that you can see all the way to the Jordan valley on the east and to the Mediterranean Sea on the west. At night the stars seem close enough to touch.

Hitch a ride out of Zefat on a nimble donkey who carries you up and down the winding paths of the Galilee heading west. Soon the mountains slope down to a broad valley filled with plowed fields, flashing fishponds, and tiny villages and kibbutzim. This is the **Valley of Jezreel**. Once it was a lonely, dangerous wilderness where jackals, vultures, and poor peasants lived. Israel's farmers have made it rich farmland.

Kiss the donkey good-by, stuff your sweater back into your pack, and jump down onto the soft earth of the valley. Pick up an orange or some pecans from under the trees, and snack as you walk. Tractors chug around the fields beside the road, and trucks rumble past carrying fruits and vegetables to market. There's a clatter of factories and the clucking of chickens from the settlements beside the road. The Valley of Jezreel is a busy, hard-working place. But you're on vacation, so stop and cool off in a kibbutz pool or play a game of basketball with some of the kibbutz kids.

Back on the road there's a haze of smog ahead. It's coming from **Haifa**, Israel's third largest city. Take a last deep breath of clean country air, and march into town. Haifa is a port on the shore of the **Mediterranean Sea**. White cruise ships, grimy cargo ships, and big, gray warships crowd the harbor. And British limeys, American sailors, and United Nations soldiers crowd the downtown streets. The city's houses are built up the slope of **Mt. Carmel**. Take the Carmelit—the only subway in Israel—up the mountain, and look down at the harbor, the ships, and the glittering sea. There's a forest at the very top where you can feed the birds and watch Israeli jets circle overhead.

Haifa started out as a port on the shore of the Mediterranean Sea. Then it grew up the sides of the Carmel mountain range. Parks, schools, hotels, and homes fill the mountaintop now, and factories and shipping crowd the shore.

Had enough resting? Go down the hill, turn south, and walk along the flat Mediterranean shore. There used to be crocodile-filled swamps along this coast. Don't worry about getting your toes nipped. Today there are only tiny lizards, sunbathing Israelis, and long-legged herons and other sea birds. The surf splashes invitingly, but the lifeguards whistle you back if you go in farther than waist-deep. The Mediterranean has a strong, hungry undertow. This warm, coastal plain is called the **Plain of Sharon**. More people live here than in any other part of Israel. You walk past towns and farms, cotton fields, fishponds, and strange plastic "tunnels." Peek in a "tunnel," and you'll find flowers and vegetables growing inside. Israel has no rain in the summer, so the farmers use plastic covers to keep the water from evaporating.

After walking awhile, an ancient ruin called **Caesarea** pops up out of the sand. Its stone columns, ancient stone roads, and

huge stadium were built by Jews and Romans 2,000 years ago. Once it was the greatest port in the eastern Mediterranean, but it had been buried in the sand for centuries and was accidentally discovered by a farmer plowing a field. There are bits of history buried all over Israel. Watch your feet. You might kick up a historic old coin or piece of pottery. Concerts and plays are performed at the rebuilt Caesarea stadium. Climb onto a stone seat to watch. Maybe a Roman emperor parked himself on this very seat 2,000 years ago.

Huge smokestacks from the **Hadera** power plant loom up a little farther on. The towns and houses are getting closer together. Soon you're walking through the suburbs of Israel's second largest city—**Tel Aviv**. You pass the bubble of a tennis stadium, a college campus with students napping on the sunny lawn, and tall apartment houses and shopping centers.

There are skyscrapers ahead! There's the haze and hum of traffic! Hop on a bus, and ride into Tel Aviv's central bus terminal. Struggle through the crowds to the noisy vegetable market and felafel stands nearby. If you're hungry, buy a huge pomegranate or a felafel sandwich—Israel's vegetarian hot dog. Pile plenty of cabbage, cauliflower, eggplant, and tehina on top of the felafel. It will keep your belly busy for miles. In the fancier part of town you can sit at an outdoor café table and watch people go by as you sip Israeli iced coffee—a little coffee with many scoops of ice cream in a tall glass.

A camel caravan walked along the quiet Tel Aviv beach in 1920.

Zionist Archives

Tel Aviv is a wide-awake, jumping place. It has concerts and dances, large shops, interesting museums, crowded beaches, puppet shows, and zoos. Would you believe that in 1909 all this was a stretch of sand dunes? A pair of knobby-kneed storks flap down to nest in the park in the middle of town. Sand dunes or city—it's all the same to them.

South of Tel Aviv and its neighbor **Jaffa** there are more sandy beaches, flat fields of cotton, and groves of shiny-leafed orange, grapefruit, and avocado trees. Take a last dip in the salty Mediterranean, and turn southeast toward the wide-open spaces of the **Negev**—the southern half of Israel.

Once only wandering tribes could live in the Negev because there wasn't enough water to supply towns and farms. The Bedouin roamed from well to well, pitching their tents on the sand and pasturing their flocks on shrubs and grass. After the State of Israel was established, pipelines were laid, bringing water from the north. There are many new towns and farms in the Negev now. Even the Bedouin are planting crops and settling down. But many of them still like to live in their black goatskin tents rather than in houses.

A tourist from Texas stopped to talk to an Israeli farmer. "What do you raise here?" he asked.

"I raise cows," the Israeli answered.

"Is that so? I raise cows, too," the Texan said. "How much land do you have?"

"Ten dunam [about three square miles]," the Israeli said proudly. "It's a good walk across my fields."

The Texan grinned. "On my ranch, I get into my car in the morning and I drive and drive and I don't reach the end of my land until nighttime."

"Tch, tch, tch," the Israeli shook his head. "I once had a car like that."

When you feel as though you've been walking forever across the flat reddish-brown earth of the Negev and the sun is melting your sunglasses and your mouth tastes like sandpaper—cheer up! **Beersheva** is just around the next clump of cacti. The city seems to pop up out of the sand. Pastel-colored apartment houses, buses, trees, and a green college campus shimmer ahead of you like a mirage.

Abraham and his family bought land in this neighborhood nearly 4,000 years ago. Today, Bedouin and other citizens of Israel buy goods and sell camels, chickens, and fine embroidery in the Beersheva open-air market. The veterinary hospital outside of town has a special camel clinic. Beersheva, like all of Israel, is a mixture of very old and very new things. On the streets you have to duck between donkeys, horse carts, and huge trailer trucks. Buy a chunk of halvah (ground sesame seeds and honey) and some almonds in the market, fill your canteen, and put on your hat. The hottest and loneliest part of your hike through Israel is about to begin.

As you walk south from Beersheva, the road stretches ahead through miles of rolling, sun-baked country, with only dusty bunches of trees here and there. It feels as though you and the tiny lizards that scuttle past your feet are the only living, breathing creatures around. But, no—there's a flock of sheep crowded in the shade of a tree by the road. A brown-skinned boy is sitting nearby, fanning a little fire. He waves. Maybe he is lonely, too. So sit down, and share a cup of tea and some halvah with him. Mmmm—the tea is good and sweet, but it would be even better with ice cubes. Moussa is the boy's name. He lives in a long, black tent on the other side of the hill. And most days he goes to school in Beersheva.

Wave good-by, and continue south on the road to **Elath**. A black bird soars high in the blue sky and then seems to hang above your head, watching you. Many birds and animals live in the Negev because it's the least crowded part of the country. If you stop to rest and sit very quietly under an acacia tree, a herd of big-eared gazelles may trot up to munch on the acacia pods, or a porcupine may waddle past. At night leopards prowl over the hills, and wolves howl at the bright stars. Israeli naturalists have caught some of the wolves and leopards and fitted them with collars that send radio signals. The naturalists use the signals to study the habits of the animals. But you might not care to meet a leopard face to face even if it is wearing a collar.

Listen closely. Do you hear running water? You're coming to **Ein Avdat**, a spring that gushes out of the rock in the middle of the desert. More than 1,500 years ago there was a city surrounded by green fields in this empty place. Farmers and scientists are learning to farm like those ancient people. They are growing vegetables and fruit trees, using only the tiny amount of water that they collect from rain and dew.

It's getting hotter and the road is steep, so hop onto a passing bus. It will carry you down into a huge crater called the **Maktesh Ramon**. You'll bounce along the bottom past rock walls in rainbow-colored layers like a gigantic sherbet pie. Geologists aren't sure how this strange crater was formed. It may have been gouged out by a giant meteor or carved by glaciers long before Abraham and Sarah's time.

The bus climbs up out of the Maktesh Ramon, and at last, after bumping, lurching and making screeching hairpin turns around the mountains, it reaches the southernmost tip of Israel, the city of Elath. King Solomon had a great port here 3,000 years ago. Today oil and other products are carried up the **Gulf of 'Aqaba** to enter Israel through the port.

If you feel hot, don't stop to sightsee. Get into your bathing suit, and jump right into the bathtub-warm water of the gulf. You won't be alone. There are hundreds of varieties of bright tropical fish whisking around the coral reefs and hiding in the fine white sand of the gulf bed. The skies are crowded, too. In the spring bird watchers peer through binoculars at storks and many other birds migrating up the valley from Africa to **Europe** and **Asia**. In the fall they watch the birds heading south for the winter.

Delicious supper smells are sizzling up from campfires along the beach. Many Israelis and tourists camp out on the beach. If you're lucky, you'll get invited to dinner. Then settle down to sing around the campfire and sleep under the stars.

In Eilat people can watch fish through the glass bottoms of boats or the glass walls of an underwater observatory. Only skin divers or snorkelers get close enough to rub noses in the clear, warm water of the Gulf of Aqaba.

In the morning it's time to start the last part of your walk. Turn north from Elath and follow the **'Arava valley** along Israel's eastern border. The Jordan valley, which you crossed at the beginning of the walk, is a more northern part of this valley. As the mountains on each side rise higher, you feel smaller and smaller. It's hot and dusty, and the water in your canteen tastes rusty. Just in time you reach **Yotvata**, a desert kibbutz. Yotvata's pampered cows live in air-conditioned barns, and the kibbutz members sell cold milk and ice cream to perspiring travelers. A great nature preserve stretches into the desert behind the kibbutz.

After more miles of walking, you see the tall towers of the **Dead Sea** potash works glimmering through the thick air. When you reach them, you are standing at the southern tip of the Dead Sea, on the lowest spot on the surface of the earth—1,300 feet below sea level. A steamy, gray lake stretches out before you, and bare, jagged cliffs loom up around the water. The fresh Jordan river water that enters the Dead Sea from the north soon evaporates. It leaves a thick, oily-feeling mixture of water, salt, and other minerals, too thick for any fish to live in.

Yuck, you think. Nothing could live here. "You'd be surprised," laugh the men at the potash works. "We have hyenas sneaking into our garbage. And we can hear wild pigs snorting around in the salt flats." The area around the Dead Sea is alive after all.

Farther up the lakeside you pass a sheer, gray hill with a flat top. It stands grimly apart, and ravens fly slowly around it. This is **Masada**, where a small group of Jews fought a brave, hopeless fight against their enemies 1,900 years ago.

Ein Gedi, a few miles farther north, is a happier place. A waterfall bounces down from the cliffs, and children yell and splash in the pools below. Look carefully to find the gazelles and wild goats that hide out in the rocks and the jungle of reeds around the water. This has always been a good place to hide. Before David became king of the Israelites, he hid from King Saul in a cave at Ein Gedi. If you want to climb around and explore some of the narrow valleys (wadis), watch out for scorpions and make sure you can scramble to high ground quickly. Water from a sudden rain that falls some place far away may come roaring down through the mountains, fill the wadi, and catch you by surprise. The desert can be a dangerous place.

After a few more miles along the Dead Sea it's time to leave the lowest spot on earth and climb into the mountains of **Judaea**. Turn west past the road to **Jericho**, where the tribes of Israel crossed the Jordan after their forty-year trek through the desert. You'd better pull out your sweater again. Jericho is in the warm, low country by the Jordan river, but you're heading up to the breezy mountaintop city of Jerusalem.

The mountains of Judaea are round and brown like huge loaves of pumpernickel bread, except where pink and tan stones break through the earth. Black cave openings gape out of the mountainsides. The Maccabees hid in some of these caves during their fight for freedom against the Greeks before the first Ḥanukkah.

Something whisks up the rock and darts into a cave. The ghost of a Maccabee? No—a small, bushy-tailed Judaean fox. Keep walking up the hills, and soon you pass a village and a gas station. Kids carrying book bags wave, and dogs bark. The lonely quiet of the desert is gone.

The buildings of **Jerusalem** begin to appear ahead. Their pink and gold stone walls glow in the sunlight. Towers, gold domes, and red-tiled roofs spread over the hills. And a great wall with a top as jagged as a line of brown teeth curves between the buildings. As you come closer, you can hear bells ringing, the growl of buses, and the honking of big-city traffic. But Jerusalem looks and feels different from the other big cities of Israel. Maybe it's because Jerusalem was the capital of the ancient land of Israel—the Biblical city where Solomon built the Holy Temple. Or maybe it's because Jerusalem is wistfully remembered in all Jewish religious writings.

The name "Jerusalem" means "city of peace," but the city has never been peaceful for long. The Turks who once ruled Jerusalem built this great stone wall to protect the city from attack. New Jerusalem spreads out far beyond the old walls.

Teak Silberman

Jerusalem is a holy city to Muslims and to Christians as well as to Jews, and it is the capital of the modern State of Israel.

Check out Jerusalem's new places: the museums, synagogues, zoos, pizza parlors, marketplaces, parks, and Israel's Knesset (parliament). And when you're ready to think and daydream and pray, go to the places that are full of history, like the last remaining wall of the Holy Temple on **Mt. Moriah**.

Your quick zigzag walk through Israel ends here in Jerusalem. But this is only the end of the beginning. In the next chapters you'll find much more to see and explore in and about Israel. So soak your feet after your long hike, take a nap, and then read on.

In the Galilee, from the top of Mt. Meron, Israel's tallest mountain, you can see four of Israel's neighbors. In the United States that would be like standing on Mt. Washington in New Hampshire and seeing Canada, Mexico, and the Atlantic Ocean all at the same time.

THE NEIGHBOR-HOOD

Far to the southeast you can see the brown hills of Jordan beyond the Jordan river. To the northeast the snowy tip of Mt. Hermon rises out of Syria. To the north are the mountains of Lebanon. And to the west you'll see the hazy blue of the Mediterranean Sea. Israel's southern border is too far away to see. It's the rocky Sinai Peninsula of Egypt.

Israel and its next-door neighbors—Jordan, Syria, Lebanon, and Egypt—are part of the Middle East. And the Middle East got its name because it is right in the middle, with Europe on the west, Africa on the south, and Asia on the north and east. It's an area with large deserts, few rivers, not much good farmland, but lots of precious oil. Most of the people living in the Middle East are Arabs and Muslims (believers in the religion of Islam).

THE NEIGHBORS

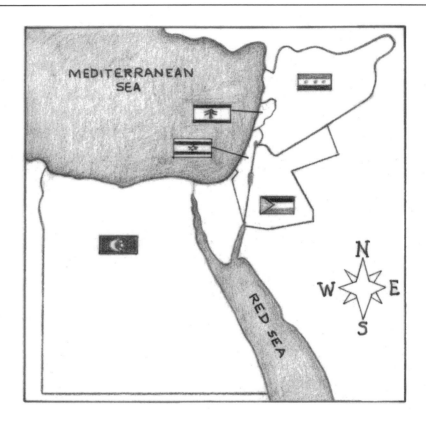

Israel has long borders with its neighbors because it is a long, narrow country. Most of the borders aren't shown on a map by neat, black lines, like the border between Canada and the United States. Instead they are dotted-line "international borders" and dashed-line "cease-fire" borders. That's because Israel and its neighbors have disagreed on where the borders should be and have often gone to war with each other over this and other matters. Only the southern border was finally agreed upon by both Israel and its neighbor to the south—Egypt.

LEBANON

Lebanon is a hilly, fertile little land on Israel's northern border. Two and a half to 3 million people of many sects and cultures are crowded inside Lebanon, and they often feud with each other. There are Druse, several kinds of Muslims, and several kinds of

WHAT'S A MUSLIM?

Muslims are people who believe in Islam, a religion that was started more than 1,300 years ago in Arabia by the fiery leader Mohammed. His teachings are written in a book called the Koran, which is holy to Muslims. It declares that there is only one God, that Allah is his name, and that Mohammed is his prophet. And it calls on Muslims to pray to Allah five times each day, to give charity, and to visit the religious shrine of Islam at Mecca in Saudi Arabia.

The Koran includes many teachings of the Jewish and Christian Bibles. Muslims, like Jews, practice circumcision and forbid the eating of pork. The Koran accepts the prophets and religious leaders of the Bible but declares that Mohammed is the last and greatest prophet, the seal of the prophets.

The first Muslims were great fighters. They marched out of Arabia thirteen centuries ago, conquered people all over Africa, Europe, and Asia, and converted them to Islam. Today there are about 700 million Muslims in the world. They are of many different races and nationalities. Islam is divided into several different branches.

Christians. In Biblical days Hiram, the king of Lebanon, sold huge cedar trees from the forested hills to King Solomon to build the Temple in Jerusalem. Today most of those ancient forests are gone. But there is rich farmland in the valleys where tobacco, oranges, and other crops are grown.

Syria borders Israel on the northeast. It is ten times the size of Israel and has nearly 10 million people. It has farmland, pastureland, natural gas, and desert. Its people are mostly Muslim of various sects. Judah Maccabee led the Jews in the battles that drove the Syrians out of Israel 2,000 years ago. Even today there is no peace on the Israeli-Syrian border. SYRIA

Jordan lies across the Jordan river on Israel's eastern border. It is almost four times as large as Israel, but most of Jordan is dry and arid. Most of the 2.5 million Jordanians are Muslims. Many are nomadic (wandering) herdsmen. Others are Palestinians who left the lands that are now part of Israel. JORDAN

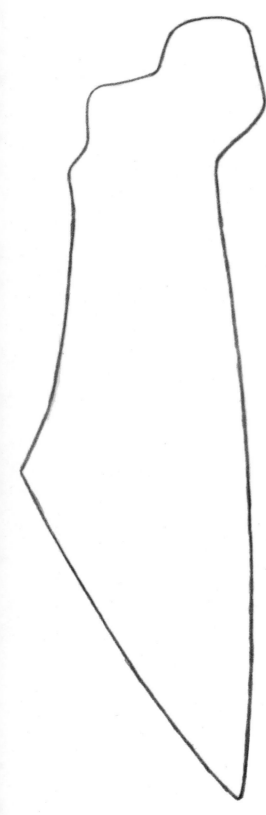

Between Israel and Jordan, on the west bank of the Jordan river, lies a hilly stretch of land. It was the center of the Biblical land of Israel and is called Judaea and Samaria by many Israelis. Forty-five thousand Jews and 800,000 Arabs live there today. It is administered by the government of Israel, as is the Gaza area, with 525,000 Arabs.

 EGYPT

Egypt is the largest of Israel's neighbors—almost forty times bigger than Israel. Most of the land is desert. Ninety-five percent of Egypt's 45 million people are crowded into the strip of rich land that is watered by the Nile river. They grow wheat, cotton, and other crops. Most Egyptians are Muslims; some are Christian. The Bible relates that the ancient Egyptians welcomed the Jews into Egypt but later enslaved them. Moses finally led the Jews out of Egypt, through the Sinai, and to the land of Israel. In 1979 Egypt became the first neighbor to sign a peace treaty with Israel.

Israel's most peaceful neighbor is on her western border. It's the blue Mediterranean Sea. Israelis have fun swimming, fishing, and sailing sunfish and other little boats in the sea. And they trade diamonds, oranges, refrigerators, and other goods through their Mediterranean ports of Haifa and Ashdod.

Trucks loaded with merchandise do not cross the borders between Israel and her neighbors. The crossing roads are blocked by barbed wire. Shells scream overhead and explode in the fields and towns on both sides of the border.

Many years ago, during another time of war, the Biblical prophet Isaiah made a promise that gives people hope for peace.

There shall be a highway from Egypt to Assyria. The Assyrians shall join with the Egyptians and Egyptians with the Assyrians, and . . . [they] shall serve [the Lord]. In that day, Israel shall be a third partner with Egypt and Assyria as a blessing on earth; for the Lord of Hosts will bless them, saying "Blessed be My people Egypt, My handiwork Assyria, and My very own Israel" (Isaiah 19:23–25).

SNOW-CAPPED HERMON

Adapted from Legends of Erets Yisrael, *by Zev Vilnay*

After God gave the Law to Israel from the top of Mt. Sinai, all the other mountains came to him and complained: "Why did you choose Mt. Sinai and not one of us?"

"Line up before Me, and each of you may explain why I should have chosen you," said God.

So they pushed and shoved until the biggest, Mt. Tabor, stood at the front and the smallest, Mt. Hermon, was at the end.

"I'm a beautiful, round mountain—the loveliest in the world," said Mt. Tabor. "Why didn't you choose me?"

"You are very beautiful," said God, "but in days to come other peoples will build places of worship on your peak. I could not give the Law to Israel from a mountain that would become the home of other religions."

Tabor turned sadly away. Then, one by one, the other mountains argued their cases. But God found a fault in each one.

At last it was the turn of the smallest, the hill called Hermon. "I'm not big or beautiful, but I stand at the northern border of the land of Israel and the fountains of the river Jordan flow from my feet," said the little hill.

God nodded. "Truly, I could have given the Holy Law to Israel from your peak," He said. "Instead I will give you another gift. I will make you the tallest mountain in the land, and your summit will always be white with snow."

A cookie map for eating

For the map-shaped pattern you will need:

tracing paper	cardboard as large as the map on page 26
pencil	tape
carbon paper	scissors

1. Using the tracing paper and the pencil, trace the outline of the map on page 26. Place the carbon paper face down on the cardboard. Tape the traced outline over it, and redraw the lines, pressing firmly.

2. Remove the tracing paper and the carbon paper. Cut out the map outlined on the cardboard.

To make 5 or 6 cookie maps you will need:

1¾ cups flour	medium-sized bowl
1 teaspoon baking powder	sifter
½ cup sugar	large bowl
¼ cup oil	measuring cups
¼ cup water	measuring spoon
1 egg	mixing spoon
raisins or chocolate bits	rolling pin
	small knife
	wide spatula
	greased cookie sheet
	rack
	small paint brush
	food coloring

tracing
carbon
cardboard

1. Preheat the oven to 350 degrees.

2. Mix the flour, baking powder, and sugar in the medium-sized bowl. Sift the dry ingredients into the large bowl.

3. Add the oil, water, and egg. Mix the ingredients with the mixing spoon until the mixture gets stiff. Then knead the mixture until the dough forms a smooth ball. Add a little flour if the dough sticks to your hands.

4. On a floured board or table, roll the dough with the rolling pin to about ¼-inch thickness. If the rolling pin sticks to the dough, sprinkle flour on the rolling pin.

5. Sprinkle a little flour on the dough. Place the pattern on the dough, and, with the small knife, cut through the dough around the edge of the pattern.

6. Use the spatula to lift each map from the board and to place it on the greased cookie sheet.

7. Repeat the procedure until all the dough has been used.

8. Mark the cities on the dough maps with raisins or chocolate bits.

9. Bake the cookies 10 to 15 minutes or until the cookies are golden-brown. Take the cookies out of the oven, and, with a spatula, place them on a rack to cool.

10. When the cookies are cool, paint them with a small paint brush, using slightly diluted food coloring as shown.

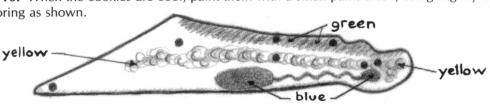

green
yellow
yellow
blue

A bread-dough map for hanging, NOT for eating

For the map-shaped pattern, follow instructions 1 and 2 at the beginning of the cookie-map section. To make 4 bread-dough maps you will need:

2 cups flour   measuring cups
½ cup salt   medium-sized bowl
1 cup water   mixing spoon
           rolling pin
           small knife
           greased cookie sheet
           small paint brush
           food coloring or acrylic paint

1. Measure all the ingredients into the bowl. Mix them thoroughly with the spoon. Knead the dough for a few minutes until it forms a smooth ball.

2. Set aside a small piece of the dough. Roll out the rest of the dough with the rolling pin until it is about ½ inch thick.

3. Place the pattern on the dough, and, with a small knife, cut through the dough around the edge of the pattern.

4. Place the dough map on the greased cookie sheet.

5. Repeat the procedure until all the dough has been used.

6. Roll the reserved dough into short, skinny worms. Wet the surface of the worms to help them stick to the map, and put them down as shown for mountain ranges.

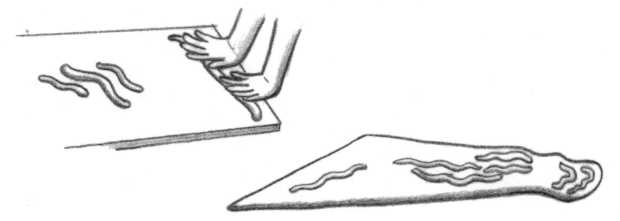

7. Bake the maps at 275 degrees until they are dry and toasty brown (about 45 minutes).

8. After the maps have cooled, paint in the lakes and river with the paint brush and food coloring, locate the cities with a dot, and decorate the maps however you wish.

Decorative maps can also be made of plaster and papier-mâché. Find out how to use these materials in a crafts book.

A mishmash of people

There are more than four million people in Israel, and on a sunny weekday morning they all seem to be out on the street at the same time. People carrying bundles, shopping bags, and babies are lined up at the bus stop. A crowd is waiting at the corner for the crossing light to turn green. Children carrying book bags are walking down the street two by two. They're going on a class trip to the museum. Men and women soldiers with guns are sitting on the sidewalk railings eating felafel sandwiches. There's a shouting, arm-waving crowd of men in the square. They're arguing about war, peace, the price of bread, religion, the government—in Israel everyone has strong opinions about almost everything.

In this chapter, you'll meet some Israelis face to face, and you'll learn some interesting facts about them.

MEET SOME ISRAELIS

Dani, an art student, is leading a group of French tourists around an archaeological site in Jerusalem.

"Before I became a guide here I led tourists on camel caravans through the Sinai desert. I love to hike in the desert. When I was younger, I would run away from high school to go hiking. Today I ride my motorbike into the desert on weekends and go walking. I also like to work with my hands. I'm studying industrial design at Bezalel art school, and I designed and built my own bed. It's made of wood slats, and it's very comfortable.

"Kids are interested in the digs here at the Wall of the Temple Mount. I explain to them that archaeology is like going down a staircase and discovering old-new places. As an archaeologist digs down through layers of earth and brick, he or she reaches earlier and earlier times. Come and join my tour sometime. I'll show you."

David, a policeman, is on duty at the Damascus Gate in Jerusalem. "I want to fight crime, and I like challenges. That's why I became a policeman. Also, my father was a policeman for thirty-seven years—first in Turkey and then here in Israel. It's interesting work. I calm people down—like when the fans get excited and start running around at soccer games. And I help to

Israel's buses are often crowded, and people must wait for them on long, slow lines. One bearded man waited and waited as his line inched along. He finally reached the bus, squeezed aboard, and handed the driver a half-price ticket—the kind of ticket used by schoolchildren.

"How did you get this ticket?" asked the driver, looking at the passenger's long beard.

"I got it before I started to wait on line," sighed the passenger.

---

protect important visitors who come to Jerusalem.

"My horse's name is Kidron. He's sixteen years old and very smart. When I call his name, he turns his head and comes to me. My son is two and a half, and he already rides Kidron. Maybe he'll be a policeman, too. But he'll decide that for himself when he gets older."

Samir, a shopkeeper, is weighing spices for a customer in the market in Old Jerusalem.

"I was born in the Old City of Jerusalem right near the Western Wall. I still live here with my parents and eight brothers and sisters. My cousin and I work very long hours to run this shop. We sell good-smelling spices that you may not know about—cumin, coriander, anise, cardamon, and others. Tourists from many countries come to sniff and buy, and I've learned words in four or five languages to speak with them. But most of my customers are local people."

Rami, a soldier, is hitchhiking back to his army post in the north.

"It's hard work being a soldier. When we train, we have to run ten kilometers (about six miles) with thirty-eight kilograms (about eighty-five pounds) on our backs. And we must carry our guns everywhere. This gun is my best friend. All the boys who were in my high-school class are in the army now, and most of the girls—except for the ones who got married. There are Arab Druse soldiers in the army and in my unit, too. They fight for Israel just as I do.

"In one more year, when I'm finished with army service, I'm going to hike around the country. There are many beautiful places to see in Israel. Then I want to study medicine. My little brother can hardly wait to become a soldier like me. Well, when I was little, I felt the same way."

Bat-Ami, a social worker, is talking to her cat Emilia on the balcony of their apartment.

"I like helping people, and I thought it would be fun to do that full-time. That's why I became a social worker. I visit and talk with old people in Jerusalem. When it's necessary, I find places for them in nursing homes or help them get special services like meals-on-wheels or nursing care. My clients and I have the most fun when we go on trips around the city. They like to visit King David's Tower, Mother Rachel's tomb, and other historic places. Afterward we have lunch together in a fancy hotel.

"Sometimes I get upset because I can't help my clients enough. They may have to wait a long time before there is room in a nursing home, or my agency may not have the money for some services. I get so upset that I have to come home and hold Emilia for a while before I feel better."

Ilan, a film editor, is cutting up long strips of film in his TV studio. "I prepare the evening news reports for TV. In Israel this is very serious work. We don't show many news stories about pets or fashions or crime. Instead, people wait anxiously to hear news of fighting on the country's borders or of problems with Israel's economy. The photographers and reporters bring the news film to me. I cut parts out, splice film together, and sometimes add music or words or animation to make it interesting and exciting. I like working with my hands as a craftsman does. It is like putting together the pieces of a puzzle. But news editing is tense work because I must always watch the clock. The film must be ready in time for the evening news broadcast. Then I can go home for supper."

Simona, a farmer, is milking a goat at the children's farm on Kibbutz Ḥatzor.

"I guess I'm partly a teacher and partly a farmer. I always loved animals and wanted to work with them. But I didn't want to work in the big chicken house or barns of the kibbutz because those chickens and calves are raised to be eaten. The children's farm is just right for me.

"Every day the children come to clean and feed their animals. They learn to be responsible for them, to love them, and not to hurt them. One boy used to chase the ducks, but he stopped when I explained that he scares them and may make them sick. And a girl was very frightened of all the animals at first. She came each day and slowly got used to them. Now she has her own pet rabbit."

Miḥal, age twelve, from Kibbutz Shamir, wrote about her hope for peace between Jews and Arabs:

Flowers of Flame

> If only the two
> Peoples were like two
> Flowers growing
> Side by side
> Like old friends
> Like two flowers of flame. . . .

Rozzy, a zoo keeper, is feeding Ricky the parrot at the Biblical Zoo.

"One day I stopped into a café for a cup of coffee. I saw a woman wearing a baby sack, but instead of a baby there was a little whiskered kangaroo inside. She told me that she worked in the zoo and she was taking care of an orphan kangaroo.

" 'Wow,' I said, 'I'd like to work at the zoo.'

" 'Do you have experience?' she asked.

" 'Oh, yes, I have a cat,' I said.

"I got the job! It's very exciting. I work in the bird section with parrots, flamingos, and swans. At first I was afraid of Ricky. She would snap and bite my fingers. But now we're friends.

"My children are very proud of me. My daughter Adina tells everybody that I work at the zoo."

SISTERS AND BROTHERS . . . OR AT LEAST COUSINS

Abraham, our forefather, had two sons—Isaac, son of Sarah, and Ishmael, son of Hagar. The Arabs are descended from Ishmael. The Jews are descended from Isaac. That makes Jews and Arabs cousins.

Even their languages come from the same family. Hebrew and Arabic have similar grammars and share many words. Each language stayed pure over the centuries because each was guided by the text of an ancient book. Hebrew is based on the Bible. Arabic is based on the Koran.

Can you think of Hebrew words with the same meaning as these Arabic words? Check your answers on page 36.

yaum al-din day of judgment	**ibn** son of	**saddik** righteous person
Al Raḥim the Merciful One	**kalb** dog	**zakat** charity
abed slave	**shams** sun	

A SPICY ISRAELI STEW

(*These numbers are given by the Israel Central Bureau of Statistics, 1988.*)

Each of the eight Israelis you just met comes from a different background. They or their parents or grandparents were Egyptian, South African, American, Polish, Moroccan, Turkish, or Palestinian. Israel is a melting pot of people from many lands. But they don't melt into one big Israeli mush. Instead they boil and bubble like a stew. Each ingredient tastes just like itself. But it also adds a very, very spicy flavor to the rest of the stew.

Here are the ingredients of the Israeli stew:

3,600,000* Jews
615,000* Muslim Arabs
102,000* Christians
75,000* Druze Arabs

More than half of Israel's Jews are of Middle Eastern, Asian, and African origin. They are called Sephardim or *Edot ha-Mizrach* (Eastern communities). Sephardim were among the early Zionists in the 1800s. But most of them reached Israel in a great wave of immigration after the state was established in 1948.

Yemenite Jews packed up their Torah scrolls and walked from their villages, across hot deserts, to Aden. Airplanes waited there to take them to Israel. Although they had never before seen an airplane (or even an automobile), they climbed fearlessly aboard. The Biblical prophet Isaiah had promised that the Jewish people would "renew their strength as eagles." And what could these giant silver monsters be, thought the Yemenites, if not Isaiah's mighty eagles?

Other Sephardim came from India, Iran, Afghanistan, Egypt, and many other lands. The streets of Israel were like an endless Purim party, sparkling with bright robes, turbans, and scarves.

Central Zionist Archives

These anxious-looking girls had just arrived in Israel from Morocco in 1948. *What next?* they seem to be thinking.

The immigrants had been merchants and craftspeople. Now they had to learn new skills and to puzzle out the mysteries of bus routes, telephones, and Western plumbing. The older people learned from their children. And the children struggled to keep up with their Western schoolmates.

A class of new Israelis studies the Hebrew alphabet.

Central Zionist Archives

Today, Sephardim are mayors, members of the Knesset (parliament), builders, singers, soccer players, and even pilots of the great silver "eagles." They are also mixing up the Israeli stew because one out of five marriages is between Jews of Sephardic and Ashkenazic backgrounds.

A little less than half of Israel's Jews are of Western—that is, European or American—origin. They are called Ashkenazim (the Hebrew word for "Germans"). Ashkenazim started the Zionist movement in the late 1800s. You can read about this in Chapters 4 and 5. Many of them built kibbutzim (collective farms) in Palestine, where they shared the work and shared the money that they earned. They even shared child care by keeping their babies and children in a central nursery. By cooperation and hard work the early Zionists hoped to build an ideal homeland.

A mishmash of people

Answers:

yom ha-din
El-Raḥamim
eved
ben
kelev
shemesh
tzaddik
tz'daka

Sticks and Stones . . .

When an Ashkenazi gets angry at a Sephardi, he calls him a Frenk, which comes from "French," because many North Africans speak French.

When a Sephardi gets angry at an Ashkenazi, he calls him a Vooz-Vooz, because Yiddish-speaking Jews say "Vooz?" which means "What?" in Yiddish.

When both of them get angry at a Jew from Germany, they call him a Yekkeh, because German Jews once dressed and behaved so formally that, even in warm Israel, they always wore yekkets ("jackets").

Labor unions, factories, and defense forces were set up in Palestine by the Ashkenazic settlers. When the state was born, they led the new government and ran the Western-style economy.

Israel has changed over the years. Today only 3.5 percent of all Israelis live on kibbutzim. There are more shopkeepers and office workers than farmers in the country. And Sephardic Jews are joining Ashkenazim as leaders of Israel.

The members of Israel's Muslim and Druse Arab minority vary widely. There are wandering Bedouins in coarse, brown robes, businessmen in suits and ties, shadowlike Muslim women hidden behind veils, erect Druse women in black velvet dresses and white kerchiefs, and boys and girls in blue jeans and sandals. They do many kinds of work—building construction, shopkeeping, farming, teaching, and more.

Before the State of Israel was established, many more Arabs lived in Palestine. Some had come from other parts of the Middle East in the years between the two world wars. Others had been born in Palestine. When the War of Liberation broke out in 1948, many Arabs fled across the borders. At the same time, Jews from Arab countries rushed to the new state. It was an unexpected exchange of peoples.

Today, Israeli-Arab children study Hebrew and Arabic in school. The adults vote in Israel's elections and serve in the Knesset. Druse Arabs are soldiers in Israel's armed forces. But many Arabs are troubled by the fighting between Israel and its neighbors. They feel loyal to their country—the State of Israel—but they also feel a tie to their fellow Arabs and their kinfolk across the borders.

Some of Israel's 98,000 Christians still speak Aramaic—an ancient language of the Middle East. These Christians are Armenian, Coptic-Egyptian, or Ethiopian. There are also Protestant, Greek Orthodox, and Catholic communities. In the mishmash of Israel's people, the Christian minority is the most varied of all. They live in high mountain villages, on the twisting streets of Old Jerusalem, and in desert monasteries. The Christian Israelis add an extra flavor to the spicy Israeli stew.

Did you ever ask your grandfather if there were dinosaurs around when he was a kid?

Did he laugh, or did he get insulted?

When Israeli kids ask their grandparents about their childhood, they get a lot of different answers. That's because Israeli grandparents come from many different places. Some grew up with camels and donkeys, some with horses and wagons, and some with Fords and Studebakers.

Read what these Israeli grandparents and their sabra (born in Israel) grandchildren have to say about their lives:

SABRAS AND GRAND-PARENTS

Chavvy Gamliel and **her grandmother**

Grandmother: ''In nineteen forty-nine I came to Israel from Yemen. Our family lived in a tent for two years. At first we had only potatoes and greens to eat. I went out to work, and my husband worked. And finally we were able to get a small apartment for ourselves and our five children. Then we started to build this fine, big house. Now I have eleven grandchildren. They visit for Shabbat and the holidays. I enjoy cooking and preparing for them. My American daughter-in-law is very nice. But I wish she would learn to speak Yemenite.''

Chavvy: ''Every two weeks before Shabbat, my two sisters and two brothers and I come to visit my grandmother in Rosh Ha-Ayin [near Tel Aviv]. On Friday night Grandma lights candles, and on Shabbat morning we eat cubana (yeast dough cooked with spices). There are only seven children in my class at school—all girls. I like arithmetic, and I like the playground with the swings and climbing bars. I showed the other girls how to bounce a ball and sing 'One, Two, Three-a-Leary.' My mother taught it to me because she's from America. Maybe I'll be a teacher when I grow up, but I haven't decided yet. My sister Naomi says I should tell the kids who read this book to study Hebrew and come to Israel.''

Yoli Peri and **her grandfather Benny**

Benny: ''When I was a boy in Brooklyn, I belonged to a Zionist youth movement. My friends and I came to Israel in nineteen forty-eight to start a new kibbutz. We roughed it at first, with no heat, electricity, or plumbing. During the first winter, there was a foot of snow. Later I went back to the United States and became a biologist. In nineteen seventy, my wife Rivka and I and most of our family moved to Israel—to Jerusalem. Yoli has lots of cousins, aunts, and uncles around. Our Passover Seder with the family and our friends is a happy, crowded event. Yoli and I garden together on the terrace. We sing music scales, too. And when she wants help, I help her with homework.''

Yoli: "I live on French Hill in Jerusalem, and I'm seven. The thing I like best at school is when the teacher reads stories to us or when she plays the piano and we sing along. There are twenty-eight pupils in my class. We have school from eight to twelve. After that we have clubs like sewing or drama. Some kids play football or soccer. But I don't—that's for boys. I like playing school or playing at housekeeping, and I love to watch 'Rehov Sum-Sum' ['Sesame Street'] on TV. Sometimes Benny does arithmetic drill with me. He made special arithmetic cards."

Abed Darusha and his grandmother

Grandmother: "Ever since I was married, fifty years ago, I have lived in this village [Iksal, near Nazareth]. I raised eight children here. I was married at twenty. It wasn't a love match. There were no love matches in those days. My father and my husband's father were best friends, and they decided that we would marry. My husband was a good man. Everybody said that he pampered me. He wouldn't let me work in the fields. I loved to cook and take care of the children and make cheese and butter from the milk of our goats. Now I have fifty-three grandchildren, including Abed. They all give me much honor. I am a hajji [she points proudly to her white kerchief]. I made the pilgrimage. [*Haj* is an Arabic word which refers to the pilgrimage to Mecca, in Saudi Arabia. Every devout Muslim is expected to go to Mecca, the center of Islam, at least once during his or her lifetime.]"

Abed: "I'm in seventh grade. I study Arabic and Hebrew, and I'm just starting English. There are thirty-six pupils in my class. We have TV programs in school that teach us math and English. We go to school six hours a day, six days a week. I like school, and I like to play soccer, but I don't like basketball. Most of all, I like animals. I have rabbits and a dog and three cats. When I grow up, I'd like to live in a village and work with animals."

Hillal Sharett and her grandmother Sarah

Sarah: I was born in Lódź, a big city in Poland. In 1936 my husband and I came to visit Palestine. I fell in love with the country and decided to come back and settle. Four years later, when the Nazis invaded Poland, my family escaped and came to Palestine. I lived in Tel Aviv and worked as a director for WIZO (Women's International Zionist Organization). Later, my daughter Devorah and her husband Ḥayyim went to build a kibbutz. I love to visit them and spend time with Hillal and my other grandchildren. I'm eighty-one now, and, as you Americans say, I'm still going strong.

Hillal: I'm a kibbutz kid, and I love nature and walking through the countryside. I like the way we share the work and property on the kibbutz. When my parents and I were in the United States, I missed the kibbutz and all my friends. We came back just in time for my group's bar and bat mitzvah. I do folk dancing and play the piano a little and work with computers at school. When I visit Grandma Sarah in the city, we talk about school and other things. When I was little, she used to tell me stories.

ISRAELIS AND AMERICANS

Americans brought chocolate-chip cookies and Weight Watchers to Israel.

Israelis brought felafel sandwiches to the United States.

There has always been heavy traffic of people, money, and ideas between Israel and the United States. In the 1860s Judah Touro, who helped build the oldest synagogue in the United States, sent money to the Jews of Jerusalem for a new housing project. Awhile later, American missionaries traveled to Palestine (later Israel) to convert the "heathen." Much, much later, in 1947, the American government helped the United Nations to decide to establish a Jewish and an Arab state in Palestine. And today, American and Israeli scientists share know-how in medical, energy, and military research.

Tourists travel back and forth all the time. Christian and Jewish Americans "ooh" and "ah" at Biblical sites and modern sights in Israel. And Israeli tourists exclaim "Wai, wai, wai!" at the Grand Canyon and Disney World. Students from both countries study at each other's schools. American Zionists send money to build hospitals, schools, and youth villages. Other American Jews go on *aliya* ("immigrate") to Israel. And some Israelis come to the United States as *yordim* ("emigrants").

Israelis love Tal Brodie, a former American basketball star who coached an Israeli team. And Americans applaud Itzḥak Perlman, an Israeli composer and violinist, who teaches and inspires American musicians. There's a lot of giving, taking, and sharing between the United States and Israel.

3 Kids in Israel

What do you think about people who live more than 6,000 miles away and speak a language you don't understand? Maybe you think they're very different from you. You may even think that you'd have nothing to say to a kid from Israel. In this chapter you'll read some of the ideas of Israeli youngsters. You'll find out about their schools, hobbies, and sports. Of course, they can't speak for all Israeli kids, just as you and your classmates can't speak for all American kids. But it's a good first look.

WHAT ISRAELI KIDS SAY

This class of fifth-graders from Kfar Saba (near Tel Aviv) answered some questions for us. Read their names from right to left:

Top row: Miḥal S., Avital, Ḥana, Naḥshon, Oren, Sagi, Dudi, Yoav, Amir

Second row down: Gai, Barak, Miḥal A., Vered, Yifat, Yuval, Gai, Shai, Ofer

Third row, seated: Orit, Noa, Aynat, Efrat, Perla, Mickey ben-Naftali (the teacher), Zaḥi, Natan, Ronen

Bottom row, seated: Irit, Tali, Galit F., Galit S., Yosef, Gil

Mihal S.

"Crafts is my favorite subject at school because the teacher isn't lecturing all the time so we can talk while we work. There's a lot of satisfaction in making things. Purim is my favorite holiday. I like to fill my belly with hamantashen and wear a costume. It's a very funny holiday."

Avital

"I love to go on trips with my parents. The best holiday is Passover because we travel to our family and sleep over after the Seder and have a long vacation. I like Michael Jackson because he's cute and he sings well."

Nahshon

"Israel is a very pretty country, but I don't like the fact there are wars every couple of years. My favorite school subject is Bible. In my free time I ride my bike, skate, and play soccer. I also like TV and radio and Michael Jackson records."

Aynat

"Math is my favorite subject because I like to use the computer. I take dance lessons after school, and on Shabbat I like to read and play with my pets."

Zadok

"When there's no school, I play tennis in the morning and then go to my uncle's to play soccer. During Passover week we go motor-boating on Lake Kinneret. I like swimming, boating, and reading. My favorite book, called *Blishi*, is about a bunch of Israeli kids who fight terrorists and help Israel. They always win."

Efrat

"I like to study English because it has a nice sound and because it is spoken all over the world, so when I travel I'll be able to speak to people. After school I play piano and go swimming. What bothers me in Israel is that the country doesn't have enough money, and also that we are at war so much and people are getting killed. 'Dallas' is the most interesting TV program because the Ewings have so many family problems to solve. Michael Jackson is my favorite singer."

Perla

"The best holiday for me is Passover because we go to my uncle's house and the whole family is together. The singers I enjoy are Yardena Arazi and Zipi Shavit. Zipi makes jokes and sings like a kid. Crafts is my favorite subject at school."

Oren

"Karate is my favorite sport. And crafts, English, nature, and gym are my favorite school subjects. I like hiking and going to Luna Park [an amusement park]. I think the rock group Genesis and actor Roger Moore are very good."

Dudi

"I like to play soccer and watch TV and, at school, to do crafts."

Yoav

"I go hiking, watch the birds, and find beautiful flowers. Israel's landscape is beautiful. But our economic problems and the problems of war and Arab and Jewish terrorism trouble me. Volleyball is my favorite game. We have a great volleyball team here in Kfar Saba. The best holiday is Yom Ha-Atzmaut. My friends and I make a bonfire to celebrate."

Vered

"I like math because it's important and gym because it's fun. I enjoy team sports like basketball and quieter things like swimming, reading, and listening to music. Avi Toledano and Ilanit are my favorite singers."

Computer science is a new, exciting subject taught at some schools. A girl from a tiny northern village, Dalit Sagi, won first prize in a Weizmann Institute science fair (like our Westinghouse competitions) for designing a computerized energy control system for industry.

Ronen

"I like math because I can do it well and I know it's going to be useful for me. I go to the library and read for hours. I like to write, too. I wrote a whole book with many chapters. It's called *The Adventures of Lassie and Her Gang*."

Tali

"I visit my grandparents or my aunts and uncles on Shabbat, and I like reading or walking with my friends. In school, gym is my best class because I like games. The best holiday is Purim. We get all dressed up and laugh at each other's costumes and give and receive Purim gifts."

Galit F.

"My best school subjects are art, sports, and dance. Science is interesting, too—to understand how plants and animals grow, how our brains and bodies work, etc. I love the TV program '*Fame*' because the stories and dancing are great. I'd love to go to a school like that."

Sagi

"I love gymnastics because I'm good at it. I don't like just sitting and studying. After school I play soccer in the field near my house and read adventure stories and go for short runs. I love Israel's warm climate because we can go swimming often. What bothers me most in Israel are the many auto accidents."

Amir

"Bible history is the most interesting school subject. After school I like to play an instrument or to play basketball or practice judo. I enjoy the Passover Seder when we tell about the time our ancestors were slaves in Egypt and we eat special foods. My favorite singer is Avi Toledano. He represents Israel at international festivals. 'Benson' is my favorite funniest TV program."

Gai

"I'm good at math, and I like to play with my brother's computer after school. I like to play soccer, too. I think Israel's army is the greatest—but I wish we didn't have so many enemies."

Mihal A.

"Most of all I like to play with my dog. I also like to visit my friends, watch TV, read adventure stories, and take naps. English is my favorite subject at school because it's an international language. And I love Israel's beautiful, quiet landscape and nice people. But I wish we would keep the country cleaner."

Yifat

"I'm a fast runner, and I like running and swimming best of all sports. Purim is my favorite holiday because we wear funny costumes and send gifts. The thing I would like most is that Israel makes peace with other lands and that we clean up the country."

Yuval

"Israel has everything from snow to desert. There are many nature preserves and parks. The most beautiful place of all is Jerusalem. But it worries me that the Arabs may capture our land and we will remain without strength and without our country. Shlomo Artzi is my favorite singer. He's a serious composer and singer—too serious for a lot of kids my age."

Yosef

"I like to play soccer after school and on Shabbat."

What do Israeli kids get for Ḥanukkah?

Shekem, a large Israeli chain of retail stores, reports that video games top the list. Next, tape players with earphones. And then books, records, clothing, and toys.

43

Kids in Israel

Gai

"I like to go to Luna Park [an amusement park], watch TV, and play with my friends. My favorite TV program has lots of fighting, shooting, and horses. Crafts is my favorite school subject."

Shai

"I love sports and fishing. And I like going to Tel Aviv."

Ofer

"At school I love to do crafts because we make nice things. At home I watch TV and read. Purim is my favorite holiday because I make a different costume each year and eat a lot and have fun."

Gil

"I love to go to soccer games and to play soccer. Michael Jackson is my favorite singer. The economy of Israel worries me."

Yifat

"I like to solve problems, so math is my favorite subject. In my free time I visit friends, watch TV, read, sleep. On Shabbat I go on picnics with my grandparents and uncles. We take trips to the Carmel [near Haifa], where the air is so clean and clear. I worry sometimes that the Arab population in Israel will grow as large as the Jewish population and then we'll have a civil war like in Lebanon."

Orit

"Reading is fun for me—and also movies. Christopher Reeve is my favorite actor because he's tall and slim and has blue eyes. I love to learn about the wild birds and animals in Israel, too."

Galit S.

"On Shabbat my favorite thing is to go skating in the park. On Passover we go to my grandparents. All my aunts and uncles come. We sing and read together, and it's a happy time. I'm in a choir, and maybe I'll be a singer when I grow up. Gym is my favorite school subject."

From death in the Holocaust to rebirth in Israel—that is the message of this sculpture in the town of Karmiel in northern Israel. Karmiel is a new town with immigrants from Rumania, Ethiopia, England, and many other lands. The building in the background is the first home for many immigrants. It is a government absorption center.

On the next page kids from Karmiel talk about themselves.

These eighth-graders from Karmiel (in northern Israel) were really proud of their language skills. They answered our questions in English.

Ofri

"I want to work with computers when I grow up. My favorite afterschool hobby is computer lessons. I'm very proud of Israel because once we Jews lived in many different countries, but now we built a beautiful land with our own hands. What I don't like in Israel is that religion is compulsory. I want to tell all American kids—come to Israel!"

Ilan

"After school I like to play basketball and work with the computer. I enjoy math in school. It's an interesting world of numbers. Genesis is the rock group I like best. I'm proud of being Jewish because Judaism is the source of all the other religions."

Yael

"I like loud music and books about adventure and mystery. When I grow up, I want to be an airline hostess. My favorite holiday is Rosh Hashanah. My family eats sweet things, we go on a trip together, and we're very happy. I'm glad to be Jewish, one of the chosen people. I wish all of you American kids would come to visit. We'll take good care of you."

Tali

"English is my favorite subject because it's interesting to be able to speak another language. I'm good at sports, so I like gym, too. I read, listen to music, and visit my friends after school. I'm proud that we developed Israel and made it such a modern country. But I worry because some people leave Israel and don't come back."

Gai

"My favorite school subject is math because I love to think. When I finish school, I want to become a doctor of children. I like to play basketball, and I enjoy Michael Jackson and the TV program 'Fame.' "

Shian

"I love nature, and I like to go hiking with friends. After school I do jazz dancing and listen to rock music. 'Little House on the Prairie' is my favorite TV program. I hope to be a teacher when I finish school."

Hili

"I like writing [language arts] in school, but I like school vacations even more. At home I play guitar and listen to the songs of Paul Young. Sukkoth is my favorite holiday. We eat in our *sukkah* for seven days."

Itai

"Mathematics, biology, and English are the most interesting subjects for me. After school I collect stamps or play volleyball. Maybe I'll be a doctor or teacher when I grow up. My favorite holiday is Lag b'Omer. We make a big bonfire and sit around it and sing and talk. We shoot with bows and arrows, too."

Rinat

"I might be a nurse or a fashion designer when I grow up. In school I enjoy English and grammar. After school I listen to Paul Young music, do homework, and go out to take a sunbath. Or I watch TV. 'Dallas,' 'Fame,' and 'Little House on the Prairie' are my favorites. I love Israel. It's a clean, beautiful country. But we have a lot of enemies who attack us."

Miriam

"I wish all American kids would come to Israel to taste our food and see our beautiful country. I will like to talk to them because English is my best school subject. My hobby is jazz. When I grow up, I hope I'll be a hairdresser."

Zvi

"I like to study history in school because I like to learn about the world. My hobbies are watching TV and doing gardening for pay. I don't know what work I'll do when I grow up, but I want to earn a lot of money. Passover is my favorite holiday. It reminds me that I come from a great people with a long history. I'm proud of Israel and its strong army. But it bothers me that some Jews are not religious."

Matti

"Here in Israel we live like a family even though we have troubles. It's a beautiful country. We didn't get it as a present. We had to fight for it. I like holidays like Ḥanukkah and Purim. My mother makes doughnuts and latkes for Ḥanukkah, and the little kids play with dreidels. Pop music is my favorite, and sad books, and TV programs like 'Fame' and 'Dallas.' "

Eran

"I like sports most of all. Computers and history are interesting, too. Sukkoth is my favorite holiday, when the whole family sits in our *sukkah* and eats all the fruits of Israel. I wish there would be peace. Then American kids would come to live in Israel, and we would build the country together."

WHAT SHOULD I DO?

These letters to Moshe's advice column in a children's magazine give us a clue to the things that worry Israeli kids.

Dear Moshe,

When my boyfriend and I are together, we don't have anything to talk about. This makes us both very uncomfortable. What can I do?

Dear Moshe,

I sit next to a popular boy at school. The teacher likes him, and he gets good marks. But he cheats and copies from my paper. If I tell the teacher, I'm afraid she won't believe me.

Dear Moshe,

There's a new immigrant girl in our class. She is always alone. Some of the kids tease her because of her accent. How can I help her?

Dear Moshe,

My mother says J.R. is a bad role model, and she won't let me watch "Dallas." But everyone in my class watches, and I feel like a dummy.

Dear Moshe,

I'm on a special program in a kibbutz. We have to wash our own floor, and I don't know how. I asked the girls to help me. But it's a religious kibbutz, and the girls aren't allowed into a boy's room. What should I do?

SOME FACTS

Education

The Israeli public school system is really many different school systems. Each religious group has its own schools, so that Muslim, Christian, and Jewish children go to separate schools. Not only that, but the system of public schools for Israeli Jews is divided into two groups—a general system and a religious system.

Sixty-five percent of Israeli-Jewish kids go to general schools, where they study math, language, gym, biology, and other subjects. History, Bible, and Jewish holidays and values are also taught, but

The writers of the Talmud did a lot of thinking about education. Here's one of their ideas. Do you agree with it?

Do not accept pupils who are less than six years old. But from that age on you can accept them and stuff them with learning the way you would burden an ox.

they are studied as culture rather than as religion. Boys and girls attend the same classes.

Twenty-eight percent of Israeli-Jewish kids go to religious schools. They study all school subjects, but stress is put on the religious teachings of the Bible and on a religious view of history. Torah study becomes a guide to daily life rather than a study of literature or history. In some state religious schools boys and girls are in separate classes.

Six percent of Israeli-Jewish kids attend private religious schools.

All subjects are taught in Hebrew in the public schools for Jewish children. English and Arabic are taught as second and third languages in many schools. School usually starts at 8:00 A.M. and ends at 12:00 noon, 1:00 P.M., or 2:00 P.M. Friday is a short school day, and there is no school on Shabbat, the Jewish day of rest. Passover and Ḥanukkah are week-long holidays from school.

Israeli-Arab kids are taught in Arabic. They begin to study Hebrew in third grade and English a little later. Their days off are Friday or Sunday. Boys and girls in most Arab towns attend school

School "work" can mean hikes and bus trips. This junior high class just visited the Kotel in Jerusalem.

together. But many Bedouin Arabs in the south still feel that girls do not need an education. Some Bedouin girls leave school early to help at home.

Another important kind of school is at the Merkaz Klita (immigrants' center). New Israelis live in these centers. The grownups go to school to learn Hebrew in the morning and study all afternoon. The children go to local schools. Sometimes they learn faster than their parents and help their parents do homework.

What do kids do after school? First, they eat. Lunch at 2:00 P.M. is the biggest meal of the day. Then they may do homework, watch TV, play soccer, or go to an afterschool club or youth group. You know all about homework, so I won't describe it. But here's some information about TV, sports, and youth clubs.

Television

You'd feel right at home in front of an Israeli TV set. Many of the programs are old American shows. There are "Fame," "Benson," "Dallas," Smurf cartoons, and others. One program looks a little like . . . sounds a little like . . . and the name, "Reḥov Sum-Sum," is a little like . . . "Sesame Street"! That's because it *is* "Sesame Street." But how it has changed in its move to Israel! Instead of Big Bird, there's a prickly, jumpy, big-hearted porcupine called Kippy. Ernie and Bert have become Arik and Benz. And the Cookie Monster is Oogie because the Hebrew word for cookie is *oogiyah*! The people who live on Reḥov Sum-Sum are Jews and Arabs and new and old Israelis, arguing and playing (mostly in Hebrew).

Israeli TV has no commercials. That makes for two problems. First, there is no time to rush to the kitchen for a snack. And, second, all American programs are too short for their time slot. But the Israelis fill in with wonderful short subjects. There are many very good Israeli-made programs that are entertaining and educational. An Arabic-language program that features sports, news, health, and farming is seen in the neighboring countries as well as in Israel. Viewers in hostile Arab countries often have questions they want answered. But they are afraid to write directly to Israel. They send their questions to Arabs in Israel, who send these questions to the TV station. Israeli viewers enjoy foreign programs, too. When they get tired of the programs on their single channel, they turn the dial and watch programs from Jordan and Lebanon.

Sports

Soccer and basketball are the most popular games in Israel. Kids play in playgrounds and empty lots. There are also young people's leagues and professional teams in the major cities. Fans get very excited at games. They shout, boo, stamp their feet, and devour tons of popcorn and ice cream. One team was penalized and not allowed to have home games for two months because its fans threw food at the opposing team.

Tennis is an up and coming sport because Israel is warm, sunny, and gets little rain. There are tennis stadiums or courts in most cities. And a few Israelis like Shlomo Glickstein and Amos Mansdorf are competing in international tournaments. Disabled Israelis play a championship game of wheelchair tennis. The rules are the same as for regular tennis except that the ball is allowed to bounce twice. And Israel's star team of handicapped volleyball players, all war veterans, won their third world title in 1983.

Maybe a new Wimbledon champion is being coached on the Karmiel tennis court.

Every few years athletes from all over the world come to compete in the Hapoel games, which are open to everybody, and the Maccabiya, which is open to Jewish athletes. Then the Israelis meet the top people in every sport from archery to weightlifting.

Youth Clubs

Everybody in Israel has an opinion about almost everything. That's true of kids in youth clubs, too. Most clubs are part of an adult organization with strong ideas about how to run the country and the government. Some are religious, some are socialist, some do scouting, some do military drills. When they aren't busy arguing, the members like to hike and camp out all across their beautiful little land. They also help at hospitals or tutor new immigrants. And some work on farms and prepare to start new kibbutzim. Boys and girls join youth clubs to have fun, but they feel a responsibility to work for their country, too.

Kids in Israel know about war. They wake up to the boom of jet planes breaking the sound barrier. They wave good-by to fathers, sisters, and brothers going off to army or reserve training. When they ride a bus, they look around carefully for suspicious packages that might be bombs. And if they live near Israel's northern border, they've had a lot of practice at sleeping in bomb shelters.

Yoash and Miki, two nursery school children from Kibbutz Shuval, had these thoughts after the Six Day War:

Yoash:

I suggest that we tell our enemies that it's better to live in peace, so they won't take our land. We need it, too—not only they—and we'll send them a flower.

Miki:

We'll tell them not to make war because our soldiers are stronger, and if they kill many fathers, then there will be lots of orphans who won't have daddies. You can't buy a daddy. If he dies, it's all over. Some Egyptian boy won't have a father, and he'll be sad all the time.

*A quarrel is like an itch: the more you
scratch, the more it itches.*
　　　　　　　—*Yiddish saying*

51

Kids in Israel

The boy and girl scouts (tzofim) of Israel are not part of an adult group. Their members are Jewish, Muslim, Druse, and Christian. You may meet Israeli scouts someday because groups of scouts come to spend summers at Young Judaea's Camp Tel Yehuda in New York and at American scout camps and other camps all over the United States.

Many high-school-aged boys and girls join Gadna. It's a youth corps of the Israeli Army. They go hiking across the country and learn to "rough it"—to cook and sleep out of doors and carry heavy packs. Youngsters from Israel's minorities are also members of Gadna. During the Six Day War (1967) and the Yom Kippur War (1973), Gadna members replaced soldiers to run farms, stores, and the post office.

Young Gadna members do a hike
in quick-step in the Jordan Valley.

Israeli Army

SABRA (BORN IN ISRAEL) GAMES

Goomee

Half of the players form a circle. A long elastic band—a goomee—is stretched between them. The other players jump over the band into the circle. Then they jump halfway out, straddling the band. And then they jump again, straddling the band and facing in the opposite direction. Finally they jump out of the circle. The goomee is raised higher and higher as the game continues until the jumping players have to do a cartwheel over it to get into the circle.

We each have the kinds of children we deserve.
　　　　　—Rabbi Naḥman of Bratzlav

Israeli kids come in all colors, shapes, and sizes—just like American kids. They have varied likes and dislikes. Some love snack foods, rock music, movies, sports, comic books, science projects, dancing, crafts, sleeping, flirting. Some don't—just like American kids.

But in some ways Israeli kids are different from American kids. A larger percentage belong to youth clubs. They seem to be more aware of differences between religious communities in their country. They worry about Israel's place in the world and about her economic problems. At a time when many American high-school kids are thinking about college applications, Israeli high school kids are thinking about which branch of the army they would like to join. Military service comes right after high school for Israelis. College comes later.

Take your own survey of how you and your classmates feel about things like school, sports, war, and peace. Compare the answers with the comments from Kfar Saba and Karmiel at the beginning of this chapter. Are you different or alike or both?

HOW ARE YOU DIFFERENT? HOW ARE YOU ALIKE?

ADRAS, Israeli tic-tac-toe

Construction workers play Adras on the ground while they wait for the rain to stop. Kids play it in the schoolyard. Here's how—

There are two players; each has three stones. The players draw a diagram like the one below. They take turns placing their stones on the intersections. One stone is used for each move. The winner is the first player to get three stones in a line at intersections in any direction.

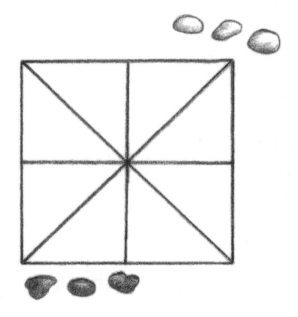

Judaeans were stubborn, independent, quarrelsome people. They disagreed with each other all the time, and they even disagreed with their rulers—the mighty Romans. There were only a few things that all Judaeans, or Jews, agreed on. They all loved their sunny, hilly homeland—the land of Israel. And they loved God, His Bible, and His Temple on Mt. Moriah in Jerusalem.

When the Romans began to interfere in Temple affairs about 1,900 years ago, the Jews rebelled. They began a brave, hopeless war against the huge Roman Empire. Finally they were beaten, the Temple was destroyed, and they were forced to leave their land.

It was very sad, but it wasn't unusual. The Romans had driven many people from their homes. Those others found new homes, forgot the old ones, and settled down. But the stubborn Jews could not forget. Every hundred years or so some of them would come back to the land of Israel. They came from Spain, Yemen, Poland, Egypt—from all over the world.

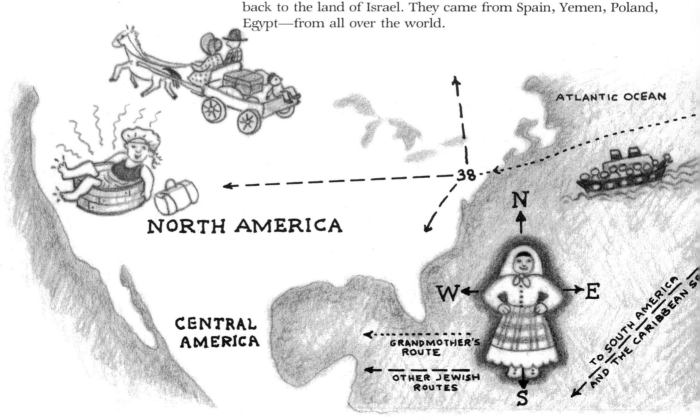

ATLANTIC OCEAN

—38—

N

NORTH AMERICA

W ← → E

CENTRAL AMERICA

GRANDMOTHER'S ROUTE

OTHER JEWISH ROUTES

S

TO SOUTH AMERICA AND THE CARIBBEAN S

trip

About one hundred years ago many more began to return. These Jews were determined to end their people's wandering. They would turn the centuries' long trip into a round trip—*from* Judaea in the land of Israel and *back* again to the land of Israel.

This 2,000 year-long round trip sounds far away and long ago. But it isn't. It's only thirty-nine grandmothers away from each of you. You can trace the trip that your family took from Judaea in the land of Israel in the first century C.E. to the United States in the 1980s. Start at the very beginning with Grandma number 1, and read your way up to your own grandmother, number 39. The first 38 grandmothers are make-believe, but the events that are described are all true. To travel along with them, follow the dotted line on the map.

B.C.E. (before the common era) corresponds to the Christian B.C.

C.E. (common era) corresponds to the Christian A.D.

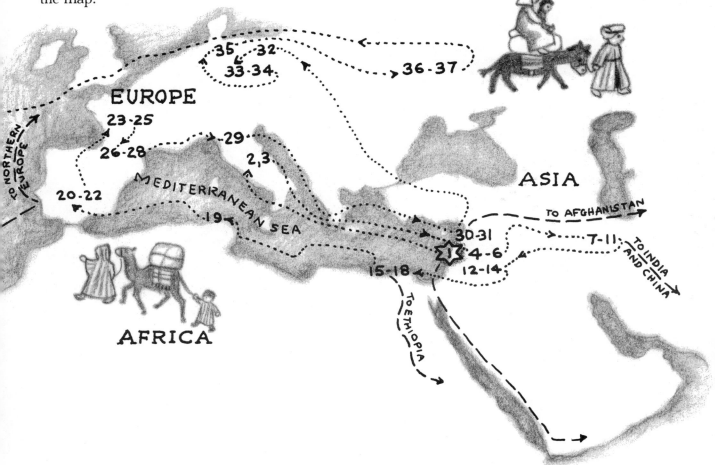

THIRTY-NINE GRAND-MOTHERS AGO YOUR FAMILY WAS ISRAELI!

80 C.E.

Grandma number 1 and Grandpa grew olives in Judaea in a village near Jerusalem. They had hidden in a cave ten years before, when Roman soldiers marched past to capture Jerusalem and destroy Jewish independence and the Holy Temple. Grandma's brothers fought in vain to save the Temple. Then they escaped to Masada to make a last stand against the Romans. Her brothers died there.

130

Grandma number 2 was captured when Bar Kokhba led the Jews in a brave but hopeless revolt against Roman rule. She was taken to Rome as a slave. Many Jews lived in Rome. They bought her and set her free. Grandma's cousins fled south to Yemen.

180

Grandma number 3 was a pretty girl who played the flute and danced at Roman banquets. She married a potter, settled down in the Jewish quarter of Rome, raised a family, made mugs and jugs, and got fat.

230

Grandma number 4, Grandpa, and their seven children yearned to go home. They sold their possessions and sailed back to the land of Israel. Grandpa was a scribe who helped to write down the Mishnah, a commentary on the Bible. Grandma and the kids raised goats and sold goat cheese in the marketplace.

280
330

Grandma number 5 and Grandma number 6 lived in Tiberias in northern Israel. They worked at the bathhouse of the hot springs where people came to cure their aches and pains. Both Grandpas were fishermen on the Sea of Galilee.

380

Grandma number 7 and Grandpa hurriedly packed their pots and children on three donkeys and fled to their cousins in Babylonia after the Romans put down a Jewish rebellion in Tiberias. In the following years Roman and Christian persecution drove most of Grandma's relatives and other Jews out of Palestine.

430

Grandma number 8 grew figs, dates, and grapes in a fertile little field in Babylonia. She was always sending packages of goodies to her son, a teacher at the famous Torah academy in Sura. He and other scholars wrote letters of advice on Torah to Jews all over the world. Babylonia had replaced Judaea as the center of Jewish life.

480

Grandma number 9 studied Torah with her father in Babylonia. Later she became Grandpa's adviser while he and his fellow scholars wrote down the Babylonian Talmud, a book of laws and lore based on the Torah.

530

Grandma number 10 had four housemaids and wore silk robes and pearls in her hair because Grandpa was an official in the court of the exilarch, the ruler of Babylonia's Jews. But she lost her wealth when the exilarch led the Jews in a struggle for religious freedom against the country's ruler. The rebels, including Grandpa, were crucified. Two of Grandma's cousins escaped on a merchant ship bound for India.

580

Grandma number 11 sold silk and damask cloth in the marketplace of Sura. Grandpa traveled from country to country, buying and selling cloth and also carrying messages from the gaon, the chief rabbi of Sura, to the Jews along his route. Jews were now living in all the countries around the Mediterranean Sea.

630

Grandma number 12, Grandpa, and their six children joined a camel caravan and happily set out for Jerusalem after soldiers of the new religion of Islam captured the city from the Christians. The Christian rulers had not allowed Jews to live in Jerusalem, but the Moslems allowed them to return.

680
730

Grandma number 13 and Grandma number 14 made delicate gold and silver jewelry and sold it in the Jerusalem market. Grandpa number 14 sailed to Egypt, Italy, and Spain, selling jewelry and precious stones.

830
880
930

Grandma number 16, Grandma number 17, and Grandma number 18 lived in Alexandria and were pious, proper women, except for Grandma number 18, who loved to belly-dance—but only in front of her sisters and girlfriends. Together they had thirty-three children and 201 grandchildren, made delicious honey pastry, and wove wool rugs.

1030

Grandma number 20 loved to sing and tell stories. She married a poet, and they crossed the sea to Cordova, Spain. Grandpa wandered about writing Hebrew and Arabic poetry and reciting for wealthy families. At that time Jewish writers, astronomers, and other scholars were welcomed in Muslim Spain. Grandma and the children wove silk tapestries for a living.

780

Grandma number 15 got a divorce from Grandpa when he became a Karaite, a Jew who refused to follow the teachings of the Talmud. The Jewish community was torn between Karaite Jews and Jews who accepted the Talmud in those years. Grandma took the children and moved to Alexandria, Egypt, where her brothers lived.

980

Grandma number 19 fell in love with a perfume salesman. They ran off to Kairouan (Tunisia), where they mixed and bottled fine perfume and had five sweet-smelling children.

1080

Grandma number 21 employed twelve weavers in her tapestry shop. Grandpa played chess with the prince of Cordova and translated writings from Greek to Arabic for the prince's library. When the Crusaders recaptured Jerusalem from the Muslims and massacred the Jews of Jerusalem, Grandma welcomed her Jerusalem cousins who had escaped the massacre. They went to work in her tapestry shop.

1130

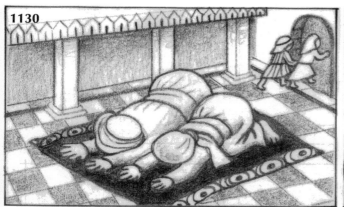

Grandma number 22 and Grandpa had to choose between becoming Muslims or being beheaded when a new, fierce Muslim ruler came to power. They converted to Islam, but their sons and daughters remained Jews and escaped to France.

1230

Grandma number 24 delivered babies and helped Grandpa tend a small vineyard. After each harvest Grandpa went to study Torah with his rabbi in northern France. Grandma collected herbs, made potions, and kept busy delivering babies.

1330

Grandma number 26 was a sturdy, broad-shouldered lady who took care of the *mikvah* (ritual bath) of her town in Spain. She wore her Jew's badge so proudly that the neighborhood children didn't dare tease her. Jews were forced to wear special hats or badges in most towns of Europe by this time.

1180

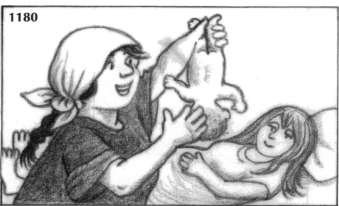

Grandma number 23 was a hard-working midwife who delivered 1,372 babies and several calves in her French village. She taught herself to read and write and once wrote for advice to Maimonides, the great Jewish physician and rabbi in Egypt.

1280

Grandma number 25 was accused of killing a Christian child at Passover—a blood libel. She and Grandpa and twenty other Jews were burned to death in the central square of their French town. Their children were taken by the Church and raised as Christians. But Grandma's sister escaped to Spain with the youngest child.

1380

Grandma number 27 and Grandpa were jugglers who traveled from town to town in a donkey cart and performed at weddings and banquets. Grandpa finally got back trouble and the donkey went lame, so they settled down and opened a small inn in central Spain.

1430

Grandma number 28, Grandpa, and their children had to hide under the straw in the stable each time anti-Jewish rioters looted their inn. Spain had become a dangerous place for Jews, they decided, and they trudged to the nearest port to take passage to Italy.

1530

Grandma number 30 and Grandpa were certain that the Messiah would soon come because so many terrible things were happening—like the expulsion of the Jews from Spain and Portugal. They packed their feather quilt and Shabbat candlesticks and sailed to the land of Israel. They settled in Zefat, where Grandpa studied Kabbalah, a Jewish holy book, and Grandma wove prayer shawls and raised chickens.

1630

Grandma number 32 lived in a small Polish town in a two-story house with a balcony. She had diamond earrings and a fur coat because Grandpa was a rich timber merchant and a tax collector for the Polish lord. Grandma also loved to cook. Two lucky students from the town's yeshiva ate Shabbat dinner at her home each week.

1480

Grandma number 29 gave dancing lessons to little Italian princes and princesses until she married Grandpa. He was a Spanish Jew who was forced to convert to Christianity. But he became a Jew again when he escaped to Italy. He and Grandma opened the first print shop in town and printed Hebrew books.

1580

Grandma number 31 became a widow when Grandpa disappeared in the wilds of Afghanistan. He had been a traveling fund raiser, collecting money for the pious scholars of Zefat from widespread communities of Jews in Europe and Asia. Grandma was very proud of her oldest son, a Torah sage. But he was invited to head a yeshiva in Poland, which was even farther away than Afghanistan. She never saw him again.

1600

Grandma number 33 lost her family in a pogrom, a violent riot against Jews in Poland. She and other survivors fled to the Jewish ghetto in Prague, Czechoslovakia. The Jewish orphan society married her to Grandpa, who was also an orphan. Grandma became a seamstress and had five children. Grandpa was a junk dealer.

1730

Grandma number 34 embroidered lions and crowns on satin Torah mantles for the synagogues of Prague. Grandpa and his brothers were money lenders. When the Jews were banished from Prague, Grandma sewed their gold into the lining of their coats. Then they walked to Berlin, Germany, to start over again.

1780

Grandma number 35 wore a wig with curls, played the harpsichord, and rode a horse sidesaddle. Grandpa had a wool-making factory in Berlin. Two of their children converted to Christianity, a third took passage to the brand-new United States, and their youngest married a pale Russian rabbinical student and went to Russia.

1830

Grandma number 36 had 12 children, 4 goats, and 20 chickens. She baked the best strudel in her small Russian town. Grandpa was a rabbi. He studied Talmud and waited eagerly for the Messiah to come and take the Jewish people back to the land of Israel.

1880

Grandma number 37 started the first school for girls in her town. One of her brothers went to Palestine and became a farmer. Another brother went to America and became a furrier. And her sister went to jail because she was a revolutionary who tried to overthrow the Russian government.

1930

Grandma number 38 came to the United States from Russia when she was a young girl. More than 2 million other Jews left the pogroms and poverty of eastern Europe to come to the United States in the early 1900s. Grandma sent money to help her cousins in Europe. But the cousins were all lost in the Nazi Holocaust during World War II.

1980

Grandma number 39 is *your grandma!* Fill in the spaces below to complete the round trip from Grandma number 1 in Judaea to your grandma—Grandma number 39.

She was born in _____ .

She works as a _____ .

She likes to _____ .

She and Grandpa have _____ children and _____ grandchildren.

America's funny man, Mark Twain, author of Tom Sawyer, found nothing funny about Palestine one hundred years ago. In Innocents Abroad he wrote, "Of all lands there are for dismal scenery I think Palestine must be the prince. The hills are barren ... the valleys are unsightly deserts. It is a hopeless, dreary, heartbroken land."

THE STORY OF MODERN ZIONISM: or, YOU THINK IT'S EASY TO BUILD A HOMELAND?

What would you do if everybody picked on you, if you were treated like an outsider in your own town or country? What if your neighbors sneered at your religion? And what if you were always afraid that they'd gang up on you and rob or beat or even kill you?

That's how it was for the Jews of Russia in the late 1800s. Many of them finally got angry enough to change things. Some joined secret revolutionary groups and fought to make Russia a democratic country. Many left Russia to find new homes in western Europe or the United States. But a few young men and women decided to settle in the ancient land of Israel, called Palestine. They felt that they would always be strangers in other lands. Only the land of Israel, which God had promised to the Jews, could become a true homeland. The young people formed a group called BILU (from the Hebrew initials of "House of Jacob, come, let's go"). In 1882 the first members arrived in Palestine, bought land, and built little villages.

Central Zionist Archives

Twelve young men and women came to the steamy Jordan Valley in 1909 to build Degania—the first kibbutz. It was hot, mosquitoes whined around them, the Jordan overflowed into their land, and Arabs attacked them in the fields. But the settlers held out. "We're strong and we're a family," they said. "We're Jewish peasants building a homeland for our people."

Theodor Herzl, a Jewish journalist from Vienna, thought there must be a quicker, easier way to create a homeland than by buying land and planting fields. He called a meeting of Jews from all over the world to plan the establishment of a whole new country, a Jewish state in Palestine. He warned the delegates to dress formally because at this meeting they would "lay the foundation stone of the house that will shelter the Jewish nation."

People came from tiny villages and from great cities like New York, Warsaw, and Berlin to that first Zionist conference in Switzerland in 1897. They bubbled with excitement and hope. Imagine! They would plan a Jewish homeland. There would be Jewish soldiers, farmers, judges—even a Jewish prime minister! In that land Jews would never be outsiders. They planned, sang, cried with joy, and threw their top hats and white gloves in the air.

But the high hopes and the dress-up clothing could not make Herzl's plan work quickly. The Turks, who ruled Palestine, were not interested in a Jewish state. For months and years Herzl argued and bargained with the Turkish sultan and European kings and politicians. Meanwhile, impatient young Jews calling themselves ḥalutzim ("pioneers") packed their knapsacks and crossed the sea to Palestine.

One young BILU member had loud arguments with his family because he wanted to go to Palestine. But deep inside he was a little worried. Here's what he wrote in his diary in 1882 before leaving: "To give up my education and take up the plow and spade in a wild country . . . to exchange all this [profession and school] for hard physical labor? A fierce struggle went on within me—it was like a fever. But now I am at peace. I know what I want."

The Zionists abroad helped the ḥalutzim by establishing a national bank and a Jewish national fund to buy land in Palestine. And after Herzl's death they continued his work of urging governments to support the plan for a Jewish homeland. It wasn't easy.

In 1917 the Zionists' luck started to change. The British wrote the Balfour Declaration, which favored a Jewish homeland in Palestine. In 1920, after Turkey had been defeated in the First World War, the League of Nations (an early version of the United Nations) agreed that the lands of the Turkish Empire should become national states. That's when Arab governments were established in Syria, Lebanon, Iraq, and Transjordan. Egypt and Saudi Arabia already had Arab governments. And all those states began to prepare for independence. The Jews of Palestine also began to prepare for independence under a British mandate.

Even then it wasn't easy. As the Jewish immigrants arrived and the country grew, with new cities, factories, and farms, more Arabs began to come into Palestine to find work. There were arguments and fights between Jews and Arabs about whose land it was. In 1929 Arabs attacked Jews all over the country. The ancient Jewish community of Hebron, burial place of the patriarchs Abraham, Isaac, and Jacob, was almost wiped out. But this time the Jews did not feel like helpless, frightened outsiders. They knew they belonged in the land of Israel, and nobody could scare them into leaving. The settlers buried their dead, organized self-defense groups, and kept planting their fields and building their towns. And back in Europe more Jewish boys and girls studied Hebrew and farming and prepared to come to Palestine as ḥalutzim.

These boys and girls danced a wild, happy hora on the Haifa dock in 1935. They had just escaped from Nazi Germany with the help of Youth Aliya, a program of the World Zionist Organization. For the next few years they would live and be educated in kibbutzim and youth villages.

Central Zionist Archives

Illegal immigrants jumped from their ship into the surf off the coast of Palestine in 1939. They were pulled ashore and hidden by waiting Palestinian Jews before the British patrols could reach them.

Central Zionist Archives

There were more attacks on Palestinian Jews in the 1930s. By then German Jews were coming to Palestine to escape Nazi persecution. The violence upset the British. They had hoped that their mandate over Palestine would give them a cosy stronghold in the Middle East. Instead they were becoming referees in a bloody battle. They decided to stop the battle by locking out most new Jewish immigrants. But the Jews kept coming, legally—with British immigration certificates—and illegally—by secret routes across borders. Not only Zionists came, but also terrified European Jews escaping from the Nazis. Nazi Germany had robbed the German Jews and thrown them into concentration camps. Now, in the late 1930s, it threatened to take over the rest of Europe.

World War II broke out in 1939. The seas crawled with submarines and warships. A few small boats jammed with refugees still made their way from Europe to Palestine. But most of the Jews of Europe were trapped, prisoners of the invading Nazi army and its murdering allies. The Jews of Palestine kept up their secret network of escape routes and sent parachutists to help Jewish resistance against the Nazis. But the help was too little, the enemy too powerful.

During the next six years the Nazis raged across Europe. They robbed, enslaved, and murdered 6 million Jews. Two of every three European Jews were lost in those terrible years.

In May 1945 the Nazis were finally beaten. The Jews who were left alive gathered in refugee camps. But the smells of Nazi death camps and the ashes of their burned homes choked the small numbers of survivors. "Europe is a graveyard. Let us go to Palestine!" they cried. And the Jews of Palestine demanded, "Let our people come home. We will help them build new lives." The British answered with a grim, gray blockade of warships that sealed the ports of Palestine.

British soldiers force an immigrant out of the hold of an illegal ship. She, and thousands of other survivors of the Holocaust, tried desperately to reach Palestine after World War II. The British caught them and held them in prison camps on Cyprus or carried them back to Europe.

Central Zionist Archives

"We shall *win because we must win.*
Ein breira *[We have no choice]."*
—an Israeli officer during the war

67

The two-thousand-year round trip

A strange thing began to happen in the ship business. People with fists full of money appeared on the docks in Europe and the United States and bought small ships. The ships were quickly outfitted and sailed to Italian, French, and other Mediterranean ports. There they secretly picked up European Jews. Then they were off again, creeping past the British blockade. On the beaches of Palestine, people waited silently. When the ships appeared they rushed into the water and passed the tired refugees from hand to hand until they reached the shore. Then buses and trucks sped them to hiding places.

But some boats did not get through. The British stopped them and forced their defiant passengers back into prison camps. Furiously, the Jews of Palestine demanded that the refugees be freed and brought to Palestine. Just as furiously the Arabs demanded that Jewish immigration end and that Palestine become an Arab state. There was shooting from the rooftops and the alleys. Bombs exploded in buses and buildings. The British were caught in the middle again. They couldn't keep peace, and they wouldn't carry out their mandate to help establish a Jewish homeland. Finally they gave up. In early 1947 they handed the problem of Palestine to the United Nations.

Like wise King Solomon, the United Nations experts found an easy solution: if two peoples want one land, cut the land in two and give each a half. But the problem could not be solved that easily.

The United Nations solution was all right with the Jews. A mini-homeland was better than none. But it wasn't all right with the Arabs of Palestine. And it wasn't all right with the neighboring Arab states. They wanted all of Palestine to be Arab.

There was no more to talk about. Many Palestinian Arabs began to pack up and leave the country as both sides prepared for war. It was a harder task for the Jews than for the Arabs. The British continued their tight sea blockade, which prevented weapons and immigrants from reaching Palestine. But they broke their own blockade by selling weapons to the Arab states around Palestine and ignoring the Arab soldiers and supplies which came into Palestine across the land borders. The Hagana, the Jewish defence force, had to produce homemade weapons and fight to keep the roads open while evading British patrols.

"We have surrounded the Jews with a ring of steel and will not rest until the last Israelite has been driven into the sea." —an Egyptian officer *during Israel's War for Independence*

The big question in May 1948 was what to call the new Jewish state— Judaea, Zion, or Israel.

"Who cares?" said some. "Let it just live and be well."

But others cared a lot. "Judaea was very important in Jewish history," they said, "but it was only a small part of the land of Israel. The name Zion may describe the land of Israel, but it's also the name of a mountain in Jerusalem. But Israel—that's something else. Israel always meant the Jewish people and their land. Jacob, the forefather of the Jews, was called Israel, meaning 'one who struggles with God.' "

That settled the matter. The struggling newborn country was named after its struggling forefather.

On May 14, 1948, the British high commissioner finally left Jerusalem. That afternoon the Jewish leaders of Palestine declared the establishment of the State of Israel. It was the first Jewish state in 1,900 years! People filled the streets of Israel dancing horas, waving flags, marching and kissing and singing. But as they celebrated, they waited and listened for the thunder of enemy guns. It was a short wait. Eight hours later the armies of Egypt, Transjordan, Syria, Iraq, and Lebanon attacked across Israel's borders.

The Haganah, renamed Zahal—the Israel Defense Forces—was now a true national army. But it faced the old desperate problem— how to fight a war without fighter planes, tanks, or artillery. It wasn't easy! The Israelis mounted machine guns on jeeps, welded metal plates onto taxicabs and buses to make tanks, and made big guns out of contraptions of pipes and wires. Pilots dropped hand grenades from Piper Cub training planes to frighten the enemy. And even though they were outnumbered, the boys and girls of Zahal dug in and seldom retreated. In such a small country, if they retreated, they would end up in the sea. Israelis fought with new hope as foreign volunteers and supplies began to arrive at the opened ports.

By the time the shooting ended in March 1949, 4,000 Jewish soldiers and 2,000 civilians had been killed in the battle to save the State of Israel. Because of their courage, the new state was not only alive, it was also strong, united, and larger than it had expected to be.

Israel's population doubled and tripled over the next few years as Jews poured into the old-new homeland from all over the world. The new people didn't find a land of milk and honey. They found tin shacks, patched tents, and muddy development towns. They struggled to learn Hebrew and new skills. And while they built their lives, the wars with the neighboring Arab states continued.

In 1956 Israel lashed back against attacks on her southern settlements by terrorists from Egypt. Zahal made a lightning-fast charge through Egypt's Sinai desert to the Suez Canal. When Zahal withdrew, United Nations forces were sent to Sinai to guard the Egyptian-Israeli border.

ZIONISM IS AN OLD, OLD STORY

At the end of the Passover Seder Jewish families lean back and sing, "To the next year in Jerusalem." Jews have sung those words at their Seders ever since they were forced to leave the land of Israel. They were always homesick, and they loved to make up stories of miraculous, dangerous ways of going home.

"Under the old-new synagogue of Prague there's a long, dark tunnel," said the Czech Jews, "and it leads directly to Jerusalem."

Algerian Jews told of an ancient cave that reached under the sea, all the way to the Holy Land. But no living person remembered where the cave opening was.

Polish Jews told a story about two spunky Zionist goats who followed a secret passageway back to Palestine. You can read about them in Chapter 13.

And the Russian Jews said, "A boiling, storming river called the Sambatyon separates us from the Holy Land. It rests only on the Sabbath, but on the Sabbath we Jews are not allowed to travel."

Clever schoolchildren had some ideas about outwitting the Sambatyon. They'd get themselves shot across the stormy river by a giant cannon, or they could tie themselves to the legs of a monster bird.

But the adults shook their heads and said, "No, we must wait until the Messiah leads us home."

In 1967 Egypt stopped Israeli ships from using the Red Sea, ordered the United Nations forces to leave Sinai, and joined Jordan and Syria in preparing to attack. In six days of hard fighting Israel smashed the three enemy armies, captured the Syrian Golan Heights, the Gaza Strip, the Egyptian Sinai Peninsula, and the West Bank, which Jordan had occupied in 1948.

Military victory did not lead to peace. "Peace is surrender!" proclaimed Egyptian President Nasser. The Arab countries and Israel hurried to buy new guns, planes, and tanks.

On Yom Kippur in 1973 Israel's enemies launched a surprise attack that nearly cut the country in half. For nineteen days artillery thundered and jets screamed overhead until the Arab armies were driven back to the 1967 borders. It was a sad victory with many dead on both sides. Again, the shooting had stopped, but there was no peace.

"It's not easy," said the Israelis. "We must stay strong and have faith. Peace will come . . . eventually." And they went ahead with the business of living. They built factories and exported polished diamonds, pretty little bathing suits, chocolate, electronic gadgets, and weapons. They built a giant water carrier to bring water from the north to the farms and cities of the dry Negev in the south. And they caught Israel's bright sun in solar collectors to heat water and make energy.

At last in 1977 there was a hopeful first step to peace. President Sadat of Egypt took the brave step when he came to Jerusalem to begin talks. Two years later, at Camp David in Maryland, Egypt and Israel finally signed a peace treaty. Israel gave back the huge Sinai desert, and Israelis jumped into buses and rode south through the Sinai to meet their Egyptian neighbors and to climb the pyramids. But shooting continued across the northern border. In 1982 and 1983 Israeli tanks rolled into Lebanon to stop the border attacks.

"We will go home one day," Jews repeated to each other hopefully during their long centuries of wandering. The following words from the Bible, written by the prophet Amos, gave them courage:

I will restore My people Israel.
They shall rebuild ruined cities and inhabit them;
They shall plant vineyards and drink their wine;
They shall till gardens and eat their fruits.
And I will plant them upon their soil, Nevermore to be uprooted
From the soil I have given them

—said the Lord your God.
—Amos 9:14

Building the Jewish homeland is not easy. The fighting goes on. Development goes on, too. High-tech factories are using robots and computers to turn out complicated products. Kids are learning their *alef-bet* on "Rehov Sum-Sum," the "Sesame Street" of Israeli TV. Engineers are designing a canal that will bring water from the Mediterranean to the Dead Sea to provide electricity. Jews are coming from all over the world to work on kibbutzim and to study in Israel's universities and religious schools—yeshivot. Israeli Arabs and Jews attend colleges and work together. Israeli Druse serve in the army beside Israeli Jews.

And in Israel's Knesset, where the laws are made, the members—Jews, Christians, and Muslims—yell at each other, debate, and struggle to run this hectic little country. When you sit up in the visitors' gallery you may need earplugs to muffle the shouting. It's not easy. But, then, who ever said it would be easy to build a homeland?

Ancient domes and towers and modern skyscrapers share the Jerusalem skyline. And a lively, varied mixture of Ḥasidim, monks, mullahs and ordinary people share the busy streets and marketplaces below.

Teak Silberman

COMING-HOME
PAPER DOLLS

Traffic was always heavy into and out of the land of Israel. There were Philistines, Canaanites, Hebrews, Babylonians, Egyptians, Greeks—and that was only the beginning. After May 1948 Israel saw the heaviest, happiest rush of traffic ever. Israelis called it "*kibbutz galuyot*," gathering-in of the exiles. Jews came home to Israel from almost 100 countries, each wearing his or her national costume.

Help Tali and Elon, the two Israeli kids on this page, try on the costumes of their new fellow Israelis. You can trace these pages or copy them on a copying machine. Color the costumes. Cut out Tali, Elon, the two stands, and the costumes. Glue cardboard to the backs of Tali, Elon, and their stands.

5 Zionism's construction crew

The construction crew that built the Jewish state started work centuries ago. First came the builders who were returning to the land to pray and die on Israel's holy soil. They settled in towns like Jerusalem and Zefat. By the late 1800s other builders began to return or to talk about returning. They had a new idea. "Why should we go to Eretz Yisrael to die? Why not to live?" they asked.

New ideas like these came from Rabbi Tzevi Hirsch Kalischer (1795–1874), who urged Jews to settle on farms in Palestine. He persuaded rich Jews to support the settlers and to found an agricultural school. Leo Pinsker (1821–1891) added a warning—that Jews would flit through the world like ghosts, always rootless, always being attacked, because they were strangers everyplace. He argued that Jews could become real people only by going back to their historic homeland.

People listened. Some of them even packed up and went to Palestine. But Zionism didn't become a national movement until

its greatest architect and public-relations expert got to work. Theodor Herzl (1860–1904) turned the dream of a Jewish homeland into a carefully planned program.

Many builders followed Herzl. Each of them has a story to tell. In this chapter you'll find a few of the stories of the old-timers— the men and women who drew the blueprints and laid the foundations of the modern state.

Some of the builders didn't live long enough to become old-timers. They worked hard, lived dangerously and bravely, and were killed while they were still young. Four of their dramatic, too-short stories are told here.

You can find out more about Zionism's construction crew in books that are listed in Chapter 14. Other Zionist leaders are listed in the index and in the mini-encyclopedia in the last chapter of this book.

THE SIMPLE, OLD MAN

Aaron David Gordon
(1856–1922)

Aaron David Gordon

- *Instead of trying to fight the darkness, men and women should try to increase the light.*

- *We are a people . . . with no roots in the soil. We must return to the soil, to independence, to nature, to a new life of work.*

- *If you don't grasp for much, you don't grasp for anything.*

Aaron David Gordon sang as he chopped up the soil with his touriya (a short hoe) and laughed at his aching muscles. All his life Gordon had worked at a desk in a dusty Russian office, and finally, at age forty-eight, he threw away his stiff collar and dark suit and came to Palestine to be a farmer.

"The old man," his young fellow workers in Palestine called him. They said it with respect because the "old man" was the strongest of them all. When they couldn't get work from the farm owners and had barely enough money to buy bread and eggplant for supper, Gordon would pull them up to dance a hora (circle dance) even though their stomachs were empty. "Ḥevra," he would laugh, "we have the soil and our independence. What more do we need? Let's dance!"

Working and dancing were not enough for Gordon. He had to shout his joy at building a homeland to the whole Jewish world. He would wake up before dawn, tiptoe out into the hall with his kerosene lamp so as not to wake the others, and write down his thoughts about a new way of life, a new religion for the Jewish people. It would be a religion of labor that would pull the Jews out of the crowded cities of Europe and bring them back to nature, to become farmers and workers in Palestine.

Life grew harder and more dangerous for Gordon and his comrades when World War I broke out. The Turks, who ruled Palestine, believed that the Jews were helping their enemies, the British. One day Turkish soldiers raided the area around Deganiah where Gordon lived. They locked all the men into a shed and dragged them out, one by one, to beat and torture them. The frightened settlers huddled together hearing the sounds of blows and screams from the next room. Suddenly gaunt, white-bearded Aaron stood up and began to snap his fingers, sway, and sing this Yiddish song:

Let my enemies torment me,
Let them drain me drop by drop,
There's a happy song inside me
That no pain will ever stop.

During those hard years many Jewish settlers died, and others left Palestine. But Gordon kept writing, urging Jews outside Palestine to come and work the land.

After a day in the fields he would sit outside his little house in Kibbutz Deganiah, and neighbors would visit and talk with him about their hopes and worries. The children of Deganiah came to hear stories and sing with the "old man." A five year old explained that she liked to come because "Grandpa Gordon is just like us, except he has a beard."

MARATHON MAN

Theodor Herzl (1860–1904)

His heart was pounding, and he was gasping for breath. Theodor Herzl was running a marathon race that he couldn't stop. The finish line was always just a step away. The prize was inches from his fingertips. He couldn't stop, couldn't even slow down—until he dropped.

When it all started, Theodor's wife thought he was crazy. He had been a successful writer and a reporter for a large Viennese newspaper. He was a tall, proud, handsome man with a wavy black beard, a man at the top of his world. But deep inside, Theodor Herzl was hurting. He felt constantly "put down" by the Jew-haters around him. He knew that poor Jews suffered even more. In Russia, Jews were beaten and killed. In Germany, they were spat upon and insulted. In France, they were unjustly thrown into jail. Why should this happen? How could it be changed?

Then he had a great idea. It was so simple, so brilliantly clear, that he knew everybody would have to accept it. Since Europe despised and rejected its Jews, he, Herzl, would lead these millions of unwanted Jews out of Europe and back to their own land—the land of Israel.

There were a few problems to be solved. He would need money from rich Jews to help settle people in the new land. He would also need approval from the Turkish rulers of Palestine and from political leaders in Europe. But why should they refuse?

Thrilled and excited, Herzl put down his ideas in a pamphlet called *The Jewish State*. Then he tucked a briefcase full of notes under his arm and began the marathon that was to last for eight years. He crisscrossed Europe, pleading and arguing with dukes and counts, with the king of Italy, the kaiser of Germany, the pope in Rome, the sultan of Turkey, and with the Jewish millionaires Rothschild and Hirsch.

Zionism seeks to obtain for the Jewish people a publicly recognized, legally secured homeland in Palestine.
—The Basel program, 1897

Theodor Herzl

- *If you will it, it is no dream.*
- *Whoever wishes to change men must change the conditions under which men live.*

The Turkish sultan gave him a medal; the king of Italy approved; the kaiser shook his hand warmly and made vague promises. Each time Herzl glowed with hope. With just a little more luck and skill and money he'd have it. He would win the great prize—permission to set up a Jewish colony. But somehow each promise broke like a bubble, leaving his hands empty.

Even while he was racing after kings and sultans, Herzl was also drawing his own people together. In 1897 he called a Zionist congress in Basel, Switzerland, to "lay the foundations of the house that will shelter the Jewish nation." People came from the great cities of western Europe and the tiny towns of Russia. They cried with hope and applauded the majestic, black-bearded leader until their hands ached. One awe-struck delegate said of Herzl, "It was as if the Messiah was facing us!"

At that congress and at the next few congresses, plans were made for a national bank and a national fund to buy land. For the first time in Jewish history a national anthem, "Hatikvah," was sung and a national flag hung overhead. It had two blue stripes, like a prayer shawl, and a six-pointed star.

But Herzl didn't believe his "little people" could establish a state. They needed the help of crowned heads, the royalty of Europe. He continued his marathon race, meeting with the sultan again and with the anti-Semitic ministers of Russia. More polite words but no results.

Slowly Herzl's heart began to fail. The marathon was endless, and the prize was always just out of reach.

Before Herzl died at the age of forty-four he felt his work had been a failure. But he brought his dream of an old-new homeland to the Jewish people. Only forty-four years later, they shaped it into a state despite the kings and the sultans.

The aim of Zionism is "to create for the Jewish people a home in Palestine secured by public law," declared Theodor Herzl at the First Zionist Congress in Basel, Switzerland, in 1897. A home—at last! The delegates cheered, shouted, and cried with joy at his words. One delegate said, "He (Herzl) was like a biblical prophet standing before us."

Central Zionist Archives

It was the nervous springtime of 1948. In only a few weeks the State of Israel would be declared. Paula Ben-Gurion took David's good suit out to be cleaned for the ceremony. Arab armies fidgeted on Palestine's borders. And the Jewish underground army—the Haganah—prepared to defend the new state while it dodged the British troops who were still ruling Palestine.

In Washington some American diplomats were getting more and more worried. It would be terrible if the Jews of Palestine were defeated and perhaps massacred. But if the Jews won their state, there would be problems with the neighboring Arab states. Whatever happened would be terrible. The diplomats could think of only one solution. They would convince the American president Harry Truman and the United Nations to put off the whole matter of statehood for months, years, maybe forever.

When the news leaked out that the plans for a Jewish state might be scrapped, Jewish leaders were horrified. They asked to speak to the president, but Truman refused to see them. It seemed as though all the work and hope and sacrifice spent to build the homeland would be lost at the last moment. Just then the strongest spokesman for the Jewish people stepped in to save the day.

Chaim Weizmann was seventy-four, tall, with a short gray beard, and wearing dark glasses for an eye ailment. Since his boyhood in a small Russian town, he had fought for a Jewish homeland at countless meetings and conferences and interviews. Now he was sick and very tired. But when Eddie Jacobson, President Truman's former business partner, managed to arrange a meeting, Chaim Weizmann came.

The president and the Zionist leader talked for a long time. In the next few weeks they exchanged letters. "The choice for our people, Mr. President, is between statehood and extermination," wrote Weizmann. And Truman became convinced that he should support the new state. On May 14, 1948, the United States was the first country to recognize Israel.

Chaim Weizmann's patient persuasion served his people many times. Thirty years earlier Weizmann was doing scientific research in England and became friendly with British political leaders. When World War I broke out, he found a process for making acetone for munitions out of corn and horse chestnuts. Weizmann spent the war years cooking up his horse-chestnut concoctions and also discussing Zionism with his "high up" friends.

THE GREAT PERSUADER, or HORSE CHESTNUTS AND A HOMELAND

Chaim Weizmann (1874–1952)

President Truman of the United States and President Weizmann of Israel were comparing their jobs one day.

"My job is very tough," said Truman. "There are one hundred eighty million people in the United States, and as president I am responsible to each one of them."

"Mine is tougher," Weizman said. "There are only one million Jews in Israel, but as president of Israel I preside over one million presidents."

Chaim Weizmann

- *To be a Zionist it is not absolutely necessary to be mad, but it helps.*
- *We are perhaps the children of dealers in old clothes, but we are the grandchildren of prophets.*

Many Britons agreed with Weizmann that the Jewish people had a right to a homeland in a small corner of the Middle East. They also felt that they (the British) had a right to keep soldiers in the Middle East after the war. Why not combine the two goals? The British could remain in the Middle East as protectors of Zionism.

In November 1917 the British government wrote the Balfour Declaration, supporting the establishment of a Jewish national home in Palestine. It was the first time any government had officially supported Zionism, and it was largely Weizmann's doing.

All of Chaim Weizmann's work was connected to his two great interests—Zionism and science. Even toward the end of his life he worked overtime at two jobs. He was the first president of the State of Israel and head of the Weizmann Institute of Science, a great research center in Reḥovot, Israel.

RABBI ON MULEBACK

Abraham Isaac Kook (1864–1935)

"Solomon overlaid the house within with pure gold, and he drew chains of gold across before the sanctuary." The small Hebrew letters on the page of Torah danced blurrily before Abraham's eyes. He turned and looked out the synagogue window, high over the rooftops of his small Latvian hometown. Suddenly, as he squinted, he saw the Holy Temple looming right out of the clouds. Broad marble staircases, carved and gilded columns, great courtyards—all shimmering and glowing in the brilliant sunlight of the land of Israel. Abraham's skin prickled with excitement. His heart was so full and happy that he felt he'd burst if he didn't rush out and gulp some cold air.

When he reached the damp courtyard of the synagogue, pale sunlight poked through the clouds and the Temple had disappeared. But it still glowed inside Abraham's head. Someday during his lifetime it might be rebuilt, he thought. And he—Abraham Isaac Kook—might serve in the Holy Temple as a priest!

He shivered, hunched against the chill, and thought more soberly. What if, God forbid, the Temple was not rebuilt soon? Well, then, he'd go to the Holy Land anyhow, Abraham told himself. He knew every corner of the land from his studies and loved it with his whole heart and soul. He could not live his life as a Jew in any other place.

One day in the year 1904 Abraham Isaac Kook, the new rabbi of the town of Jaffa in Palestine, sprang from the harbor boat onto the soil of the Promised Land. An Arab brushed past him pulling a bony cow. "Oy, an Israeli cow!," cried Abraham and threw his arms around her neck. He wanted to hug everybody and everything. He was home at last!

The rabbi's joy was quickly mixed with trouble. To his surprise he found that the Jews in the Holy Land seemed always to be fighting with each other. Hebrew-speaking Jews fought with Yiddish-speaking Jews. European Jews looked down on Jews from Arab lands, and Arab Jews returned the compliment. Elderly, orthodox Jews who had come to Palestine to pray and die were suspicious of young pioneers who never prayed and wanted only to be farmers.

"Atheists in short pants who never lay tephillin and women with uncovered heads who wear bloomers and work in the fields should be thrown out of Palestine," argued Rabbi Kook's fellow orthodox Jews. "They're an insult to the land!"

Rabbi Abraham bought a mule and rode off to see for himself. He met the "nonbelievers" on the kibbutzim and farms and spoke with them about Bible and history. In the cool evenings the rabbi sometimes dropped his dignity and joined in a wild, stamping hora.

His congregants were shocked. "How can you dance with nonbelievers?" they asked. "They should be cast aside."

Rabbi Kook smiled and said, "These nonbelievers have God in their hearts. The commandment to love each other is more important than the commandment to hate those who disobey Jewish law. Besides, we need people of all kinds to help us to build the land."

And to end the argument, at least for a while, Rabbi Kook would give this example: "In the Great Temple in Jerusalem there was a Holy of Holies that only the high priest could enter. And he entered only once a year after purifying himself. But the Temple, the House of God, was built by simple masons and carpenters. Even the Holy of Holies was built by ordinary people, no holier than any of us."

At the end of the First World War, Rabbi Kook became Ashkenazic chief rabbi of Palestine. Now he had a new headache— resolving differences between the Jewish community and the British.

The Talmud gives two kinds of advice about leadership:

- *If there is no man [leader]—you must become the man [leader].*
- *It is better to be a tail among lions than a head among foxes.*

Rabbi Abraham Isaac Kook

- *A people can have no future if it cuts itself off from the roots of its past.*

But his hardest work was to bring his argumentative fellow Jews together. As a deeply religious Jew who was also an enthusiastic Zionist, Abraham Isaac Kook became a bridge between many different groups in the Jewish community. "We can love each other even while we disagree with each other," said the gentle rabbi.

THE BIG TALKER

David Ben-Gurion (1886–1973)

Little David Green had a big head with fierce eyes, a bull-dog chin and a short, skinny body.

"Tch, tch, tch," clucked his aunts and uncles in the small town of Płońsk in Poland, "a big thinker or a big talker he may be, but a big worker—never!" When David was fourteen and began to organize young people in his town to become farmers in Palestine, the aunts and uncles smiled to themselves. He was a great talker, but could he ever become a real pioneer with a pick and shovel and hoe?

David surprised them. He stubbornly forced his body to do anything he thought was important. When he was twenty, he became a farm worker and road builder in Palestine. When thieves attacked their settlements, David and his comrades learned to ride horses and shoot. When their employers paid starvation wages, they organized a political party and a labor union (the Histadrut) to fight for their rights. And during World War I, David and his friend Itzḥak Ben-Zvi came to the United States and recruited members for a Jewish Legion that helped the Allied armies.

David took a Hebrew surname, Ben-Gurion, to tie himself even more closely to the Hebrew homeland. David Ben-Gurion was certainly a big talker. But he was ready to back his words with actions.

In 1948 David's determination helped the Jews of Palestine to take a heroic, dangerous step. The British rulers of the land were leaving on May 14, and the State of Israel was to be declared the next day. But six Arab armies were waiting to attack the new state.

"It will be a bloody massacre. We'll drive the Jews into the sea!" blared the Arab radios.

Countries like the United States that had supported the new state became nervous. "Wait. Let's talk some more," they suggested. "You'll be crushed if you declare a state now."

Jews were worried, too. "It's suicide. We'll lose everything—our farms, our lives," some said.

"We've already waited two thousand years. We can be patient and wait a little longer," said others.

Advice, fears, and warnings hammered at David Ben-Gurion. As secretary of the National Council of the Jews of Palestine, he knew how risky the situation was. The Jews were outnumbered 30 to 1. But he had learned long before that risks must be taken and talk must be backed by action. He and the other members of the council stuck by their decision. On May 14, 1948, the State of Israel was established. As its first prime minister, David Ben-Gurion had to lead the country into a war for independence.

A new frontier opened when Ben-Gurion retired from politics. For years he had told everybody who would listen that Israel must develop the Negev. Now, although he was nearly eighty, he backed his words with action again and moved from the big city to the tiny desert kibbutz of Sdeh-Boker. Visitors who came to see the former prime minister had to follow him on one of his kibbutz jobs, trotting from station to station and measuring the dewfall and temperature.

A big talker *and* a big worker was little David.

David Ben-Gurion

- *Israel has straightened the backs of Jews everywhere.*

- *A homeland is not given or received as a gift . . . nor bought with gold or held by force . . . it is created by the sweat of the brow. The true right to a country springs from work.*

The sand dunes and rolling hills of the Negev cover half of Israel's pre-1967 territory. David Ben-Gurion felt that the future of the country would be built here in the south. After a happy Friday night spent singing and eating with the other members of the Negev kibbutz, Sdeh-Boker, he said, "I regret the forty years I wasted in government offices."

Ehud Ryden

THE MOTHER OF ISRAEL

Henrietta Szold (1860–1945)

Henrietta was the oldest of five daughters, and she wanted so much to be a boy. "Nonsense," said her father, a Baltimore rabbi. "You're as good as a son. Maybe better." They studied together, and she helped him with his writing and research. Together they started a school to teach English to Russian-Jewish immigrants. Later Henrietta helped to found the Jewish Publication Society and led a women's Zionist group called Hadassah. She even studied at an all-male school—the Jewish Theological Seminary. Henrietta was the first woman ever to attend. But she had to promise that since she was a woman, she would not expect to graduate as a rabbi.

There it was. Being a woman in the late 1800s always seemed to stop her from doing big, important things. She knew that women had important work to do like homemaking and raising children. But as the years went by, she remained unmarried. By 1921, when Henrietta was sixty, she felt as though her life was nearly over and she hadn't done a thing with it! She couldn't imagine that her happiest and busiest time was just about to start.

Henrietta's organization, Hadassah, had set up health clinics in Palestine before the First World War. After the war Hadassah built more clinics as well as hospitals, laboratories, and a nursing school. Henrietta came to Palestine to visit and stayed to direct the work. Only a few years later she took on a much harder task, one that would mean life or death to thousands of children.

Hitler had come to power in Germany and began to threaten and arrest German Jews. Reḥa Freier, a German-Jewish leader, persuaded parents to let their children travel to Palestine, where they would be safe. She crisscrossed Germany and nearby countries like a Pied Piper, pleading with worried parents and gathering boys and girls for the trip. It became Henrietta's job to take care of the children when they reached Palestine. She met them at the ship and found housing, youth leaders, and schools for them in kibbutzim and children's villages. She coaxed money from Hadassah and other organizations to pay the children's expenses. And she argued and bargained with the British to allow the children into Palestine. Each year more and more desperate parents sent their children to Henrietta. If only the British had allowed more entry certificates, thousands more children would have been saved.

On her seventy-fifth birthday Henrietta Szold was too busy to stop and rest, even for a day. "I have a great, new work ahead of

me," she said. "I must get young people out of Germany, and after that out of France, Lithuania, and Russia. What does age mean? Nothing!"

This huge rescue operation was called Youth Aliya. It saved 170,000 European boys and girls in the 1930s and 1940s. Many of them never saw their parents again. The gentle lady with soft, brown eyes and white hair who met the children at the dock became a second mother to them.

Henrietta Szold's "foster children" grew up in youth villages and kibbutzim. These boys and girls lived at the youth village of Ben Shemen in the 1940's.

Central Zionist Archives

"The eggs think they know more than the chickens! Raḥel, you're a silly, stubborn child," scolded Mrs. Lishansky. "You're only fifteen years old. You don't know what you want."

Raḥel's round cheeks and pug nose were flushed. Her curly brown hair bristled indignantly. "I know exactly what I want. I want to learn to be a farmer, and then I want to go to Palestine and become a ḥalutza [pioneer]."

Her father looked up from his prayer book. "So how will you buy bread to eat while you're learning, my little ḥalutza?" he asked with a smile.

"I'll give Hebrew lessons, I'll sew, I'll . . . I'll manage. Don't worry."

SHE KNEW WHAT SHE WANTED

Raḥel Yanait Ben-Zvi (1888–1979)

Dawn

by Raḥel (a young pioneer of the early
1900s)

A jug of water in my hand
And on my shoulder—basket, spade
and rake.
To distant fields, to work, I make my
way.

On my right the great hills raise
protecting arms.
Before me—the wide fields
And in my heart, my twenty Aprils
sing.

Be this my way until my life is done,
With the dust of your road, my land,
And your grain waving golden in the
sun.

A few days later Raḥel packed her things, marched to the station of her small, Russian hometown of Malin and took the train to the big city. Soon she was making speeches, attending meetings, organizing groups of young people to go to Palestine as Zionists, and giving Hebrew lessons on the side. But Zionism was against the law in Russia. Within a year Raḥel was arrested for antigovernment activity. After six months in prison her father met her at the prison gate.

"My poor child, you're so pale and thin," he said. "Now you'll come home and stay home."

"Russia is not my home," she answered stubbornly. "I'm going home to Eretz Yisrael."

More years of work and study passed. Then, finally, Raḥel set sail for Palestine with a few rubles in her pocket and several loaves of black bread under her arm.

The new land was a hard place. Malaria raged in the country-side, jobs were few, but Raḥel was so happy to be in Palestine that she floated above the troubles. She got busy organizing workers to strike for better pay, collecting guns for the new Jewish self-defense organization, and taking long hikes over the hills and valleys of her old-new homeland. She even found time to get married to another young Zionist, Itzḥak Ben-Zvi.

At last, in 1919, Raḥel became a farmer. She found land near Jerusalem with plenty of water and camel dung to use for fertilizer, and she began to plant tree seedlings. Children from a Hadassah orphanage came to help her. Soon Raḥel's seedlings were planted on bare, rocky hills all around the city. Then she had a new idea: Why not turn the tree nursery into a farm school for girls? With the help of Pioneer Women, a group of American Zionists, Raḥel opened her school on a broad hilltop.

Lonely children began to come to Raḥel's school from Europe in the years before World War II. They had escaped the Nazi terror but had to leave their parents behind. Raḥel became a mother to her students as well as to her own two children. They studied, planted trees, raised chickens, and built a homeland together.

In June 1948, Raḥel's school faced a deadly danger. The State of Israel was established, and enemy armies attacked across the borders. The school, with its 100 children, was on the front line of the battle. They couldn't run away. If they ran, the enemy would take their school, and the beautiful hilltop would be lost to the

Jewish state. The girls dug trenches and piled up sandbags. They studied by candlelight while shells screamed over their heads, and they waited. When the fighting ended, the farm school was still part of Israel.

Many years earlier, Raḥel had told her mother, "I know exactly what I want." Then she went out and worked to make it happen. In 1952 Raḥel's husband became the second president of the State of Israel. Raḥel put away her work boots, scrubbed the earth from under her fingernails, and learned to serve tea like a proper first lady. Maybe she didn't exactly *want* to do that. But it would have made her mother very proud of her after all.

THE REBEL

Vladimir Jabotinsky (1881–1940)

Vladimir grabbed a club and joined other young Jews to put down an attack against the Jews of Odessa, Russia, in 1903. For the next thirty-seven years it seemed as though he never stopped fighting.

During the First World War he argued with the British government and convinced them to establish a Jewish Legion which fought in Palestine. The British soldiers could never learn to pronounce his name and dubbed him "Lieutenant Jug-a-Whiskey." After the war he led a Jewish self-defense unit in Palestine. When his unit tried to stop Arab rioting in Jerusalem, the British threw him into jail. But the fight that he carried on for the rest of his life, against the British and against other Zionist leaders, was the fight for a Jewish state on both banks of the Jordan river.

When Great Britain became the mandatory power in Palestine (the country in charge of helping Jews to establish a homeland), it chopped off the eastern part of Palestine and set it up as a new Arab kingdom. Leaders of the World Zionist Organization weren't happy that the hoped-for homeland was cut to one-third of the size the League of Nations had intended. But they accepted the change. One-third was better than nothing.

Jabotinsky furiously accused Zionist leaders of giving away the homeland. "The Jordan flows through the center of Israel, not along its frontier!" he cried. He and his supporters formed the Revisionist party and the Betar youth organization to fight for a "complete" land of Israel.

When Jabotinsky went abroad in 1929, the British refused to allow the "troublemaker" back into Palestine. He kept fighting

from Europe and the United States. During the 1930s when riots, murders, and attacks on buses happened daily in Palestine, the Haganah, the underground army of the Jews of Palestine, struck back only against the individuals or groups who had committed the crimes. But Jabotinsky's followers formed an underground force called the Irgun Tzvai Leumi to hit back hard against any Arabs or Britons for each attack. Both groups quoted the Bible to justify their actions: "Thou shalt not kill," said the Haganah; "Thou shalt give life for life, eye for eye . . . burning for burning," said the Irgun.

Jabotinsky's anger against the British and against cautious Zionist leaders grew when he visited Poland in 1936. He saw Jews who were starving because the government would not allow them to work. Yet these Jews couldn't escape because no other country would let them in. Jabotinsky met with political leaders all over Europe. He got sympathy but no help. Finally his followers began an underground railway to Palestine for Polish Jews. The Palestinian Jewish community continued and expanded the rescue work.

In a 1939 white paper the British finally and openly smashed the hopes of all Zionists. They decided to cut Jewish immigration to Palestine and to establish it as an Arab state. There was an explosion of protest from Zionist leaders. And Jabotinsky's response was a call to battle: "The only way to liberate our country is by the sword!"

The rebel and fighter died in New York in the middle of a campaign for a Jewish army. In the new State of Israel his followers became a powerful political party that still fights for a "complete" land of Israel.

Vladimir Jabotinsky

- *Palestine, astride the Jordan, has room for a million Arabs, for another million of their children, for several million Jews, and for peace.*

SHE FOUGHT FOR PEACE

Golda Meir (1898–1978)

Bang, bang, bang . . .

Eight-year-old Golda blinked sleepily awake. Her father was hammering boards across the window, blocking out the blue, early morning light.

"Papa, why are you . . ." she began.

"Be quiet, Goldele," he said, "and get dressed. Hurry!"

Her older sister helped her dress and hugged her tightly. Golda could feel her shivering. "It's a pogrom," her sister whispered.

When the house was nailed tight, the family huddled in the dark kitchen and waited. The pogrom sounds came closer. Screams, the crash of breaking glass, shouts of "Kill the Jews—get the Christ killers!" And then the sounds moved past and were gone.

Soon after, Golda's family left Russia, crossed the ocean, and settled in Milwaukee, Wisconsin. But Golda never forgot that terrible morning. Fifteen years later, when she was twenty-three, she decided to go to Palestine to help build a Jewish homeland.

"But why?" asked her friends.

"Because we Jews must have our own land," Golda said. "I am determined to save other little Jewish children from this kind of experience."

In Palestine, Golda and her husband Morris joined a kibbutz—a collective farm where many members share the work. When the farm work became too hard for Morris, they moved to the city and Golda began to work for the Histadrut, a large labor union. Even though she had two young children, she found herself working long hours. "I know I won't bring the Messiah," she laughed at herself as she hurried from meeting to meeting, "but when jobs need to be done, I *have* to do them."

Her most dangerous job came in 1948. It must have made her shiver with fear, just as she had during that long-ago pogrom. War was coming in 1948 between the new State of Israel and the Arab states on Israel's borders. One Arab leader, King Abdullah of Transjordan, had promised not to attack Israel. Somehow Golda had to reach Abdullah, deep in enemy territory, and find out whether he would keep his promise.

Golda disguised herself in the loose dress and veil of an Arab woman. She drove across the border with an Arabic-speaking Israeli who carried false identity papers. Time after time they were stopped by Transjordanian soldiers. Golda shrank deeper into her seat each time. If the soldiers spoke to her, they'd quickly discover that she couldn't speak Arabic, and then she and her driver would be lost!

The trip was a success—they reached Abdullah. But it was also a failure—the king refused to promise peace. They made the dangerous trip back with sinking hearts, knowing that Israel would face attack from Transjordan as well as from her other neighbors.

When Golda was seventy-five, and prime minister of Israel, she

Golda Meir

- "When will the Arab-Jewish problem be solved?" a reporter asked Golda.

  "When the Arabs love their children more than they hate us," she answered.

- Golda was puzzled by the Americans who came to help Israel during the 1967 Six Day War. "Why do you come to us in war and not in peace?" she asked. "You were ready to die with us. Why don't you come to live with us?"

faced a great crisis. In 1973 Israel's Arab neighbors launched a surprise attack. The country was nearly cut in half before the army was able to rally and drive the enemy out. Many young Israelis were killed and wounded.

"How could the government be caught by surprise? They were asleep, stupid, careless!" people cried. Golda left the prime minister's office in disgrace. She was tired. It was time to go home and play with her grandchildren, bake cookies, visit friends. But she had a sad, unfinished feeling. Would there always be war, Golda wondered? Would her hope always be disappointed—that Jewish children have a safe home, free of attack?

In the last years of her life the hope grew strong again. Anwar al-Sadat, president of Egypt, who had been Israel's archenemy, came to Israel to talk about making peace. Laughing and crying with joy, Golda shook his hand. "What took you so long?" she asked.

FOUR WHO DIED YOUNG

Ḥaviva Reich (1914–1944)

Oranges bumped gently against Ḥaviva's head. She was hidden in a peaceful, green treetop world, and she sang out loud as she plucked oranges and plunked them into her bag. I'm a ḥalutza, she thought happily. Me—a country girl from the Carpathian Mountains—I'm finally building a homeland in Palestine!

Those months in the orange grove at Kibbutz Maanit were the happiest in Ḥaviva's life. But World War II was blazing in Europe, and terrible news began to arrive from Ḥaviva's hometown and other areas. As the Nazis advanced, Jews were being arrested and thrown into concentration camps. In Carpathia a few young people had escaped from the camps and were hiding in the mountains.

"The fellowship of men fighting for a common cause is surely the perfection of camaradie. Without it nothing can be achieved."

—Yitzḥak Sadeh
Palmaḥ commander

Now, when Ḥaviva walked out to the grove, she could no longer hear the birds sing and smell the crisp, shiny leaves. She imagined the crack of bullets and shivered with the fear and despair of her trapped friends. At last she made a decision. I'll have time to work in the orange groves, to have a family and raise my children, she thought. Now I must go back and fight.

In September 1944 Ḥaviva and four other parachutists from Palestine were dropped into the numbing cold of the Carpathian Mountains. They pushed through the snow and met the Jewish youngsters in a town in rebel territory. One of the young people described the meeting later in a letter: "You sent us new life. Just in time the parachutists dropped from the sky and brought us hope and happiness."

Ḥaviva organized the young people into a fighting group. When the Nazis and their allies began to close in on the town, she and her group set up camp high in the mountains with tents, food, and a wireless set. They fought bitter cold and snow to make lightning-fast hit-and-run attacks against enemy troops. But the Nazis drew closer. The small band couldn't hold them off. Finally, Ḥaviva and some of the others slipped out of camp and headed across the mountains to join the Russian troops. As they rested, exhausted and freezing, in the deep forest, they heard the sounds of advancing troops and commands shouted in Russian. They rushed out and found, to their horror, that they had fallen into the hands of the Ukrainian SS, Russian allies of the Nazis.

The group was executed by a firing squad.

After the war Ḥaviva's identity tag and the tags of three other parachutists were dug up from a mass grave. The story of her struggle and her death was pieced together from the reports of survivors. One of them said, "When it was impossible to live any longer, Ḥaviva showed us how to die."

Eliahu Hakim
(1927–1945)

A great booming explosion shook the houses above Haifa port in November 1940. Eliahu Hakim ran out onto the balcony of his home and saw billows of smoke rising from one of the ships in the harbor. Black dots bobbed in the water, and desperate screams rose faintly. Eliahu's brother raced up the stairs and out onto the balcony with binoculars. "It's the *Patria*," he cried, "the ship of refugees from Europe that the British wouldn't allow into Palestine. It's blown up!"

The boys watched with clenched fists as British navy boats darted around the sinking freighter picking up survivors, debris, and the torn bodies of men, women, and children. Later the British announced that 250 "illegal Jewish immigrants" had died in the explosion. All the surviving "illegals" would be deported as soon as the authorities could get another boat. On that November day thirteen-year-old Eliahu learned to hate the British for shutting his homeless fellow Jews out of Palestine.

Without telling his family the slim, black-eyed boy joined a small, secret group called the Freedom Fighters for Israel (Leḥi). The group was fiercely determined to force the British to leave, with bombs and bullets if necessary. His family would have been horrified. Like most Palestinian Jews, they were against violence. In spite of the *Patria* tragedy and attacks on settlements and buses by Arab terrorists, they felt it was wrong for Jews to fight British cruelty or Arab terrorism with Jewish terrorism. The members of Leḥi disagreed.

Eliahu kept his thoughts and his work secret from his parents. The tiny group of Freedom Fighters was now his true family. He became an expert shot, carried out attacks on British police, and smuggled guns and ammunition. Finally, when he was seventeen and an experienced fighter, he was given his most dangerous assignment. He was to go to Egypt to kill Lord Moyne, the British minister of state in the Middle East. Lord Moyne had always opposed Jewish immigration. When there was a chance to save 1 million Hungarian Jews from death in the Holocaust, Lord Moyne refused to consider the offer. He represented the British government's decision to destroy the Jewish homeland. For this reason the Freedom Fighters for Israel had sentenced him to death.

At noon on November 7, 1944, Eliahu Hakim and Eliahu Bet Tzouri, another member of the Freedom Fighters, waited behind the shrubs at the home of Lord Moyne in Cairo, Egypt. At 12:30

P.M. the minister's car pulled up. The two Freedom Fighters sprang out, raced to the car, and fired one, two, three shots into the minister's body. The young assassins sped off on bicycles but were quickly captured. Lord Moyne died that evening.

Four months later in Cairo, Eliahu Hakim, seventeen, and Eliahu Bet Tzouri, twenty-two, were sentenced to die on the gallows. They stood straight and proud and sang the Jewish national anthem, "Hatikvah," as they waited for death.

Reuven Sadeh (1937–1967)

"Come this way," Reuven called, going up a narrow mountain trail. "I'm going to show you a fantastic view."

"Are you kidding? This trail would scare a mountain goat!" protested one of the group of visitors from the big city.

"You and your desert, Reuven," grumbled another. "It's just going to be a rocky wadi like all the others."

"No, this one is the prettiest ever," Reuven said excitedly as he scrambled far ahead.

Groaning and puffing, they finally made it to the windblown mountaintop and gasped. At their feet a gash opened in the mountain. Its wall was jagged rock in shades of gray, red, and gold, and speckled with bright wildflowers. Twisting and tumbling, it cut through the mountain and led to the blue, shimmering surface of the Dead Sea.

"Well?" asked Reuven. His thin face glowed, and his blue eyes sparkled—as proud as a father showing off his new baby.

"Fantastic," sighed the visitors. In spite of blisters and aching muscles, they had to admit that Reuven Sadeh's desert was a special place.

Reuven, Dina, and Nir plant a tree on their first Tu Bi-Shevat (arbor day) in the bare, new town of Arad.

It wasn't really Reuven's desert. It just seemed to be because he knew every hill and valley within miles of his small town of Arad. Reuven and his wife Dina were the pioneers of Arad. They came when the red Negev hills were bare, the roads were bumpy, dusty tracks, and Bedouin Arabs living in black tents were their only neighbors.

Reuven had wandered all his life. His family went from Poland to Spain, Portugal, Morocco, and finally Israel after the state was established. "When I came to Israel, I found everything I had never had before," Reuven wrote to a friend. "I owe very much to this land, and I hope to pay my debt." He served as a paratrooper in Israel's army and in 1960 settled in Arad to build a home and a town.

Dina and Reuven lived in a small prefabricated house and began to raise their black-haired sturdy sons, Nir and Ran. Reuven worked at a marble quarry with Bedouin tribesmen. On his long walks in the desert he often stopped at a neighbor's goatskin tent for a visit and a tiny cup of thick, sweet coffee.

In the next six years the town of Arad grew quickly. Dina and Reuven began to build a permanent home. It was almost finished by Israel Independence Day, 1967. The townspeople had a happy Independence Day party and a stamping, shouting hora that Nir and Ran and all their friends joined.

A few weeks later the Six Day War broke out between Israel and the neighboring Arab states. Reuven and the other men rushed to join their units.

"*Mazal tov* on your new house," called his paratrooper buddies as they collected their gear at the army base. "First thing after the war we'll go to Arad for a housewarming!"

"And I'll show you some beautiful spots in the desert," Reuven said eagerly.

But for Reuven there would be no housewarming. He was killed fighting at the Lion's Gate in the wall of the Old City of Jerusalem.

The desert was a lonelier place after June 1967.

Insignia of Israel's paratroopers

There was the stillness of death on the rocky hillside as Yoni and his men crawled forward. Their noses stung with the ugly smells of war—gunpowder, burned flesh, and the scorched metal smell of smoldering tanks. Above them, in the town of El Shams on the Golan Heights, the guns of the Syrian enemy waited. Someplace in between they had to find wounded Israeli soldiers and drag them back to safety.

"Don't come closer," a voice called weakly in Hebrew. "The Syrians are firing. They'll get you, too."

They followed the sound and quickly reached two wounded Israelis in a trench. Covered by the guns of his squad, Yoni ducked down and ran from one burned-out tank to another searching for more wounded. He found only blackened bodies. They loaded the two soldiers onto stretchers and crept back down the hill.

It was one week after Yom Kippur, 1973. The Israeli army was fighting to beat back a surprise Arab attack that had nearly cut the country in half. And at the age of twenty-seven Yonatan Netanyahu, paratroop officer, was fighting in his second major war.

Yonatan Netanyahu (1946–1976)

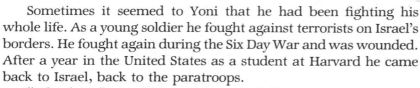

Sometimes it seemed to Yoni that he had been fighting his whole life. As a young soldier he fought against terrorists on Israel's borders. He fought again during the Six Day War and was wounded. After a year in the United States as a student at Harvard he came back to Israel, back to the paratroops.

"Why do it?" one of his friends argued. "If you stay alive, you're going to be a general. But if you go on like this, you'll be killed."

Yoni laughed and said, "If I make it to thirty, I'll have a chance."

He didn't want to fight or die. He wanted to finish school, marry, have children, and raise German shepherd puppies. But he stayed in the army because he feared for the safety of the land of Israel. Once Yoni wrote to his parents, "We are compelled to cling to our country by our fingernails, with our bodies, with all our strength. Only if we do that will Israel remain the State of the Jews." If not, he warned, the Jewish state might again be swept away and the Jewish people would again be homeless wanderers.

The Yom Kippur War ended in victory for Israel. But it was a sad victory. Yoni lost many friends. He was tired. But he went back to work, first as a tank commander and then as commander of a paratroop unit. He drove his men as he drove himself—running with them, sleeping on the ground beside them, and being first to face enemy fire.

In July 1976 a terrorist band hijacked an Air France plane that carried 150 Israeli passengers. (You can find out more about the rescue at Entebbe in Chapter 6.) In Entebbe, Uganda, 2,000 miles from Israel, the plane landed, and the Israelis were held for ransom. Only with luck and with a daring, split-second army-paratroop operation could Israel hope to rescue its people. Yonatan Netanyahu was called on to help plan and lead the rescue.

Yoni was shot and killed at the terminal of Entebbe airport as he directed the rescue squads. He had just made it to age thirty.

News of the Entebbe rescue reached the United States on the Fourth of July, 1976, when bicentennial barbecues and fireworks were in full swing. Many Americans raised the blue-and-white flag of Israel beside the Stars and Stripes for a joyous double celebration of freedom and independence.

Mount Tavor in the Valley of Jezreel.

Ranan Burstein

WHAT IF . . . ?

"What ifs" are teasing, tantalizing questions that we can never answer.

What if Ḥaviva, Reuven, Yoni, and Eliahu had lived out their lives? Would they have changed Israel?

What if the "old-timers" had made different choices at turning points in their lives? Would there be an Israel today?

What if *you* were Golda, David, Aaron, or one of the other "old-timers"? How would you have chosen?

GOLDA MEIR: Should I keep teaching and raise a family here in Milwaukee? Or should I start from scratch in Palestine?

DAVID BEN-GURION: The danger is so great—we're sure to be badly hurt, maybe destroyed. Should we put off declaring the State of Israel? Or should we risk everything right now?

RAḤEL YANAIT: I paid my dues. I went to jail for Zionism. Should I go home to Mama and Papa and use my skills to open a school for girls? Or should I become a laborer in Palestine?

THEODOR HERZL: Should I keep writing witty plays and essays and earn a good living for my family? Or should I follow this dream of creating a new life for the Jewish people?

AARON DAVID GORDON: I'm no youngster anymore. Should I sit at my desk in Russia and write books that inspire young people to become farmers in Israel? Or should I myself go and show them how?

"We are compelled to cling to our country by our fingernails . . . only if we do that will our country remain the land of the Jews."

Yonatan Netanyahu

Soldiers and agents

Israel is a tiny country with many hostile neighbors. To stay alive she must have powerful armed forces. The Jews living in Israel before the state was established also had to fight to protect themselves. In the section in this chapter called "How Israel's Army Grew" you'll find out about Israel's defenders, from the musta-chioed, sword-bearing horsemen of the 1890s to the khaki-clad recruits of the 1980s.

Terrorists who attack schools, buses, and passenger planes are another great danger to the country. Israeli agents gather infor-mation on terrorism and other activities that may affect Israel's safety all over the world. They send it to their intelligence office, the Mossad, where the information is reviewed and passed on to the government and the armed forces. "Operation Noah's Arks" is the name of a dangerous mission that Jewish soldiers and agents carried out. You'll find that story and others in this chapter.

Finish off by practicing some superspy skills of your own at the end of the chapter.

The northern tip of Israel is like a finger pointing up. That finger was almost chopped off in 1920 when Arab bands attacked Tel Ḥai and other northern settlements. Joseph Trumpeldor, the hero of the Jewish brigade, led a small group of men and women in defending their set-tlements. He was fatally shot in the battle. As he lay dying, he whis-pered, "It is good to die for our country."

A great roaring lion carved out of stone stands at Tel Ḥai to remind visitors of the soldier-farmer who loved his land so much.

*"Our army does not depend on size
. . . but rather on quality. . . . We want
courage and boldness instilled in the
men. . . . We want officers who say
'Follow me!' not 'Forward!' "*
—Moshe Dayan,
formerly Zahal chief of staff

HOW ISRAEL'S ARMY GREW

First came the shomrim: In the bad old days, one hundred years ago, Jewish settlements were often robbed and attacked by passing Bedouins (wandering tribesmen) or by neighboring villagers. A few strong, bold men like Joshua Stamper and Yussuf Ibn Daud became shomrim (watchmen) for the frightened settlers. Yussuf was a Jewish Bedouin from Syria. He galloped against the enemy with his headdress streaming behind, swinging his sword and shouting bloodthirsty curses in Arabic. Yussuf scorned firearms. "A rifle is for women," he said. "The lance and the sword are the only weapons for a man."

When nearby tribesmen took over the fields of Petah Tikva, a Jewish village, Yussuf challenged the leader to a duel. They charged at each other furiously. Yussuf's lance struck the leader from his horse, and the tribesmen gathered their gear and fled, never to return.

Next came Hashomer: By 1907 there were Jewish farms and settlements all over Palestine. A few daring horsemen like Joshua and Yussuf couldn't cover the country. New settlers from Russia, including David Ben-Gurion and a young woman named Manya

Shoḥat, formed an organization of guards called Hashomer. The guards trained hard and became great horsemen and sharpshooters who went to any farm or village that needed protection. They spoke Arabic, hunted and feasted with Arab friends, and kept the peace not only by fighting but also by talking. For instance, once, when a Bedouin stole a rifle from the wagon of a guard, the guard stole a bull from the Bedouin's field.

The Bedouin came to the guard's tent and asked politely, "Have you perhaps found a bull wandering in your field?"

The guard answered just as politely, "Have you perhaps found a rifle that fell off my cart and rolled into your tent?"

The two exchanged "finds" and remained friends.

Alexander Zaid lived with danger. He became a shomer, a guard, when he was twenty-five. He built a small house and farm for his family out in the countryside and patrolled the Jewish villages on his horse. A Bedouin's bullet killed him when he was forty-five. This statue of Zaid and his horse looks down on peaceful farms from a hilltop near his home.

Then came the Jewish Legion: When World I began in 1914, Turkish and British armies fought bitterly over the lands of the Middle East. The British won Jewish help when they promised to support a Jewish homeland in Palestine. Fearless, one-armed Joseph Trumpeldor, a veteran of the Russian army, and silver-tongued Vladimir Jabotinsky persuaded the British to allow a Jewish brigade to fight in the British army. Many Hashomer members joined and fought in Europe and Turkey. When the war ended, the battle-hardened men of the brigade came home to face new dangers and challenges.

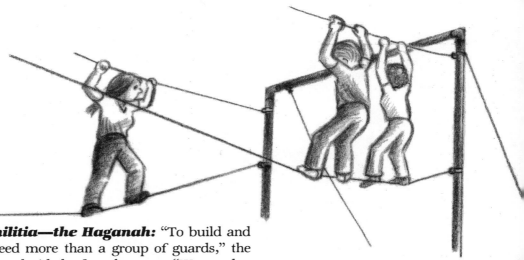

At last, a homeland militia—the Haganah: "To build and protect a homeland we need more than a group of guards," the leaders of Jewish Palestine decided after the war. "We need a democratic militia of all the young Jews of the land."

The Haganah ("defense," in Hebrew) was formed in 1920. Young men and women joined their local units, learned to shoot with whatever ancient guns they could get, and drilled and hiked across the countryside. In that same year Arab riots broke out all over Palestine. When the Haganah fought to stop the riots, the new British rulers banned all private armies and confiscated the Haganah's tiny stock of weapons.

The Haganah went underground. Members met in secret, smuggled weapons across the borders, and held training exercises late at night, far out in the countryside. Boys and girls became lookouts on the streets and rooftops to warn when British soldiers came near.

By 1936 terrorist violence was tearing Palestine apart as Arab militants fought to stop Jewish immigration. Bombs exploded on city streets. Buses were ambushed on the highways. Orchards and fields were set afire. And Jewish villages were attacked. At last the British called for the Haganah's help. They even allowed Orde Wingate, a British captain, to train young Palestinian Jews in night-fighting tactics to stop the Arab raiders. Moshe Dayan, Yigal Allon, Yitzhak Rabin, and other eager youngsters learned Wingate's lessons so well that they became leaders of Israel's army a few years later.

Haganah fighters battled against Arab terrorists with all their might, but they refused to attack peaceful Arabs. Other Jews argued that all Arabs were enemies. "An eye for an eye and a tooth for a tooth," they cried, using a phrase from the Bible. These Jews broke away from the Haganah. They formed a small secret army called the Irgun Zvai Leumi (Etzel) and an even smaller, more violent group called Loḥamei Ḥerut Yisrael (Leḥi) to fight against the British and the Arabs.

The Haganah goes to war: In 1939 the powerful army of Nazi Germany invaded Poland and began World War II. At the same time, the Nazis carried on another war—a war of annihilation against the Jews of Europe. Haganah members fought the Nazis as soldiers in the British army and later in a special Jewish brigade. They parachuted into Europe to try to lead the broken Jewish communities. But their efforts failed. The killing of Europe's Jews went on for six terrible years.

Finally, in 1945 the Nazi armies were beaten. The death camps were opened, and the surviving Jews of Europe were free to go. Many wanted only to go home, to their own people, to Israel. But a new enemy blocked the way—Great Britain. The British had cut off all Jewish immigration to Palestine. Now the Haganah and the smaller groups were forced to fight a tough new war.

Haganah people formed a group called Briḥa ("escape"), which led refugees on underground escape routes across Europe to reach the seaports. From the ports they sailed ships packed with refugees through the British blockade to Palestine. Inside Palestine, Haganah crews blew up bridges, roads, and radar stations to prevent the British from blocking arriving immigrants. Units of Leḥi and Etzel ambushed and attacked British soldiers and bombed British headquarters.

British camps and prisons were filled with Jewish fighters and refugees, but the war went on. Each day it grew angrier and bloodier. At last Great Britain gave up. On May 14, 1948, the British withdrew from Palestine. The Jews of Palestine immediately declared the establishment of the State of Israel. And on May 28 the first Jewish national army in 2,000 years was formed to replace the Haganah. It was called Tz'va Haganah Le-Yisrael, the Israel Defense Force—Zahal for short.

Zahal today: You can read more about the battles of Zahal in Chapter 3. Here's some information about how Zahal works.

Zahal has nearly 170,000 full-time soldiers in an army, a navy, and an air force. There are men and women, Israeli Jews and Israeli Druse Arabs.

Recruits are called up at age eighteen. They start off with tough basic training—push-ups, twenty-mile hikes, and target practice. Some recruits, including many new immigrants, go to Haganah schools to learn to read and write Hebrew and to study history and current events.

Soldiers serve in Zahal's regular forces for two and a half to three years. When they finish, some go to college, others take jobs, and some just lie around on the beach. But they're not finished with Zahal. They've just begun.

After regular service each soldier becomes a member of the reserves. There are 400,000 reservists. They report to their units for one or two months of reserve duty each year. They must be well skilled in their military jobs because they may be called up on a moment's notice in an emergency.

Male reservists may be called to active duty until age forty-five and to less strenuous jobs until age fifty-five.

Women have a shorter army service period than men. They do reserve duty until age thirty-five or until they marry. After basic training women serve in Zahal in such jobs as teaching, driving, and radio operating.

Naḥal is a special unit of Zahal whose members do basic military training and then serve as soldier-farmers on isolated border settlements.

High-school kids train in Gadna, Zahal's youth corps. You'll find more about Gadna in Chapter 3.

Israel's national army can keep a citizen busy from high school until grandparenthood. As one tired reservist said, "Every Israeli civilian is a full-time soldier temporarily home on leave."

Israel's generals have unusual hobbies. One of the generals, Motta Gur, writes children's stories. (You'll find a story by Motta Gur in Chapter 13.) Others have been archaeologists and Bible scholars. During the Six Day War a scholarly general led his troops along a trail he knew only from the Bible. It went from Jerusalem to the border of Jordan, where the troops caught enemy soldiers by surprise.

SECRET AGENTS FOR ISRAEL

The Nili Spies, 1916

A reed tickled the back of Sarah's neck, and her left foot had fallen asleep. She squirmed into a better position behind the sand dune, never taking her eyes off the dark tumbling surf of the Mediterranean. Would the British ship really come? After all the months of waiting, would she and her friends finally be able to help the British in the war against Turkey?

She felt for the packet of maps and other information that her group had gathered secretly, right under the noses of the Turks. It was wrapped in oilcloth and tucked down among the reeds.

"I see a light!" hissed the boy crouching beside her.

The signal. Sarah looked down the beach. It was empty. She snatched the packet and plunged through the reeds to the water's edge.

A dark head bobbed in the surf. Soon a swimmer struggled out of the water—a thin, young man, breathing hard. "Nili," he said.

"Netzach Yisrael lo yishaker," Sarah answered.

He pulled a dripping package from his belt. She gave him her packet in return. Then, with a "Jolly good" and a quick smile, he turned and dove into the surf, heading back to the British ship that waited offshore.

Sarah's best friend, Avshalom Feinberg, tried to reach British headquarters in Egypt by crossing the Sinai desert. He was killed by Bedouins. Fifty years later, when Israel occupied the Sinai desert during the Six Day War, Avshalom's grave was found. A palm tree had grown from a date pit in his pocket and shaded the lonely burial place.

The year was 1916. The First World War raged across Europe, and a British army battled the Turkish rulers of the Middle East. Most of the Jews and Arabs of Palestine were too frightened to take sides. They hoped only to be left alone, to stay alive. But Sarah, her brothers, and other young people from the village of Zikhron Ya'aqov hated the Turks. They were cruel rulers who had killed thousands of Turkish Armenians. Our own people, the Jews of Palestine, might be next, thought Sarah and her friends. The youngsters decided to risk their lives to collect information that would help the British in their war against Turkey. They formed a spy group called "Nili." And on that dark night Sarah and her friends delivered their first packet of information to a British navy ship.

For the next eight months the work went smoothly. A British boat crept up the coast from Egypt every few weeks. Sarah and her friends waited for it on the beach below Zikhron Ya'aqov. The boat delivered instructions and money, and picked up the information that Nili members had collected. A coop of carrier pigeons was hidden behind one of the village houses. The pigeons carried emergency messages that couldn't wait for the boat.

It was a lost carrier pigeon that doomed the Nili spies. The bird was flying back from British headquarters in Cairo and fluttered down, too soon, into the arms of a Turkish policeman. The police quickly found the coded message on the pigeon's leg. They could not understand the words, but they knew the meaning—someplace nearby spies were at work.

Two weeks later a Nili member was arrested, and the police began to question him. Sarah knew they were finished. She sent a last desperate message to Egypt asking that a ship be sent immediately to pick up her people. But when the ship arrived, the beach was empty. It was too late.

One after another, Sarah and other members were arrested and tortured. The Turks wanted to know the names of all the members, their contacts, and the information they had gathered. The prisoners were silent. The police grew exasperated and decided to move them to a central prison for more "efficient" questioning. Sarah was given a few private minutes at home to change her clothing. She quickly wrote a farewell note saying, "I haven't the strength to suffer any more—I wanted to save my people." And then, using a gun she had hidden long before, she shot herself.

After the First World War the British said, "It was very largely the daring work of young spies . . . which enabled the . . . [British] Field Marshal to accomplish his undertaking . . . the leader of the spy system was a young Jewess, a Miss Sarah Aaronsohn."

Eli's lonely mission, 1965

"My heart yearns for you, my desert love," wailed the radio. It was almost drowned out by sounds of glasses clicking and loud laughter and talk in the warm living room of Amin Kamil Taabes in Damascus, Syria. Amin, a tall, dark-eyed, smiling man, was a busy host. He filled glasses, brought out another tray of honey pastry, and joked with his guests. But most of all, he listened.

When the last guest left, Amin drew the curtains, locked the door, and sat and wrote. Then he went into the cluttered kitchen and lifted off the top of his electric food mixer. Inside the base there was a powerful miniature radio transmitter. Softly Amin began to transmit a coded message to Tel Aviv.

Amin Kamil Taabes, the popular Damascus businessman, was Eli Cohen, an Israeli Jew and an agent of the Mossad.

Eli was born in Egypt and came to Israel in 1956. A few years later he began to work for the Mossad, collecting information inside Syria. It was a very important job. The Syrians, Israel's neighbors to the northeast, were fierce enemies. They held the Golan Heights, which loom above Israel's Jordan valley. From the heights they had been shooting into Israeli villages along the river. If war broke out, they could rapidly sweep down and cut Israel in half. The Israelis had to know Syria's plans. Only a spy in Damascus could give Israel the early warning that might save her life.

To become Amin Kamil Taabes, Eli first went to Argentina, where many Syrians live. He became known as a young Syrian businessman, handsome, friendly, and always ready to throw a party, lend some money, or argue politics at a sidewalk café. When Amin finally went "home" to Damascus, his social life became even busier and more glamorous. The propaganda minister, high air-force and police officials, and the president himself were his friends.

Amin and his friends visited Syrian fortifications on the Golan Heights. He looked down on the green fields, fishponds, and villages of Israel and took many snapshots of the "Zionist enemy." His wife and three children lived only a few hours away in Tel Aviv. He was so close, but yet a long, lonely distance away. At other times Amin and his friends eagerly discussed new weapons and battle plans over tiny cups of Turkish coffee.

Late at night Amin became Eli. He spent hours putting his information into secret code and transmitting it to the Mossad in Tel Aviv. He hid plans and photos in the false bottoms of backgammon sets and the hollow legs of furniture. Eli's company exported them to Switzerland, where Mossad agents were his best customers.

By January 1965 Eli had nearly finished his work. In a few months he would return to his wife Nadia and his three children in Israel. As he transmitted late one night, the door of his apartment suddenly burst open. A squad of men charged through with guns drawn. "Secret police!" shouted the leader. "You are under arrest."

An accident had betrayed Eli Cohen. The operator at the nearby Indian embassy had complained that an unknown transmitter was interfering with his messages. "Unknown" could mean only one thing—a spy. Syrian police cruised the area with listening equipment until finally, on a night when there was an electricity blackout and few sets were operating, they traced the signal to the house of Amin Kamil Taabes.

The Syrians hanged Eli Cohen as a spy in May 1965.

Two years later his lonely sacrifice paid off. The Six Day War broke out, and Israeli planes attacked the Golan Heights. Because of Eli's reports, they knew every ridge, rock, and gun emplacement. After the planes wiped out many fortifications the tanks stormed up the cliffs, carefully avoiding mines, traps, and trenches, and drove the Syrians back.

Eli's brave, late-night messages from a dangerous city had prepared the Israeli army and saved hundreds of lives.

The Golan Heights in the background loom over the fields and orchards of the Jordan Valley. Before the Six Day War in 1967, Syrian gunners sat in forts on the mountaintops and fired down into Israeli villages in the valley.

Noah's Arks, 1969

"They can't do this to us," the Israeli cabinet minister spluttered. "The French have no right to stop shipment of those missile boats. We paid for them, we helped design them—they're ours!"

"What's worse is we need them. Without those boats Egypt controls the sea. She can blast Tel Aviv or Haifa right off the map," another minister added gloomily.

The people around the table chewed their fingernails and doodled on their pads until the firm voice of the chairman sliced through the gloom. "There'll be no blasting off the map. We'll find a way to make the French change their minds."

"What if we can't?" asked the gloomy minister.

"Then we'll call in the Mossad. They'll find a way."

For the next few months during 1969 Israeli officials pleaded with the French government to keep its promise and to send Israel the five missile boats being built in the port of Cherbourg.

"*Non*" was the answer. "France has decided to stop sending war supplies to the Middle East."

"But our enemies buy from other countries. They can buy all they need," the Israelis argued. "We buy only from you. You leave us empty-handed."

"*Non. Absolument non!*"

It was hopeless. Another way would have to be found.

Israel's intelligence branch, the Mossad, was called in. Within two weeks they planned and began a five-step operation. The code name was "Noah's Arks."

Step 1: Mordecai Limon, Israel's chief arms buyer, called Félix Amiot, manager of the Cherbourg shipyard. "Israel does not want the missile boats anymore," he said. "You may find another buyer and pay us back for our costs."

Step 2: A few days later Mr. Amiot had a happy surprise. A Mr. Siem, director of a Norwegian shipping company, offered to buy the speedy little boats for oil exploration near Alaska. "We need them quickly," Mr. Siem said, "so urge your government committee to okay the deal soon."

The committee eagerly approved.

Step 3: Young "Norwegian" sailors began to arrive in Cherbourg. They inspected the boats and, night after night, tested the motors. After a while the townspeople stopped noticing the roar of motors.

It was nearly Christmas, and the days were cold and blustery. But one sailor spent freezing hours on the shorefront examining a seldom-used eastern channel from the port out into the English Channel. The "sailor"—Ezra Kedem, an Israeli naval commander—was worried. It was a tricky passage, full of rocks. But they could move through it without being seen. It would give the boats a head start. They had to risk it.

Step 4: While the people of Cherbourg trimmed their trees on Christmas eve, the boat engines began to roar again. At midnight, as the church bells rang, the missile boats slid away from the docks. One by one they threaded their way through the dangerous eastern channel and moved out to sea. Hardly anybody noticed.

Two days later the news reached Paris.

"Where are they going? To Alaska?" asked the newsmen.

"Where are they going?" government officials demanded from Mr. Amiot in Cherbourg. Mr. Amiot could only shrug. How should he know?

Three days later the boats were spotted entering the Mediterranean, heading east toward Israel. It was too late for the French. The speedy little boats could outrace any French navy ship.

Step 5: The missile boats arrived in Haifa to a cheering welcome. The arks had landed at Mt. Ararat. The Mossad closed its Noah's Arks file.

Hijack: seven days and fifty-three minutes, 1976

The first day, Sunday, June 27, 1976:

It happened so quickly. One minute the passengers of Air France flight 139 from Tel Aviv were lowering their trays and sniffing lunch smells from the galley. The next minute they heard screams and scuffling and found themselves facing three hard-eyed men and a woman, all carrying guns. A strange voice blasted from the plane's speaker: "This is Captain Basil el-Koubesi of the . . . Palestine Liberation Forces. This plane has been hijacked!"

Who? Why? The passengers stared at each other in shock and then felt the plane tip as it turned off its course and headed south.

Sandwiches and coffee were being served at the Sunday-morning meeting of the Israeli cabinet when an aide hurried in with a note. Prime Minister Rabin glanced at it, then stopped chewing and reread it slowly. "*Haverim* [friends]," he interrupted the conversation, "there's trouble. An Air France plane with many Israelis aboard is missing over the Mediterranean."

The room was quiet until one minister asked the dreaded question, "Hijacked?"

"We don't know yet."

The second day:

The Air France jet bounced to a stop on an airport runway in the steamy African night. It sat and waited as the sky brightened and the sun rose. At midday the hijackers drove their hostages past armed Ugandan soldiers to the terminal building. A huge, broad-shouldered black man wearing a uniform covered with medals stood smiling in the doorway. "*Shalom,*" he said, "I am Field Marshal Doctor Idi Amin Dada, president of Uganda. You will be my guests until your governments agree to the demands of the Palestine Liberation Forces. For your sake I hope they will agree quickly."

Isser Harel, a chief of Israel's Mossad (intelligence office), loved opera and mystery stories. He thought most spy novels were stupid. "My boys make heroes like James Bond look like amateurs," he said.

"The plane was hijacked by members of the Popular Front for the Liberation of Palestine," Prime Minister Rabin told a cabinet committee. "We don't yet know what they want."

Phone calls from worried relatives began to jam the lines to government offices. "Bring our people home, whatever the cost," they pleaded.

The third day:

Mosquitoes whined through the terminal. Some hostages dozed. A few children were kicking a soccer ball. Everybody tensed when a blond hijacker with pale-blue eyes appeared in the doorway. "We will divide you into two groups," he shouted through a bullhorn. "Passengers whose names I call will go into the next room." One by one he read 150 names—the names of all the Israeli passengers. As they moved through the doorway under terrorist guns, one passenger, a survivor of the Nazi death camps, relived a dreadful memory. Many years before, when he and his townspeople were brought to the Nazi camp, they were divided into two groups. One group was killed immediately; the other—his group—was allowed to live. Would he be as lucky this time?

"Here are the hijackers' demands," announced the prime minister in Tel Aviv. "To save the hostages we must free fifty-three terrorists from Israeli jails and bring them to Entebbe, Uganda, within two days, by July first at one P.M."

All the ministers spoke at once.

"No, we can't agree. If we give in to blackmail, there will be hijackings every day!"

"What else can we do? Risk the lives of helpless children and old people?"

"Rescue them. Send in the army."

"Impossible! Entebbe is two thousand miles away."

In the end they agreed. There was no choice. They would have to deal with the hijackers.

But when the others had gone, Prime Minister Rabin and Defense Minister Peres made another decision. They would deal with the hijackers as agreed, but at the same time they would search for a way to fight them.

"If you can't bite, don't show your teeth."

—Yiddish saying

The fourth day:

The Israeli hostages watched through grimy windows as the forty-nine non-Israeli hostages left the Entebbe terminal to board planes for Paris and freedom.

"Happy landings!" said Idi Amin. He shook each person's hand.

The Ugandan troops and terrorist guards moved closer to their remaining prisoners. The Israelis felt more alone than ever.

Only one day was left before the hijackers' deadline.

Israeli officials prepared a list of terrorists to be exchanged for the hostages. It would be sent to Paris in the morning.

Crowds of families and friends of the hostages gathered at government offices crying, "Give the hijackers whatever they want. Save the hostages!"

Later in the day the non-Israeli hostages arrived in Paris to a happy reception and to welcome-home parties. But first they met quietly with Israeli agents and told them everything they knew about Entebbe airport. How many doors, windows, soldiers, terrorists it had—everything.

Lights burned through the night in Tel Aviv as Israeli experts from the army and the Mossad studied maps and diagrams, planned air routes, and worked out timing. At last they straightened up and rubbed their tired eyes. "A rescue is possible," they agreed.

The fifth day:

Idi Amin's splendid white uniform gleamed in the dusty terminal as he scolded the weary hostages. "Your government is stubborn," he said, "I got you a little more time. The new deadline is Sunday. But, believe me, you're in great danger."

The terrorists at each doorway watched grimly. They were tired, too.

"Israel surrenders!" screamed the headline of the *New York Post*. The Israelis had finally agreed to talk about exchanging prisoners for hostages, reported the news story, but the hijackers had warned the Israelis that time was running out.

In Tel Aviv the planners of the rescue operation also knew that time was running out. The plans were not done, but the men would have to start training. Paratroopers would be needed, men from the Golani brigade, and a topnotch commander. "Call Yoni Netanyahu," they ordered.

The sixth day:

As if heat, fear, and mosquitoes were not enough, some of the hostages became ill. Seventy-five-year-old Dora Bloch choked on a bit of food. Against her will she was rushed to a hospital in a nearby town. The terrorists paced tensely past the doorways.

Talks on exchange of hostages and terrorists dragged on between diplomats in Paris and Uganda.

On a deserted landing strip in southern Israel a sandbag model of Entebbe airport was built. A huge transport plane was pulled up nearby. Again and again soldiers with their guns ready raced from the belly of the plane to the sandbag terminal.

"Faster!" yelled Yoni, the operation commander, "A hand grenade takes four seconds to explode. We have to surprise the terrorists and shoot them before they can kill the hostages."

The rescue was rehearsed and timed step by step and second by second. Speed and surprise were crucial. Any slip-up could mean failure.

The seventh day:

The rescue plan had been kept secret even from many of the Israeli cabinet ministers. They settled into their seats that afternoon, glumly prepared to discuss the exchange of hostages that would take place the next day. Instead, the chief of staff rose and unrolled a large map. Pointing to the black dot marked "Entebbe," he said, "We have an alternative to blackmail. If you agree to this plan, Israel's fighting men will attack Entebbe airport and bring the hostages home. Here's how we'll do it. . . ."

The plan was risky. The ministers were worried. Yet, raising trembling hands, they agreed. Minutes later, four Israeli transport planes loaded with trucks, guns, medical equipment, fighting men, doctors, and a shiny Mercedes automobile lifted off from the Sinai desert, circled into the slanting afternoon sun, and headed south toward Africa.

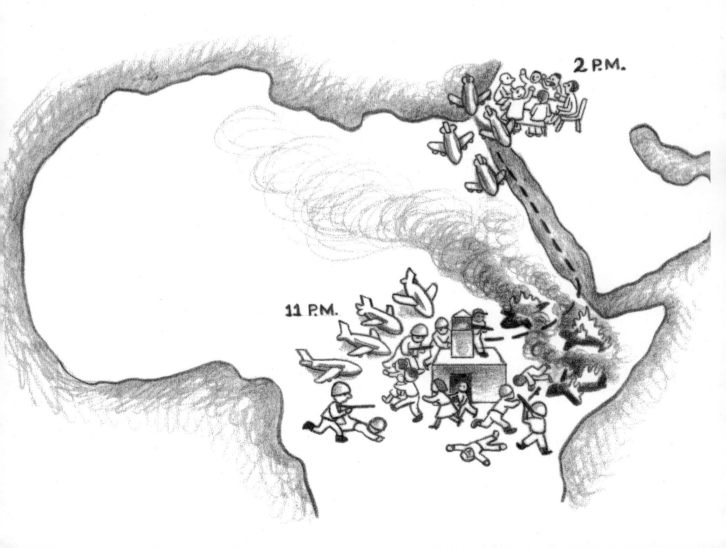

In Paris the negotiators finally reached an agreement for the exchange. The Israeli representative called Tel Aviv. "What shall we do now?" he asked.

"Keep talking," answered the prime minister's aide and hung up.

After nine hours and 2,200 miles of flying, the giant transports swooped down to their target through flashes of lightning. Entebbe airport. It was 11:00 P.M. They were on schedule.

The first transport rolled to a stop, and its great doors swung open. The Mercedes carrying Yoni and eight others raced out toward the terminal building where the hostages were being held. Two land rovers followed. Men from the other transports poured out to attack the control tower and clear the area for a quick takeoff.

A hail of Israeli bullets cut down the shocked terrorists at the terminal doors. Then, shouting in Hebrew, "This is Zahal [the Israeli army], we've come to take you home," the Israelis raced into the building to free the dazed hostages. In the dark parents grabbed their children; husbands, wives, and friends found each other. Within minutes, while shooting was still going on between Israelis, terrorists, and Ugandan troops, the hostages were led to the transports. Stretchers carrying the casualties were rushed to waiting doctors. Explosions shook the windows, and orange flames lit the sky as paratroopers blew up the Ugandan planes on the airfield so the planes could not be used to attack the heavily loaded transports.

Fifty-three minutes after touchdown, the Israeli planes were roaring out of Ugandan air space. They would stop to refuel and then turn north for the long flight home, to freedom.

Yoni, the thirty-year-old commander, died in the operation. Three hostages also died. A fourth, Dora Bloch, who had been taken to the hospital, was dragged from her bed the next day and shot by Ugandan soldiers. It was a sad price to pay for the daring rescue. Thousands of Israelis greeted the freed hostages at Ben-Gurion Airport, kissing, hugging, and throwing flowers. They were wildly happy but not amazed. Zahal, after all, was expected to do the impossible.

Only Idi Amin, who heard the news at breakfast, was really amazed. It ruined his appetite.

Codes

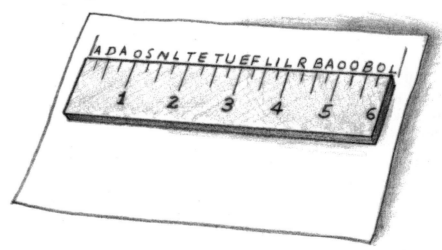

Pretend you're a secret agent with information about a new enemy weapon or a battle plan to attack your country. Would you rush to the nearest phone and call headquarters? Or would you write a letter and send it Express Mail? Of course not! Your information wouldn't be a secret anymore if you did that—or would it? It *would* if you and headquarters had worked out a disguised language—a code—that only you two could figure out. If an enemy agent read your coded message, he or she would find only gobbledegook or a simple, harmless letter to a friend.

Start practicing for a career as a secret agent by using the following codes with your friends:

Inch code. Write a three- or four-word message. Place a ruler on a sheet of paper. Draw a line on the paper at each end of the ruler. Write the letters of the message above each half-inch mark on the ruler. Place a dot above the last letter of the message. Fill in the spaces between the message letters to confuse outsiders. Your partners will line up a ruler with the end marks and read the message.

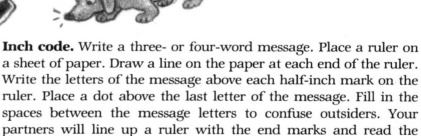

The message is "Don't tell Bob."

Textbook code. Here's a teacher-proof way to pass notes at school. Write out your message. Copy it into your textbook by putting a light dot under the letters that spell out the message. Then exchange textbooks with your partner.

In the meantime the work of the pioneers continued to transform the little land into a flowering garden and industrial center. Trucks rumbled along the roads to the busy city food markets. The waters of the Jordan river were harnessed, and their power was used for electricity in homes, schools, and factories.

The message is "Wait for me after school."

Mask code. Make up a short message. This example has seven words. Cut six slots on the lines of two sheets of paper. Give one slotted sheet to your partner. Place the second slotted sheet on a paper and write one word in each slot. Remove the slotted sheet and fill in a fake message around your words.

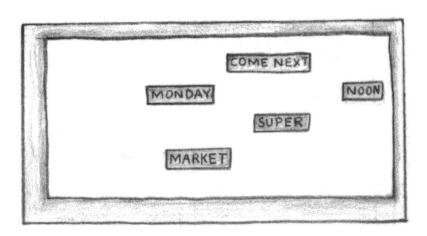

Here's the fake message—the real message is underlined:

A BIG SNOW STORM IS DUE TO <u>COME NEXT</u> WEEK. LET'S GO SLEIGH RIDING ON <u>MONDAY</u> OR TUESDAY AFTER<u>NOON</u>. MAYBE YOU WANT TO TRY MY NEW <u>SUPER</u>-FLYER. IT'S THE FASTEST SLED IN THE TOY <u>MARKET</u>. BRING YOUR NOTEBOOK, AND WE'LL DO OUR MATH HOMEWORK LATER.

Holidays are the same

Israeli Jewish kids spin groggers at Purim, play dreidel at Hanukkah, and steal the afikomen at Passover, just like American Jewish kids. So what's the difference?

One big difference is that in Israel the holiday feeling is everywhere—on the street, in school, in the synagogue, and at home. Special holiday foods crowd the shelves of the food stores. Holiday programs fill the radio and TV schedules. Street fairs and parades tie up traffic and keep everybody entertained—except the drivers. Best of all, students don't have to bring notes to the teacher explaining that they were absent for a Jewish holiday because the schools are closed on most Jewish holidays.

Here's another big difference. Since Israelis come from many countries, they bring different customs with them. Israeli kids from Canada can enjoy the Moroccan Passover Mimouna party. Israeli Yemenite kids can taste European Purim hamantashen. And Israeli kids from Brooklyn can get scared out of bed by the Eastern custom of banging pots at midnight before Rosh Hashanah.

New ways of enjoying the holidays have grown from life in Israel, too. Thousands of Israelis march up to Jerusalem on an Israel Independence Day hike. Children wearing crowns of flowers and carrying baby chicks get tractor rides to celebrate Shavuoth. And there's an Adloyada parade, a Bible quiz, and more.

The holiday feasts and processions of Israel's Muslim and Christian citizens add even more variety to the country's celebrations.

Just read the chapter, and you'll see—it's different!

SHABBAT

The seventh day of each week

Empty the cat's litter box, wash your hands, polish the candlesticks, set the table, comb your hair. From the minute you get home from school on Friday afternoon it's work, work, work until, at last, the sun starts to set. Then it's time to light the Shabbat candles and start enjoying the best day of the week.

For observant Jews all over the world Friday evening and the whole next day are a time for prayer at the synagogue, reading, taking walks with friends and family, and feeling the special peacefulness of the day of rest.

In Israel the Shabbat feeling is even stronger because the bus driver, the storekeeper, and everybody else in the neighborhood

... but different

share it. By Friday, noon, there are long lines of people at the bus stops carrying bags of freshly baked ḥallahs (Sabbath bread) and bouquets of flowers. They're hurrying to get home early for the holiday. In midafternoon the shutters of stores begin to rattle down, and cooking smells drift out of busy kitchens. The buses stop running at sundown in some Israeli cities and don't begin to run again until Saturday night. As the streets grow dark on Friday evening, dressed-up families stroll to the synagogues to welcome the Sabbath queen.

The next day—the Sabbath—is peaceful and prayerful for some Israelis, but not for all. Those who are less religious go to beaches, parks, and soccer games to enjoy their one day off. Sunday is an ordinary workday.

At dusk on Saturday the closing prayers are said, the lights are turned on, and the sweet quiet of the Sabbath ends. Buses begin to roar through the streets, café shutters roll up, and stores open. And half of Israel goes walking on the main streets of town while the other half sits at café tables "noshing" and calling "*Shalom. Mah nishma?*" ("Hi. What's doin'?") to their friends. For both religious and nonreligious Israeli Jews the Sabbath is the warmest, friendliest day of the week.

Kirschen draws a cartoon for *The Jerusalem Post* each day. Ever since he arrived in Israel from the United States, he has been helping Israelis to poke fun at their troubles.

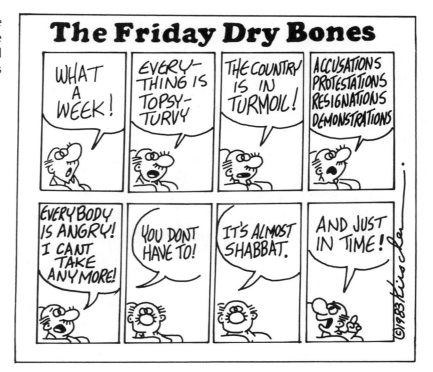

The Friday Dry Bones

WHAT A WEEK!

EVERYTHING IS TOPSY-TURVY

THE COUNTRY IS IN TURMOIL!

ACCUSATIONS PROTESTATIONS RESIGNATIONS DEMONSTRATIONS

EVERYBODY IS ANGRY! I CANT TAKE ANY MORE!

YOU DONT HAVE TO!

IT'S ALMOST SHABBAT.

AND JUST IN TIME!

©1983 Kirschen

ROSH HASHANAH AND YOM KIPPUR

Where would a Jew be on Yom Kippur? In the synagogue!

This fact saved the State of Israel on Yom Kippur day in 1973. Three enemy armies invaded Israel in a surprise attack. Quickly the Israeli soldiers were called from their homes and synagogues. And because there was no other traffic on that quiet holiday, they swiftly reached their army units.

Driving off the enemy took a little longer.

A legend tells us that the gates of heaven are open from the Rosh Hashanah holiday until Yom Kippur, as God listens to our prayers and decides our fate for the next year. We have a lot of thinking to do during those days in the synagogue. And if we get sleepy or bored, the loud cry of the shofar snaps us back to attention. Many people spend all of Yom Kippur at the synagogue fasting and praying. At the end of the holiday we dip ḥallah and apple in honey and wish each other a good, sweet year.

A lot of thinking goes on in Israel, too, at the beginning of the Jewish year. And some people don't wait for the cry of the shofar to start them off. In the darkness of dawn before Rosh Hashanah, Jews from North Africa open their windows and bang loudly on their pots and pans. This doesn't put the neighbors in a religious frame of mind, but the pot bangers hope it will chase away any evil spirits who want to mess up their new year. It also wakes people up to go to the early sliḥot prayer before the holiday.

On Yom Kippur traffic stops all over Israel. The roads and streets are empty and hushed. Toward the end of the long Yom Kippur day, tired Jerusalemites wearing white robes and dresses go to the Kotel, the Western Wall. They pray as the sun sets and the first stars appear. It is a last plea for a good new year before the gates of heaven close.

Ranan Burstein

Ḥasidic Jews pray beside the huge stones of the Kotel, the ancient Western Wall of the Temple Mount. Some people write notes or prayers and put them in the cracks between the stones. They hope that their prayers will rise from this holy place and reach God quickly.

What year is it? In Israel that's a hard question to answer.

According to the Jewish calendar, which counts from the Biblical date of the Creation, it is almost the year 6000. According to the Muslim calendar, which counts from the date Mohammed (the Muslim prophet) came to Medina to preach his new religion, it's only the mid-1300s. And according to the Christian (Gregorian) calendar, which is used in Western countries, it is the late 1900s.

What month is it? That's even harder to answer.

Each Jewish or Hebrew month has a Hebrew name. The month begins with the appearance of the new moon. An extra month, Adar Bet, is added every few years to keep the shorter lunar year from slipping behind the solar year. Otherwise months would come out at different seasons. Passover might turn up in midwinter and Ḥanukkah in midsummer.

Muslim months have Arab names. Like Hebrew months, they begin with the new moon. But Muslim holidays do come out in different seasons. The month-long fast of Ramadan may be an easy midwinter fast or a hot, cranky midsummer fast.

The Gregorian calendar is based on the sun and rolls smoothly along with only one special arrangement—an extra day, February 29, every four years.

Here's how to convert the general (Gregorian) year into the Jewish year: add 3,760 to the general year between January 1 and Rosh Hashanah; add 3,761 to the general year between Rosh Hashanah and January 1. For example: 1986 (general calendar) + 3,760 = 5746 (Hebrew calendar).

Now, can you figure out the Hebrew year in which you were born?

The masthead of Israel's English-language newspaper, *The Jerusalem Post*, carries the date in Arabic, English and Hebrew.

THE JERUSALEM POST

Vol. LIV, No. 16311   Friday, September 5, 1986 ● Elul 1, 5746 ● Moharram 2, 1407   NIS 1.40 (Eilat NIS 1.22)

Don't try to borrow a book from the library or go shopping during Sukkoth week. All the schools and many businesses are closed for the holiday. The beaches and parks are full. There isn't much space left at this campground at Ein Gedi on the Dead Sea.

Teak Silberman

SUKKOTH AND SIMHAT TORAH

What looks like a house on the outside and has a leaky, leafy ceiling and dangling fruits and vegetables on the inside? It's a *sukkah*—the little house we build in our backyards or in the synagogue yard to celebrate the Sukkoth holiday. We eat meals in the *sukkah* and remember that the Jewish people once wandered through the desert and lived in tents and *sukkahs*. When a hanging apple or cucumber bumps your head, be grateful for our rich harvests of good foods. And remember Israel's harvest when you wave a green branch and a lemonlike fruit (the lulav and etrog) in the synagogue.

Simḥat Torah, at the end of the week of Sukkoth, is a party for the Torah. We finish reading the scroll of the Five Books of the Torah. Then we take all the Torahs out of the *Aron* (closet) of the synagogue and carry them around and around in a dancing, singing parade. After the parade one Torah is unrolled to the first chapter of the first book, and we start reading all over again.

In the days of the Bible, Sukkoth was one of three holidays when the Jews loaded up their donkeys and came to the Temple in Jerusalem. They would bring gifts of their harvest for God and His priests. It was a happy time because it came at the end of the great fall harvest, when the storehouses were packed full of figs, olives, wine, grains, and vegetables. The pilgrims feasted, sang, and prayed for rain to water the winter crops.

Modern Israelis are busy harvesting at Sukkoth, just like their ancestors. The markets are full of fruits and vegetables. House-keepers carry home heavy shopping bags for the holiday meals in the *sukkah*. And the first things on the Sukkoth shopping list are a perfect, golden etrog and a tall, rustling lulav.

During the four workdays between the beginning and end of Sukkoth, Israelis come to the Kotel from all over the country. The Temple is gone, but the people share the joy of the holiday at its last remaining wall. And on Simḥat Torah the Torahs of many Jerusalem synagogues are carried to the Kotel. Men, women, and children dance through the streets as they follow the Torahs. And people throw candies to the dancers from their balconies.

Near Sukkoth time Jews from Ethiopia add another holiday, a day of fasting called Sigd. It celebrates the giving of the Torah from Mt. Sinai and the return of the Jews from Babylonia. Priests wearing white turbans lead their people to the top of a hill. Together they recite the Ten Commandments and the words of the prophets. A holiday feast ends the day of fasting.

ḤANUKKAH

The days are so short in midwinter that it's dark when you get up for school and it's dark again when you get home. Just in time you take down the Ḥanukkah menorah, and for eight nights you and your family brighten the darkness by lighting Ḥanukkah candles. The family sings "Maoz Tzur" and tells the story of Judah Maccabee and his army who fought for freedom against the Syrian rulers of the land. Everybody knows about the miracle of the oil, when a tiny jug of oil—enough for one night—burned for eight nights in the Holy Temple in Jerusalem. There are presents for the children and dreidel games and latkes (pancakes) and holiday parties. Right after Ḥanukkah, though it's still winter, the days start getting longer. The bold Ḥanukkah candles must have scared away the dark.

The people of modern Israel are fighting to keep their country free, just as the Maccabees did in ancient Israel. At Ḥanukkah they feel very close to Judah and his stubborn followers. Although it often rains in December, they climb up to the mountainside village

Dreidel rules:

Each player gets an equal number of pennies or nuts and puts one in the center for the pot. The players take turns spinning the dreidel. If it lands with the נ *(nun) up, the player gets nothing; with the* ג *(gimmel) up, the player takes all the coins in the pot and everybody must put another one in; with the* ה *(hé) up, the player takes half the coins from the pot; with the* ש *(shin) up, the unlucky player gives one coin to the pot.*

The nun, gimmel, hé and shin stand for the Hebrew words "A great miracle happened there." But the Hanukkah story happened in Israel, so Israelis say, "A great miracle happened here." They change the shin to a pé (פ). *It represents the Hebrew word po, which means "here."*

of Modin, where Judah was born. Runners light torches at Modin and carry them down the mountain. The burning torches are handed from runner to runner until they reach the Kotel in Jerusalem. There, the torch from Modin lights the ḥanukkiya, the eight-branched menorah atop the ancient wall.

Big electric ḥanukkiyot shine from the tops of office buildings and kibbutz watchtowers. And small Ḥanukkah candles flicker in windows all across the land. Ḥanukkah torches blaze on Masada, where other fighters for freedom once lived. For eight days all of Israel sparkles with lights.

Like in the United States, kids get presents and make presents to give to their families. They play dreidel and eat latkes and soofganiyot (doughnuts). There's no school for the eight days of the holiday, so many Israelis escape the chilly rain by going south to the Dead Sea and sunny Elath.

THESE LIGHTS ARE HOLY

told by a soldier who fought in Israel's War for Independence

Shaika was a newcomer to Israel. He had barely lived through the Holocaust in Europe. Now he was fighting near Jerusalem in Israel's War for Independence.

The road to the city of Jerusalem had been cut by the enemy. Trucks that tried to bring food and other supplies were fired on and destroyed. If the army did not find a new route quickly, the city would starve. Bulldozers climbed into the hills above the old road and began to clear a new passage. But when they came near an abandoned Arab village, the bulldozers were attacked by Arab snipers hidden in the hills. Shaika and the other soldiers watched helplessly as the bulldozers stopped in their tracks. The army couldn't silence the snipers because they couldn't find the snipers' nests.

It was the afternoon before Ḥanukkah. Shaika pulled out the bag of Ḥanukkah candles he had brought in his pack. Suddenly he had an idea. He hurried to his commander and said, "Let me sneak into the village late this afternoon. I'll light these candles on the window sill of the two-story house. When it gets dark, the candles will shine out. The snipers will think we're in the building, and they'll blast it. Then we'll know where they're hiding.

The commander nodded. "It might work. But, Shaika, it's dangerous. There are mines on the paths to the village."

"Don't worry," said Shaika. "I'll go across the fields."

Carrying a rifle, the Ḥanukkah candles, and matches, Shaika crept toward the village under cover of the rocks and bushes. Finally, breathless, he reached the door of the two-story building. His hand was at the knob when he saw a thin wire wound around it stretching back into the house. The door was booby-trapped! If he had pulled it open, it would have exploded.

Softly Shaika said the blessing of "gomel," for one who has been saved from danger. He backed away, found a broken window, and squeezed inside. As the sun was setting, he placed his candles near the window that faced the enemy, lit them, and said the blessing. Then he crept back to his unit, silently singing "Maoz Tzur."

Night fell, and the hill was dark. Only the candles shone brightly in the window of the two-story house. They were a perfect target. A flurry of shots rang out from the sniper hideouts on the hill.

"We have them pinpointed!" cried the commander.

That night Israeli army units forced the snipers out. Shaika's Ḥanukkah candles had helped to clear the road that would save Jerusalem.

TU BI-SHEVAT

You dress in layers like an onion to keep warm because it's always raining or snowing out. What a strange time to think about birds and bees, flowers and trees. But exactly at the coldest time of the year in the United States, Jews celebrate the new year of the trees —Tu Bi-Shevat. Your religious school teacher brings in raisins, nuts, long brown carob pods, and other fruits of Israel. Everybody says the blessing over the fruit and takes a taste. Watch out for your braces when you try the carob or dried fig. It's tough.

Even in Israel you might need your boots and raincoats at Tu Bi-Shevat. But the smell of spring is in the air. Birds are coming home from their winter in Africa, and buds are growing fat on the trees and bushes. The most eager tree of all, the almond tree, ignores the rain and bursts into blossom in time for the holiday.

Israeli kids put away their math and history books for a day and go out into the fields and hills to plant tiny young trees. Hiking groups celebrate the new year of the trees by exploring the woods and countryside. And everybody blesses the fruits of the land and has a Tu Bi-Shevat feast, as Jews did long ago. But the ancients would never recognize some of Israel's new fruit. Today's mangoes, pineapples, bananas, kiwi fruit, and even oranges never grew in King Solomon's orchards.

Nimrod, Yaeli, and Elad are planting a walnut tree on Har Ḥalutz (pioneer mountain) in northern Israel. They sing this Hebrew song as they work:

The almond tree is blooming and the sun shines bright
Birds atop each roof call out— the holiday's in sight.
Tu Bi-Shevat has come, the festival of trees,
Tu Bi-Shevat has come, the festival of trees.

Ehud Ryden

You and I are landowners! Because of the Jewish National Fund, we own a piece of Israel. The fund was started in 1901 to buy land in Palestine for the whole Jewish people. The owners would often sell only swampy soil or barren, rocky land to the Jewish National Fund. So farmers worked to drain off the extra water and to clear the rocks. Then they planted trees and crops and watched the land come to life.

All that work cost money—a lot of it. In faraway New York City, boys and girls with blue-and-white collection boxes ran from car to car on the subways and asked the passengers for money to help plant trees in Palestine. Many people filled JNF boxes at home with a few pennies each day. Today many people still have boxes. They also plant trees by buying tree certificates from the JNF for Mother's Day, Father's Day, and other special times.

By 1984, JNF had planted date palms in the desert, pine trees on the hills, and eucalyptus in the swamps—165 million trees to green the land of Israel.

When you visit Israel, call JNF and ask to plant your own tree. They'll help you do it any time—not just at Tu Bi-Shevat. If you want to buy a tree certificate in the United States, write to the Jewish National Fund Inc., 42 East 69 Street, New York, New York 10021. They'll let you know what to do.

PURIM

Nobody will "shush" you in the synagogue at Purim. Stamp your feet, laugh out loud, and spin your grogger (noisemaker) while the Purim *Megillah* (scroll) is being read. It tells about Mordecai and his niece Esther, a brave Jewish girl who married King Ahasuerus of Persia. When Haman, the king's chief minister, wanted to kill the Jews of the kingdom, Esther risked her life and saved them.

It's a mitzvah (a commandment or good deed) to make so much noise that nobody can hear the name of evil Haman when the *Megillah* is read. And it's a mitzvah to eat, drink, and celebrate until you're so mixed up that you can't tell the difference (in Hebrew: *adloyada*) between wicked Mordecai and lovable Haman. Whoops . . . I mean between lovable Haman and wicked . . . no, no . . . between wicked Mordecai and . . . oh, well . . . see what I mean? At Purim people also have costume parties, give gifts to poor people, and bring dishes of food treats (*shalaḥ manot*) to friends.

All these things happen in Israel, too—and more. For weeks before Purim the store windows are crowded with costumes and masks. On the eve of the holiday the *Megillah* is read in the synagogues and also on Israeli TV. Then thousands of Queen Esthers, Hamans, Supermen, pirates, Smurfs, and monsters swarm into the streets and onto the buses in a great, country-wide Purim masquerade.

On Purim day the towns and cities have Adloyada parades with giant dolls, floats, clowns, and dancers. Costumed kids dance along and hit each other with squeaking plastic hammers. Others carry covered *shalaḥ manot* dishes with hamantashen (prune- or poppy-seed-filled pastries), colored eggs, and marzipan cakes to their friends and relatives. Special treats are delivered to army camps, to shut-ins, and even to prisons.

Tel Aviv has a Purim marathon race, which gives people a chance to run off their bellyfuls of hamantashen. Jerusalem and Haifa have street fairs with mimes and puppet shows and, above all, food booths. It's an eat, drink, and be-a-little-crazy holiday.

"The Jews have so many Hamans but only one Purim" complains a Jewish proverb. But Jewish folklore tells of many times when communities were rescued from danger. Each was called a "Purim." Here is a story of the Purim in the town of Hebron in Palestine.

THE HEBRON PURIM

adapted from Legends of Judea and Samaria by Zev Vilnay

Many years ago a cruel sheik ruled over Hebron. One day he called together the leaders of the Jewish community and commanded, "Bring me 50,000 piasters within three days. If you fail, I will enslave half of you and burn the other half!"

The Jews of Hebron were poor. Their souls shrank with fear when they heard this demand. They rushed to the synagogue and fasted, wept, and prayed to God for help.

That same night the sheik had a dream. Three old men stood over him and demanded 50,000 piasters. If they did not get it, they would kill him. Terror-stricken, the sheik pulled a purse filled with gold and silver from the treasure chest under his bed and gave it to them.

Moments later the caretaker at the synagogue heard a noise at the gate. He jumped up, afraid that the sheik's soldiers were coming to destroy them. To his surprise a hand pushed through the bars of the gate, flung in a purse, and disappeared.

The purse contained exactly 50,000 piasters.

Three days later the soldiers burst into the Jewish quarter and demanded the money. The leaders of the community gave the soldiers the mysterious purse. When it was brought to the sheik, he recognized it as the purse he had given to the old men in his dream. He realized that God had helped the Jews, and he cried, "Behold, the Guardian of Israel neither slumbers nor sleeps."

Because of this miracle, the Jews of Hebron appointed the fourteenth day of the month of Kislev as a day of joy and gladness—a Purim day.

PASSOVER

Here comes the great spring holiday of freedom. You'd better freely pick up your socks, clean the crumbs and apple cores out of your pockets, help with the vacuuming, and straighten your room. If you don't do it freely, your parents will *make* you do it. Because at Passover everything must be clean and fresh and special. There are special dishes, special foods, new clothing, and two wonderful Seder meals when the story of the holiday is told.

We read the Haggadah, an ancient book of stories, songs, and prayers, at each Seder. It tells how God helped the Jewish people to escape slavery in Egypt and go off into the desert. As we read, we try to imagine how hard slavery must have been, and we think about people who are still struggling for freedom today. It's a thought-filled holiday, but it's a fun holiday, too. The kids start the Seder off by asking four questions. Then, while the grownups are busy reading the answers in the Haggadah, the children try to steal the afikomen that the Seder leader hid away. After the meal they watch carefully to see the invisible prophet Elijah sip wine from his glass. The Seder ends with singing until late at night. And afterward there's a week of holiday still to come.

Israeli kids aren't as lucky as American kids at Passover. That's because Israeli families only have one Seder. And that means there's only one chance to ask the Four Questions and steal the afikomen. Of course, there are also good things about Passover in Israel. For instance, many families pack a tent and their Seder meal and go south to the Negev or Sinai deserts. They have a Seder under the bright desert stars, just as the Jews did during their years of wandering. A little sand in the soup or on the matzo makes it even more real.

The sweet smell of spring is everywhere because wildflowers are blooming and barley is ripening in the fields. The Bible tells us that Passover was one of three holidays when Jews came to Jerusalem bringing gifts of their harvest. Many modern Israelis come to the Kotel in the middle days of the holiday. They are not bringing baskets of barley; they are bringing their hopes and prayers.

Too quickly the holiday is over. But Jews from Morocco have a lively holiday called the Mimouna that stretches the fun of Passover for another day. Families come to the parks with blankets, beach umbrellas, and baskets full of food. Many wear the embroidered vests and dresses and the jingling head gear of their old country. They light cooking fires, and soon spicy smells of roasting lamb and liver fill the air. While the picnickers wait to eat, they bounce to the rhythms of clay drums, cymbals, and tambourines. Musicians begin to twang a melody on round-bellied uds (pear-shaped guitars). Soon grandmas, young soldiers, and anybody who feels like it get up to dance while others clap along.

Israelis miss out on one Seder, but they make up for it with the music and feasting of the Mimouna.

YOM HA-ZIKARON AND ISRAEL INDEPENDENCE DAY

Happy holidays fill the Jewish year. But there are also days when Jews sadly remember the tragic times in their history. Tishah Be-Av is the day on which the Temple in Jerusalem was destroyed—once in 586 B.C.E. and again in 70 C.E. The Jews were expelled from Spain on the same day in 1492. Yom Ha-Shoah reminds Jews of the deaths of 6 million of their people in the Holocaust during World War II.

In Israel, as in every other Jewish community, the fast day of Tishah Be-Av, on the ninth of Av, and Yom Ha-Shoah, Holocaust Remembrance Day, on the twenty-seventh of Nissan, are days of prayer. Special verses from the Bible are recited in the synagogue on Tishah Be-Av. On Yom Ha-Shoah the Yizkor memorial prayer is recited for the lost Jews of Europe. On the eve of Yom Ha-Shoah a siren blast reminds Israelis to stop work and drivers to pull over to the side of the road for a moment of silent remembering.

Here's a Jewish holiday that doesn't go back 4,000 years. It started in 1948 when the State of Israel was born. In American synagogues on Israel Independence Day, a prayer is said for Israel. There are fairs, birthday parties, and parades. The biggest is the huge Israel Day parade that rolls up Fifth Avenue in New York City, with floats, dancers, flags, and marching bands.

Israelis love parties and parades, too. But before they begin their Independence Day celebration they have some important, painful remembering to do. The day before Israel Independence Day (Yom Ha-Atzmaut in Hebrew) is a memorial day, called Yom Ha-Zikaron, for the men and women who died while defending the country. There are two minutes of silence on Yom Ha-Zikaron. All work stops, and buses and cars pull to the side of the road and wait. Later people bring flowers and wreaths to cemeteries and war memorials. Israel is such a small country that each family has lost a friend or a relative in its years of war. A woman at a cemetery said quietly, "Without Yom Ha-Zikaron we would not have Yom Ha-Atzmaut. Our soldiers died so that Israel could live."

At sundown sirens blast across the land. Yom Ha-Zikaron has ended. The celebration of Yom Ha-Atzmaut can begin. Torches blaze into the night sky from Mt. Herzl in Jerusalem. For weeks youngsters have been gathering wood for their own bonfires, and now holiday fires are lit on hillsides all over the land. People sing and tell stories around the fires till dawn. Those who don't like campfire songs and ants in their shish kebab spend the evening dancing at flag-covered bandshells in the city parks.

The next day, Israel air-force jets roar overhead in tight formations. There are breathtaking free-fall demonstrations by air-force parachutists and soccer games and flower-decked, flag-waving parades. In Haifa dance groups wearing costumes in a rainbow of colors parade and perform.

A high point of Israel Independence Day is the Bible Quiz. Youngsters come to compete from all over the world. And Israelis rush home from parades and parties to watch the quiz on TV.

By afternoon a stream of dusty, tired people begins to pour into Jerusalem. They are Independence Day hikers who have walked through the country for three days, sleeping out of doors along the way. Jerusalemites greet the hikers with clapping, cheering, and hot showers.

The last big event is a song festival and contest which features Israel's biggest stars. It is broadcast live, like the Bible Quiz, and Israelis end the day arguing about who should win.

Settlers dance a hora around the flag on Israel Independence Day. They live in a new *mitzpeh* (lookout) village on a Galilee mountain.

Teak Silberman

No more curls for this three-year-old, except for the curly earlocks (*payess*) that hang in front of his ears. On Lag B'Omer the tomb of Simeon ben Yoḥai at Meron becomes the hair-cutting center of Israel.

Central Zionist Archives

LAG B'OMER

Drop your books! Get out the soccer ball or archery set, and head for the green outdoors. Lag b'Omer is a springtime holiday for all students. It celebrates the day that the students of Rabbi Akiva recovered from a serious illness in ancient Judea.

In Israel, Lag b'Omer is a happy time for everybody except three-year-old boys. Religious families don't give haircuts to their little boys until the Lag b'Omer after their third birthday. Then they bring the children to the small town of Meron in the Galilee and have a mass haircutting. There's lots of crying (the little boys) and lots of singing and dancing (the grownups).

Why do they come to Meron? It is the burial place of Simeon ben Yoḥai, a great rabbi who died on Lag b'Omer. A parade of pilgrims carries a 150-year-old Torah to Meron from the nearby town of Zefat. The people light bonfires, have picnics, and enjoy the outdoors—even the close-clipped three-year-olds.

Bonfires are lit in empty lots all over Israel at Lag b'Omer. It is also a busy time for weddings because, except for Lag b'Omer day, weddings may not be performed during the seven weeks between Passover and Shavuoth.

SHAVUOTH

Butterflies are making the rounds from flower to flower as we go to the synagogue for Shavuoth. Flowers decorate the synagogue, too. We sniff the sweet smell as we stand with the congregation and recite the Ten Commandments. At Shavuoth we enjoy the first fruits and flowers of springtime, and we remember the gifts of the Torah and the Ten Commandments that the Jewish people received at Mt. Sinai.

During the seven weeks between Passover and Shavuoth many of the fruit trees have flowered in Israel and new fruit is beginning to grow. Cows are enjoying the fresh grass and giving more milk. And the markets have Shavuoth "specials" on milk, cheese, and butter because it's a custom to eat dairy foods on the holiday.

In Biblical days the farmers decked their oxen and donkeys with flowers and brought their first fruit to the Temple in Jerusalem for Shavuoth. Many kibbutzim celebrate the holiday with a parade of their own first fruit. The children decorate wagons and tractors with flowers. Then they climb aboard, along with baby lambs and calves, new chicks, and baskets of wheat and fruit. The tractors chug through the kibbutzim while everybody sings and claps. There's a great Shavuoth party afterward that always includes milk and honey biscuits because, as the Bible says, Israel is "a land flowing with milk and honey."

Many Israelis follow the custom of studying the Holy Books together during the whole night of Shavuoth. A table loaded with cake, fruit, and chickpeas helps to keep them going until dawn. In Jerusalem at dawn the tired students pile out of their synagogues and homes, many parents carrying little children in pajamas, and make their way to the Kotel, the last wall remaining from the Holy Temple. They stream down the stairs and fill the large square in front of the Kotel as the sun rises over the Judaean hills. Then they recite Shavuoth prayers in the place where Jews had once stood with their flower-decked gifts of first fruits.

ISRAEL'S MINORITIES CELEBRATE

On Friday, the Muslim Sabbath, Muslims come to their mosques for the noon prayer. They wash at the fountain in the courtyard, leave their shoes at the doorway, and enter the cool, dimly lit room. There they kneel on the carpeted floor, pray, and hear a sermon from the prayer leader. During the week the voice of the muezzin (caller) sounds above the city noises five times a day, reminding Muslims to pray. Those daily prayers can be done privately, but the Sabbath (Friday) noon prayer is a community prayer.

The Muslim year begins with the holiday of Muharram, which celebrates the Prophet Mohammed's escape from the hostile city of Mecca to friendly Medina more than 1,300 years ago. Ten weeks later Mawlid-al-Nabi arrives, a feast day in honor of Mohammed's birthday. Families set up tents in the yard to house visiting kinfolk from all over the land, and the women prepare mountains of rice, lamb, and vegetables. Verses that tell the story of the prophet's life are chanted from the Koran. Children listen as they lick special holiday candy made in the shapes of dolls or knights on horseback.

The ninth month of the Muslim year, Ramadan, is a time when devout Muslims fast all day. They eat only after sundown and again in the early dawn. "Fasting purifies the soul and makes us feel sympathy for the poor," explained a Muslim shopkeeper. Ramadan ends with an explosion of gaiety, hospitality, and good food in the holiday of Id-al-Fitr. People dress up in their best clothing, poor people receive alms, and children get sweets and gifts.

There are many other holidays and feast days in the Muslim year. They honor Muslim saints as well as Biblical leaders like Abraham, Isaac, and Moses.

Church bells peal out all over Israel on Sunday morning, the Christian day of rest. They are loudest of all in Jerusalem, which has churches of every Christian denomination. On Christmas and Easter the Christian community is joined by visitors from all over the world. Pilgrims gather in Manger Square in Bethlehem on Christmas Eve. The ringing of the bells is joined by the music of hymns and prayers coming from the huge, ornate Church of the Nativity. The pilgrims in the square watch the services on a large TV screen and joyously pray along. And visiting choirs from many countries sing carols.

Before Easter sad-faced and sobbing pilgrims walk along the narrow street called Via Dolorosa, ("Road of Grief"), in the Old City of Jerusalem. The New Testament describes this street as the pain-filled route Jesus followed, carrying the cross. But on Easter morning all the church bells of Jerusalem ring out, and the holiday ends in happy celebration.

PUT AN OASIS ON YOUR WINDOW SILL

Jewish holidays are linked to the seasons of the land of Israel. As the Jews planted and harvested, they gave thanks to God and celebrated.

Celebrate a holiday by planting a desert oasis or an orchard right on your window sill. You can use dwarf palm trees or the seeds of a fruit that grows in Israel such as an orange or a grapefruit.

Palm-tree oasis

You will need:

potting soil
container, 4 inches or 5 inches deep and about 10 inches square—available at a plant nursery or in the disposable-bakeware section of a food store

dwarf palm plant, available at a plant nursery
small pocket mirror
cup of sand or small pebbles
miniature plastic camels and people

1. Sprinkle 1 inch of soil in the container.

2. Leave the palm in its pot. Place the pot to one side, on the soil in the container. Fill the container with soil as high as the soil level in the pot.

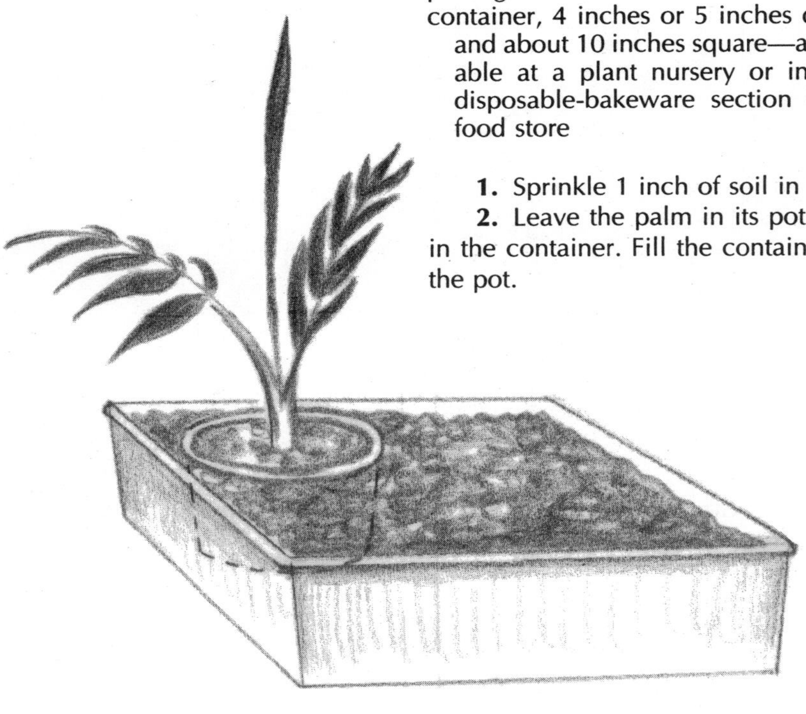

An orange grove is called a pardes in Hebrew. The word was borrowed from the Persians. Later the English borrowed the Persian-Hebrew pardes and changed it to paradise.

There's a bit of paradise at Yeshiva University in New York City—a Biblical garden with date palms, pomegranate and olive trees, papyrus, flax, and many other things that are mentioned in the Bible.

3. Lay the mirror on the soil in the center of the container.

4. Sprinkle the sand or pebbles over the edges of the mirror and around the palm.

5. Place miniature plastic camels and people beside the palm, or make your own oasis dwellers out of clay, plasticene, or bread dough (see page 29).

An oasis needs water, so remember to follow the nursery's instructions and water your palm when necessary.

When the palm outgrows its pot, you can lift it out and plant it directly in the container.

Be a patient farmer. Keep watching, and water when necessary. Fruit seeds have hard coats and take many weeks to sprout.

Citrus grove

You will need:

8–10 orange seeds or grapefruit seeds (If you use the seeds of Jaffa oranges from Israel, you'll have a real Israeli orchard.)
cup of water

container, 3 or 4 inches deep
potting mixture: one-half soil, one-quarter perlite, one-quarter peat moss
pebbles

1. Soak the seeds overnight in a cup of water.

2. Fill the container three-quarters full with potting mixture. If the container has no drainage holes, put a layer of pebbles at the bottom.

3. Plant the seeds ½ inch deep in the potting mixture, water the mixture lightly, and put the container in a warm place. Keep the soil moist.

4. In three or four weeks, when the seedlings appear, move the container to a bright but not sunny place. In another two or three weeks, you can move it to a sunny window sill.

Eventually, your seedlings will grow into trees, so be prepared to replant them in larger and larger containers.

Ben-Zion Dorfman

Orange trees are new immigrants to the land of Israel. Olive, date, fig and pomegranate trees are sabras with roots going back to Bible times. This naked fig tree is waiting for the winter to end. By Passover it will be covered with leaves and flowers.

MAKE AN ISRAEL INDEPENDENCE DAY PARTY

- Set up a sandbox archaeology dig in the backyard. Bury any weird things you can think of—a frisbee, a pencil, coins, keys, pots. All your guests can become archaeologists and make "finds." Each "archaeologist" has to explain his or her find and the civilization it comes from. Give prizes for the dumbest, funniest, most scientific, and most imaginative explanations.

- Have an Israel quiz. Make up questions from the information in this book. Or, instead of a Bible quiz, play "Who Am I?" Pin the name of a Bible character on a player's back. The player must guess who he or she is by asking questions that can be answered with "yes" or "no." For example: "Was I in Egypt at the time the Jews lived there as slaves?" "Did I lead them out of Egypt into the desert?" That was too easy, wasn't it? So try this: "Did I have twin sons—one who became a hunter and one a farmer?" "Did I prepare a delicious stew to trick my husband?" Or this: "Did I win a very important beauty contest?" "Did I risk my life when I invited my husband to dinner?"

- Have a barbecue or campfire in the park or backyard. Toast marshmallows or frankfurters. Or make an Israeli dish. (You'll find recipes in Chapter 9.)

- Teach an Israeli song or dance. Tell an Israeli story (Look in Chapters 10 and 13.)

- Make a gooey birthday cake, and decorate it with candles and little Israeli flags. The flags are easy to make. Draw them with a blue marking pen, and tape them to plastic straws: Light the birthday candles, make a great wish for all of you and for Israel, and blow!

8 Crafts

Bezalel, the first great Jewish craftsman, got his orders from Moses. And Moses got them directly from God. The Bible tells how Bezalel labored in the desert to make a pure gold menorah and an ark for the Ten Commandments. Since that time, Jewish craftspeople have made jewelry, crowns, fine pottery, mosaics, and many other precious things. But, like Bezalel, they worked hardest on the tools of their religion. Crowns for the Torah, jeweled and embroidered ark curtains, and carefully carved spice boxes and charity boxes were the richest possessions of every Jewish community.

Muslim and Christian craftspeople decorated their places of worship with ceramic tile designs, great hammered brass trays and lamps, and carved olivewood screens. The new land of Israel inherited these craft traditions.

In 1906, when the early ḥalutzim (pioneer settlers) were living in tents and fighting malaria mosquitoes, a school of arts and crafts was founded in Jerusalem. It was named Bezalel after the Biblical craftsman. During the next eighty years Bezalel turned out many artists, craftspeople, and industrial designers. Graduates of Bezalel and other artists are making beautiful objects beside the Mediterranean in the village of Ein Hod, high in the mountains in Zefat, and elsewhere.

Try some of the projects in this chapter, and you'll be a craftsperson, too. You won't be as great as Bezalel because you won't get your orders from Moses. But you'll have fun.

D'vora makes mugs and pitchers at her workshop in a *mitzpeh* in northern Israel. She's not the first potter to work here. Bits of ancient pottery have been found in the earth nearby.

Jews face Jerusalem and the Temple mount when they pray. Muslims face Mecca in Saudi Arabia. Both peoples place a special mark on the wall that faces their holy city. Jews make a woven hanging or picture called a mizraḥ, meaning "east" or "toward the sunrise." Muslims cut a niche into the wall and call it a mihrab.

Mizraḥ

You will need:

pencil
tracing paper
masking tape
light colored cloth (an old clean sheet will do)
dressmaker's carbon paper

crayons
2 brown paper bags
ironing board
iron

1. With a pencil, draw a design on the tracing paper. You may copy some of the symbols on pages 150 and 151 or make up your own.

2. Tape the cloth to a flat surface.

3. Place the carbon paper face down on the cloth. Place the drawing on top of the carbon paper, and tape it in place.

4. Draw over the design, pressing firmly. Remove the tape, drawing, and carbon. The design should appear on the cloth.

5. Color in the design with the crayons. For a bright picture, press firmly and don't leave white spaces in the colored area.

6. Tear open a brown bag. Place it flat on the ironing board. Place the crayon design face down on the bag. Put the other bag, which has also been flattened, over the design.

7. Run a hot iron over the bag for several minutes. The heat will melt the crayon wax and spread the color.

stretch the cloth
as you tape it

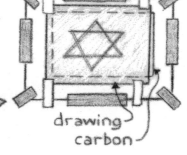

drawing
carbon

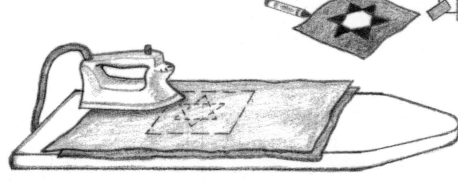

Magen David decorations

CHAIN
   You will need:

rectangular sheets of white or colored paper   scissors

1. Fold the paper in half. Fold it in half again.

2. Cut up to the fold from the shorter open edge, as shown.
3. Cut out the triangle, as shown.
4. Unfold the cut paper.
5. Repeat steps 1–4 for each triangle. Link the triangles together to form a chain.

Folded edges

open edges

PINWHEEL
   You will need:

scissors   crayon or marker
2 sheets of construction paper   thumbtack
   of different colors   long pencil with eraser tip
paste

1. With the scissors, cut a triangle out of each sheet of colored paper.
2. Paste the triangles together, as shown, to form a star.
3. With a crayon or marker, write "ISRAEL," putting one letter in each point of the star.
4. Push the thumbtack through the center of the star into the eraser tip of the pencil. Tap a point, and the star will spin.

HANGING STAR

You will need:

scissors	stapler or tape
cardboard or oaktag	string

1. With the scissors, cut two Jewish stars of the same size out of the cardboard or oaktag.

2. Cut a slit in each star, as shown.

3. Fit the stars together, as shown.

4. Staple or tape the string to a point of the star, and hang the star up.

You can decorate the stars with glitter or marker designs.

slit

Paper cuttings can be very complicated. They can also be very simple. Either way they're pretty.

Paper cutting

Interesting designs are made by folding paper and cutting through the fold. Many years ago Jewish craftspeople in Europe used cut-paper designs for greeting cards and decorations. Today they are being made again.

You can use your cut-paper design for a greeting card, a mizraḥ design, or a window hanging.

You will need:

1 sheet of strong, medium-weight paper, such as typing paper
scissors (advanced cutters can use a crafts knife)
paste or rubber cement

black or colored paper, or cellophane for backing (if you use cellophane, you will need a cardboard frame to hold the paper stiff)
marking pens or crayons

1. Fold the paper in half. Fold it again into quarters.
2. Cut in from the edges of the paper to make cut-out designs. Be sure to leave *some* of the folded edge uncut, otherwise you will cut the sheet in half.
3. You may unfold the paper to see how the design looks. Then refold the paper, and continue cutting. Try the cutting ideas on this page for mizraḥ designs or holiday cards.
4. When you are finished cutting, glue the design to the black or colored paper or cellophane backing.
5. Decorate your design with the crayons or markers, if you wish.

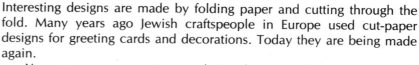

folded
edges

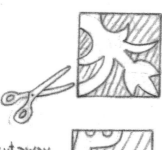

cut away
striped
area

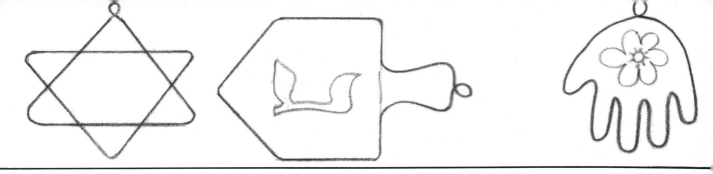

The people of the Middle East were the first to make glass. Archaeologists found many delicate glass perfume bottles and oil jars in Israel.

You can make translucent (foggy, not clear) glasslike decorations from white glue. Hang a glue zoo, a Magen David, or a dreidel in your window.

You will need:

pencil
paper
tape
cardboard
wax paper, larger than your decoration
white glue, such as Elmer's Glue-All

small disposable container
food coloring
pop stick or plastic knife
small paintbrush
gold or silver gift-wrapping cord or plain cord (must be pliable—not stiff)

1. With a pencil, draw a simple design, without sharp corners, on the paper. Copy the designs on this page, if you wish. Tape the paper to the cardboard.

2. Tape the wax paper over the design.

3. Pour glue into the disposable container. Add a drop of food coloring. With a stick or knife, stir the glue until it is evenly colored.

4. Dip the paintbrush in the glue, and trace the outline of your design on the wax paper.

5. Place the cord along the line of glue, making a loop at the top, as shown.

6. Pour the colored glue inside the cord outline, as high as the top of the cord. Fill the whole space—have the glue touch the cord outline.

7. Allow the glue to dry until it is clear and hard (about three days).

8. Peel off the wax paper, and hang your decoration in the window or around your neck.

You can use a marker to draw on your glass glue after it has hardened.

Glass-glue decorations

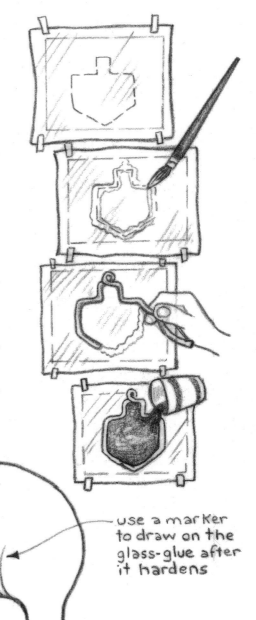

use a marker to draw on the glass-glue after it hardens

Abraham prepares to sacrifice Isaac
1. brown   2. orange   3. gold   4. yellow

Throughout Israel people have found pictures on ancient floors and walls. They were made by placing small ceramic (clay) tiles of different colors beside each other. Today colorful and complicated tile designs decorate the walls of mosques. Israeli artists and craftsmen use tile in furniture, floor surfaces, and wall decorations.

Mosaic tile

This picture is part of the tile floor of a 1,500-year-old synagogue. It was found by farmers digging a ditch near Kibbutz Bet Alfa. It shows the patriarch Abraham preparing to sacrifice his son Isaac.

You can copy the picture on a copying machine or trace it and transfer it to drawing paper with a carbon sheet. Then color it by the numbers.

COLORED PAPER MOSAIC TRAY OR PLAQUE

You will need:

scissors
paper
Styrofoam tray, paper tray or dish, or sheet of cardboard
colored crayons

sheets of colored construction paper cut into ½-inch squares
white glue or paste
sheet of clear, adhesive-backed plastic film, large enough to cover the surface of the tray or plaque

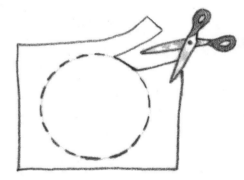

1. Using the scissors, cut the paper to the size of your tray or board.

2. With the crayons, draw and color a simple design, using the colors of your construction paper, or copy a design from this page.

3. Spread a thin layer of white glue or paste over part of the tray or board. Using your drawing as a guide, place the colored squares side by side on the paste.

4. Repeat step 3 on another part of the tray or board. Do a section at a time until the design is complete.

5. Let the glue dry overnight.

6. Peel the paper off the adhesive-backed plastic. Lay the plastic over the mosaic surface. Press it flat, and trim the edges.

glue

CERAMIC TILE TRAY OR PLAQUE
You will need:

scissors
paper
metal or wood tray, or piece of plywood
 or composition board
colored crayons
tile cement, from a crafts store or home-
 supplies store

small tiles, ½-inch square,
 from a crafts store or home-
 supplies store (some should
 be brightly colored; some
 should be one background
 color)
liquid grout in a tube
sponge or damp rag

1. With a scissors, cut the paper to the size of your tray or board.

2. With the crayons, draw and color a simple design, using the colors of your tiles.

3. Spread tile cement over part of the tray or board. Using your drawing as a guide, press the tiles into the cement, leaving a small space between the tiles for grout.

4. Repeat step 3 on another part of the tray or board. Do a section at a time until the design is complete.

5. Squeeze the grout into the spaces between the tiles. With a damp sponge or rag, gently wipe the extra grout off the tile surface.

6. After 24 hours, when the grout is dry, clean the tile surface again with a damp rag or sponge.

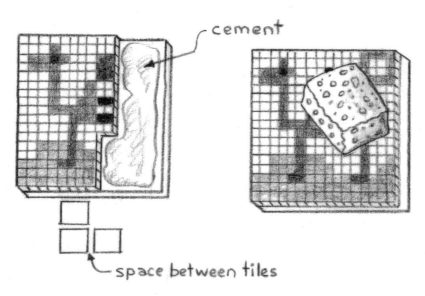

cement

space between tiles

Hiker's stick

This is a project for older children, those able to handle a sharp knife. An adult should be nearby.

The ancient Israelites wandered in the desert. Their descendants wandered over the whole world. And modern Israelis love to wander up and down the land of Israel.

Make a fancy stick to help you on your own hikes.

You will need:

penknife or pocketknife
sturdy tree branch, long enough
  to lean on with your elbow bent
paint (optional)
brush (optional)

newspaper
tape
can of clear plastic spray
  from a paint or hobby store

1. With a penknife or pocketknife, whittle (cut) some of the bark from the branch, leaving a design. Take care! Be sure to cut away from your body and away from the hand that is holding the stick.

2. With some paint and a brush, you may paint designs or your name in the whittled spaces. Or you may leave them white.

3. When the paint is dry, spray the stick with the clear plastic. Tape newspaper on the wall behind the stick. Be sure to spray out of doors or in a room with an open window.

SYMBOLS

What's an ancient Jewish symbol? A Jewish star—right?

Wrong.

Abraham did not wear a Jewish star around his neck. And King David did not have a Magen David (Jewish star) on his shield. The six-pointed "Jewish" star wasn't Jewish at all until about 500 years ago, when people began to use it as an amulet or a synagogue decoration. But it became officially Jewish in 1897, when the Zionists sewed it onto their new blue-and-white flag.

The granddaddy of all Jewish symbols is the seven-armed menorah. It was first made by the Biblical craftsman Bezalel. Pictures of menorahs are found on ancient gravestones, pottery lamps, and buildings. And today a menorah is shown on the official seal of the State of Israel.

Here are some symbols that have been used on Jewish objects for centuries. You may want to draw some of them on your crafts projects.

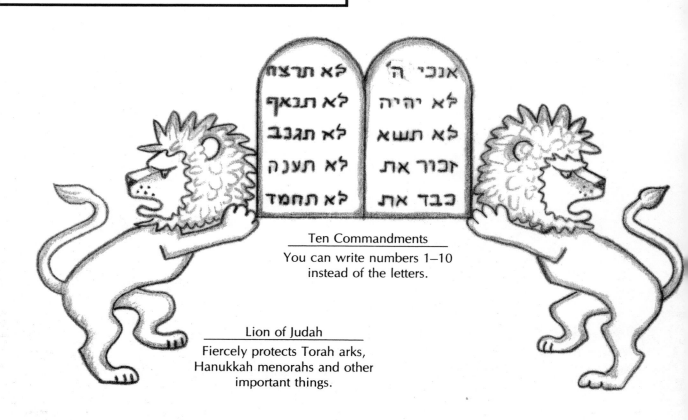

Ten Commandments
You can write numbers 1–10 instead of the letters.

Lion of Judah
Fiercely protects Torah arks, Hanukkah menorahs and other important things.

Hamsa
A good-luck charm shaped like a hand, the name comes from "hamisha," "five" in Hebrew.

Stamp of the State of Israel
The menorah looks like the gold menorah of the Holy Temple.

Pomegranates
Seed-filled fruit, native to Israel. The design decorates coins and the headpieces of Torah scrolls.

Shofar
Ancient trumpet made of a ram's horn.

Flag of the State of Israel
The colors are blue and white.

Lulav
Branches of willow, palm and myrtle, used at Sukkoth.

Milk and honey and more

Take a pinch of northern cooking, a tablespoon of western cooking, a dash of southern cooking, and a smidgeon of eastern cooking. Chop it all together; add lots of garlic, honey, olive oil, and chicken fat; and you've got—*Israeli cuisine!*

From the four corners of the world Jews returned to Israel after the state was established. They brought their pots and pans and favorite recipes. The aromas of frying eggplant, roasting lamb, simmering cholent, baking honey cake, and many other dishes rose into the air from stoves all over the country. Migrating birds must have gotten tipsy with the strange mixture of smells. But the Israelis tasted each others' foods and smacked their lips. Soon peppery Yemenite shakshooka turned up on the supper table of Jews from Brooklyn, Moroccan Israelis noshed on Russian blintzes, and Viennese pastry sat beside Turkish baklava on café tables.

The Chinese and the Jews are thought to be the two oldest peoples in the world. But the Chinese nation is 400 years younger than the Jewish nation. Since there are Chinese restaurants in all of Israel's cities an Israeli wise-guy asks, "How could the Jews live without Chinese food for 400 years?"

One combination of foods is purely Israeli-born—a "sabra" in the national cuisine. It is called the "kibbutz breakfast." Only a hard-working farmer can cope with it. In the early dawn the farmers gulp down tea with bread and jam and hurry to the fields to do some work before the sun gets hot. Several hours later they come back to the dining hall, hungry enough to eat everything in sight. Here's what they find on the long dining-room table:

1. sliced tomatoes, cucumbers, green peppers, and onions
2. grated carrot salad
3. green and black olives
4. mounds of cottage cheese and squares of hard cheese
5. soft-boiled and hard-boiled eggs
6. pickled herring
7. chunks of halvah (sometimes)
8. yogurt and sour cream
9. hot cereal
10. white rolls, black bread, margarine, and jelly
11. coffee and tea

Three or four hours later it's lunchtime, the heaviest meal of the day. Chicken, fish, or meat is usually served. After lunch, as you can imagine, most people have to rest for a while before they go back to work. Supper, in the evening, is just like breakfast—tomatoes, olives, cheeses, herring, cereal, and more.

בְּתֵאָבוֹן
חֲבֵרִים!

On the next few pages you'll find recipes for Israeli foods that were brought from all over the world. Before you try them, please read these **kitchen-safety rules:**

1. Make sure there's an adult around in case you need help. Some recipes are hard to do.

2. Wash your hands.

3. Do all cutting on a cutting board. Cut away from your body, not toward yourself.

4. Turn pot handles in over the stove so you won't bump into them accidentally.

5. Keep *dry* potholders handy to hold hot pot handles. (The heat goes right through wet potholders.)

6. Turn off the stove and oven when you finish cooking.

Marak perot

**Fruit soup from Russia
serves 6**

Maybe it was their tart fruit soup and borscht (beet soup) that gave the early Russian-Jewish pioneers strength to drain swamps and clear rocky fields.

You will need:

5–6 cups of cut-up fruit:
   3 plums, 10 cherries (sour cherries are best), 4 peaches (apples, pears, apricots, or grapes are also good to use)
1 tablespoon of honey or sugar
⅓ teaspoon cinnamon
water
1 cup sour cream or yogurt

cutting board
knife
large saucepan
measuring cup
measuring spoons

1. Remove the pits from the fruit. Peel the peaches (an easy way to do this is to drop them in boiling water for a minute, remove them with a slotted spoon, place them in cold water, remove them and peel them).

2. Cut the fruit into bite-sized pieces. Place the fruit in the saucepan. Add the honey or sugar and the cinnamon. Add water until it *almost* covers the fruit.

3. Bring the mixture to a boil, turn the heat down to simmer, cover the pot, and cook the soup for 10 to 15 minutes or until the fruit is soft.

Serve fruit soup cold, topped with a heaping spoonful of sour cream or yogurt.

When the early pioneers were too poor to buy bread, they could still afford eggplant. So they learned from the Turks how to fry, bake, cook, chop, stuff, and pickle eggplant.

You will need:

1 medium-sized eggplant	baking pan
½ cup lemon juice	large bowl
2 small cloves of garlic	knife
2 sprigs of parsley	cutting board
2 tablespoons tehina sauce (see page 159)	measuring spoon
salt to taste	blender, or chopping bowl
pepper to taste	and chopping knife

1. Preheat the oven to 375 degrees. Place the eggplant on the baking pan, and bake until it is soft—about ½ hour.

2. Place the eggplant in the bowl, and let it cool. Peel it, and cut it into chunks.

3. Add the lemon juice to the eggplant.

4. Peel the garlic. Cut the garlic and the parsley into tiny pieces. Add them to the eggplant.

5. Add the tehina sauce, salt, and pepper.

6. Blend the mixture in the blender, or chop it in the chopping bowl until it is smooth.

Serve salat ḥatzeeleem cold, and decorate it with tomato wedges, olives, and sliced scallion tops.

Salat ḥatzeeleem
Eggplant salad from Greece
serves 8

prick the eggplant before you bake it—otherwise it may explode!

Pita sandwiches
enough for 4 people

Pita is a flat bread that opens like an envelope. It is usually filled with felafel, which are deep-fried balls of mashed chickpeas. Tehina, a sauce made of sesame seeds, is poured on top. You can make felafel from a packaged mix or use the felafel recipe in this chapter. The pita, felafel mix, and tehina can be bought at a kosher butcher store, supermarket, or a store that sells foods from other countries.

Jewish Israelis learned to make these spicy sandwiches from their Arab neighbors. They add onions, fried cauliflower, pickled beets, and other toppings, and eat their felafel sandwiches on the run, just as we eat hot dogs.

You will need:

½ onion	vegetable peeler
1 cucumber	knife
1 green pepper	cutting board
2 tomatoes	large mixing bowl
4 pitas	mixing spoon
16 felafel (see recipe on opposite page)	
tehina sauce (see recipe on page 159)	

1. Peel the onion and the cucumber. Cut the green pepper in half. Scoop out the seeds and white ribs, and throw them away. Slice the tomatoes. Cut all the vegetables into narrow strips. Then cut the strips into little pieces. Put them in the bowl, and mix the ingredients thoroughly.

2. Slit the top edge of each pita, as shown in the illustration. Pull the sides apart to make an open "pocket." Fill each pocket with one quarter of the vegetables. Add 4 felafel.

3. Pour tehina sauce over the filling in each pocket.

Felafel
makes 16 balls

You will need:

1 cup cooked or canned chickpeas (garbanzos), drained	can opener
1 clove garlic	large mixing bowl
½ teaspoon salt	potato masher
⅛ teaspoon pepper	knife
⅔ cup fine bread crumbs	cutting board
2 eggs	measuring cups
2 tablespoons oil	measuring spoons
oil for deep frying, enough to fill the pot about 3 inches	mixing spoon
	pot for deep frying
	slotted spoon or frying basket
	plate
	paper towels

1. Mash the chickpeas in the large bowl. Cut the garlic into tiny pieces. Add the garlic, salt, pepper, and bread crumbs to the chickpeas. Mix the ingredients together. Add the eggs and oil to the mixture. Mix the ingredients thoroughly.

2. Heat the oil in the pot to 375 degrees, or until little bubbles rise to the surface.

3. Shape the mixture into 16 balls, each about 1 inch in diameter. With the mixing spoon, gently place a few of the balls in the oil—don't drop them in because the hot oil may splash. Fry a few at a time until they are golden brown—about 5 minutes.

4. Remove the felafel with the slotted spoon. Drain them on a plate covered with paper towels.

If you want to mix your own felafel, here is a recipe to use. Whether you buy a mix or make your own, be sure to ask an adult to help with the deep frying. Splattering oil can burn you.

Tehina sauce
makes about 1 cup

You will need:

¾ cup tehina	measuring cups
⅓ cup lemon juice	measuring spoon
⅛ teaspoon garlic powder	small mixing bowl
⅓ cup water (approximately)	mixing spoon

1. Put the tehina, lemon juice, and garlic powder in the bowl. Mix the ingredients until you have a smooth sauce.

2. Add the water, 1 teaspoon at a time, until the sauce is thin enough to pour.

3. Pour tehina sauce over pita sandwiches, or use the sauce as a dip for raw vegetables.

Tehina is a paste made from sesame seeds. You can buy a can of tehina in stores that sell felafel or pita and then turn it into tehina sauce.

Israel is a Garden of Eden for noshers (snackers). As you stroll down city streets, you can buy and munch on felafel sandwiches, beef and chicken burgers, pizza, shashlik (lamb) sandwiches, salted bagels, pumpkin seeds, freshly squeezed orange juice, prickly sabras, or one of a dozen flavors of ice-cream cones.

Humus and tehina

makes 4 cups

All over the Middle East people eat ful (fava beans—large brown beans) and humus as a main dish. They scoop it up with little wedges of pita.

You will need:

large clove of garlic
¾ cup tehina (ground-up sesame seeds available in a can in health-food or specialty stores)
1 tablespoon olive oil or other cooking oil
2 tablespoons chopped parsley
juice of one large lemon
dash of pepper and salt
3 cups cooked or canned garbanzos (chickpeas)
½ cup water (approximately)

vegetable knife
measuring cup
measuring spoons
medium bowl
blender

1. Peel the garlic, and cut it into several pieces.
2. Mix the tehina, oil, parsley, lemon juice, salt, and pepper to make tehina sauce, as shown on page 159.
3. Place all the ingredients in the blender, add water, and blend. The mixture should be as thick as apple sauce. If it is too thick, add more water, a little at a time, and blend the ingredients until the consistency is right.

Pile your humus-tehina on a platter, garnish with olives and parsley, and serve it with pita.

Jews from Yemen were early Zionists. Many came to Palestine before Herzl and the BILU. Their spicy, peppery vegetable dishes make Israeli tongues tingle.

Shakshooka

An egg-and-tomato dish from Yemen
serves 4 to 6

You will need:

5 ripe tomatoes	cutting board
½ large green pepper	knife
3 cloves of garlic	medium bowl
1 medium onion	large frying pan with a lid
oil for frying, about 2 tablespoons	spatula
salt to taste	
red pepper to taste	
6 eggs	

1. Cut the tomatoes into cubes and the green pepper into thin strips. Place them in the bowl.
2. Peel the garlic and onion. Cut them into tiny pieces.
3. Heat the oil in the frying pan until it sizzles.
4. Add the onion and garlic. Turn the heat down to medium, and fry the vegetables until they turn golden-brown.
5. Add tomatoes, green pepper, salt, and red pepper. Cover the pan, and simmer the mixture over low heat until the tomatoes are soft.
6. Carefully crack open the eggs (try not to break the yolk, and drop them on the vegetables. Cover the pan and keep cooking the mixture at the lowest heat for 10 more minutes or until the eggs are set.

Serve shakshooka on a platter or in warm pita.

"He brought us to this place and gave us this land, a land flowing with milk and honey."
—Deuteronomy 26:9

Blintzes from Romania

makes 7 or 8 blintzes

"In Romania life is good," say the words of a Yiddish folksong. Even in Israel, Jews from Romania love the rich foods of their fertile old home—lots of eggs, cream, cheese, and fruit.

For the blintz leaf (wrapper) you will need:

1 egg	medium bowl
½ cup milk	measuring cup
¼ teaspoon salt	measuring spoons
½ tablespoon salad oil	fork
½ cup flour	6-inch skillet
oil for frying	paper towels or an old, clean dish towel
	large frying pan or baking pan
	spatula

1. Break the egg into the bowl. Add the milk, salt, and oil. Beat the ingredients with the fork until the mixture is blended.

2. Add the flour to the bowl, and mix the ingredients until all the lumps are gone. The mixture should be as thick as heavy sweet cream.

3. Oil the skillet lightly, and heat it. Turn the heat to medium.

4. Pour 2 tablespoons of batter into the skillet. Quickly tilt the skillet from side to side until the batter coats the whole bottom. Let the batter lightly brown on one side until firm—this takes less than a minute.

5. Turn the blintz leaf out on the paper towels or dish towel, brown side up. Repeat the process until the rest of the batter is used up.

tilt from side to side

For the blintz filling you may use cheese *or* blueberries.

For cheese filling you will need:

1 cup farmer cheese or drained cottage cheese	measuring cup
	measuring spoons
1 egg	medium bowl
1 teaspoon sugar	mixing spoon
¼ teaspoon cinnamon or ½ teaspoon vanilla extract	

Mix all the ingredients together in the bowl.

For blueberry filling you will need:

3 tablespoons sugar	measuring spoons
1 tablespoon cornstarch	medium bowl
¼ teaspoon nutmeg	mixing spoon
1½ cups blueberries	measuring cup

1. Mix the sugar, cornstarch, and nutmeg together in the bowl.

2. Add the blueberries, and mix gently until the blueberries are well coated with the dry ingredients.

To make the blintzes you will need:

filling	teaspoon
blintz leaves (wrappers)	frying pan or baking pan
2 tablespoons oil or butter	spatula

1. Place a heaping teaspoon of one of the fillings towards one end of the blintz leaf. Flatten the filling slightly. Roll up the blintz like a jelly roll. Fold each end into the center to seal. Repeat until all the filling and all the wrappers have been used.

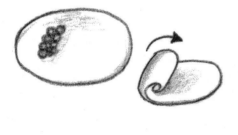
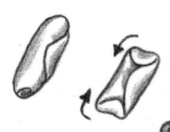

2. Now you can (a) fry *or* (b) bake your blintzes.

(a) Heat oil in a frying pan until the oil sizzles. Place blintzes in the pan with the folded-over edge down. Fry the blintzes over medium heat until they are golden brown. Turn the blintzes over, and brown the other side.

or:

(b) Heat the oven to 400 degrees. Place the blintzes in a buttered baking pan with the folded-over edge down. Bake the blintzes until they are golden brown—about 15 minutes.

Serve the blintzes hot with sour cream or yogurt.

Schnecken
makes about 12 buns

In Europe these yeast buns were made before the Sabbath from the same dough that was used for ḥallah. Today an old man sells them on the street in front of the supermarket in Nahariyya. One bun can keep you going from breakfast till supper—almost.

For the dough you will need:

¼ cup oil	measuring cup
½ teaspoon salt	measuring spoons
2 tablespoons sugar	large mixing bowl
½ cup warm water	mixing spoon
1 package dry yeast	2 small bowls
½ cup lukewarm water	fork
2 eggs	pastry board for kneading
3½–4 cups flour	clean dish towel
	rolling pin
	sharp knife
	8-inch × 12-inch baking pan

More Filling Suggestions

Instead of sugar, you can use ½ cup apricot or cherry jam, or ½ cup chocolate bits, or ⅓ cup honey (for very sticky buns).

For the filling you will need:

¼ cup butter or margarine, melted
½ cup brown sugar
½ cup walnuts, chopped
½ cup raisins
1 teaspoon cinnamon

1. Place the oil, salt, and sugar in the large mixing bowl. Add the warm water. Mix the ingredients until the sugar has dissolved.

2. Mix the yeast and lukewarm water in a small bowl until the yeast has dissolved.

3. Break the eggs into the large bowl, add the yeast and mix.

4. Add the flour 1 cup at a time. Mix the ingredients after every cupful. Continue mixing until the ingredients form a ball.

5. Spread a little flour on the board, on your hands, and on the dough. This will keep the dough from sticking. Put the dough on the board, and knead it for about 5 minutes.

To knead—press down on the dough with the heels of your hands, and push it away from you. Fold it over, and give it a quarter turn. Press, push, fold over, and turn again and again . . . until the dough is smooth and springy.

6. Pat a few drops of oil on the ball of dough to keep it from drying out. Place the dough in the bowl, cover it with the towel, and put it in a warm place to rise.

7. When the dough has doubled in size (after about 1 hour), place it on the board and knead it for a minute. Divide the dough into two parts.

8. Roll the dough, one part at a time, into rectangles about 10 inches wide and 16 inches long.

9. Drip the butter or margarine evenly over each rectangle of dough. Divide the sugar, nuts, raisins, and cinnamon in half. Sprinkle the filling over the two pieces of dough.

10. Roll each piece of the dough up like a jelly roll, starting from the long edge. Cut each roll into 1½-inch-long pieces. Place the pieces cut side down in the greased baking pan, leaving space between the pieces.

11. Let the dough rise in a warm place for ½ hour.

12. Heat the oven to 375 degrees. Bake the schnecken for 25 minutes or until the buns are golden brown.

You can also make ḥallah from this dough. Follow steps 1 through 6. After the dough has doubled in size, divide it into three pieces. Roll each piece into a long strand, braid the three strands, place the ḥallah in a pan, and let the loaf rise for ½ hour. Then bake the bread in a 375-degree oven for about 30 minutes.

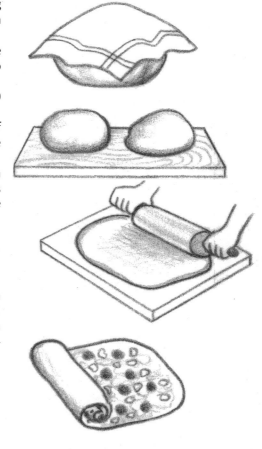

Kipferln

Half-moon cookies from Austria
makes about 24

In the 1930s German and Austrian Jews brought practical business know-how to the Jewish community of Palestine. They also opened little coffee houses, where people played chess, read newspapers, argued politics, and ate delicious cakes and cookies.

You will need:

⅓ cup butter, softened to room temperature	medium bowl
⅓ cup sugar	measuring cup
1 teaspoon pure vanilla extract	measuring spoon
⅓ cup finely chopped almonds	mixing spoon
1⅓ cups flour	cookie sheet
½ cup confectioners' sugar	spatula
	small, shallow bowl

1. Preheat the oven to 350 degrees.

2. In the bowl, mix the butter, sugar, and vanilla until the mixture is fluffy.

3. Add the nuts and the flour. Mix the ingredients with the spoon and with your fingers until the mixture is blended and forms a ball. Add a teaspoon of water if the mixture is too crumbly.

4. Make balls of dough about as big as walnuts. Roll them between your hands into long ovals. Then curl them into half-moon shapes.

5. Place the cookies on the ungreased cookie sheet, and bake them until they are golden brown—about 12 minutes. Cool the cookies.

6. Place the confectioners' sugar into the shallow bowl. Roll the cooled cookies in the sugar.

A few years ago American immigrants had to wait for "care packages" from the United States before they could make their favorite cookies. There were no chocolate bits to be found in all of Israel. Today chocolate bits are sold in the supermarkets, and there are even chocolate-chip cookie stores.

Chocolate-chip cookies
From the United States
makes about 48

You will need:

½ cup (1 stick) butter or margarine	large bowl
½ cup sugar	measuring cup
¼ cup brown sugar, firmly packed	measuring spoons
1 egg	mixing spoons
1 teaspoon vanilla extract	small bowl
1¼ cups flour	teaspoon
1 teaspoon baking soda	cookie sheet
6 ounces chocolate chips	spatula
½ cup chopped nuts or raisins	

1. Preheat the oven to 375 degrees.

2. Let the butter or margarine soften to room temperature. In the large bowl mix the butter or margarine and the sugars together until they are blended.

3. Beat in the egg, and add the vanilla. Mix the ingredients well.

4. In the small bowl mix the flour and baking soda together thoroughly. Add them gradually to the mixture in the large bowl, mixing them until the ingredients are evenly blended.

5. Add the chocolate bits and the nuts or raisins. Mix the ingredients well.

6. Drop the dough by the teaspoonful onto the greased cookie sheet. Bake the cookies until they are golden (about 8 minutes).

Take one!
Bi-tay-a-von (good appetite)!
To say 'bitayavon', just rhyme it with 'hurray pa won'.
bi-tay-a-von
hur-ray-pa-won

Hit songs of one hundred

Boys and girls in the early Zionist ḥalutz (pioneering) groups clapped their hands, stamped their feet, whirled in horas, and shouted their Hebrew songs loudly enough to rattle the windows. The words of some songs came from the Bible and the prayer books. Some of the tunes came from Russian, Yiddish, and German melodies. But they all blended into a happy Zionist medley.

When the ḥalutzim came to Palestine, they continued to sing about their love of the homeland and of becoming farmers. And in spite of their aching backs from swinging picks and pushing plows, they kept dancing horas, too.

New songs were sung when the State of Israel was established. There were songs about war and songs about newly settled parts of the country such as the Negev and Elath. New immigrants from Yemen, North Africa, India, and elsewhere brought with them different and exciting dances and music as well as sparkling performers.

Modern Israeli songs draw from many sources—Europe, the Middle East, and American jazz and rock music. Religion and patriotism are still important subjects, as are love, sadness, hope, joy, and anger. Israelis hear new songs at their Ḥasidic Song Festival and Israel Music Festival. Records and tapes of many new songs cross the ocean and are taught and sung at American-Jewish camps, schools, and centers.

years

This song of yearning and hope for a homeland became the anthem of the Zionist movement in 1897.

SONGS

Hatikvah

כָּל עוֹד בַּלֵּבָב פְּנִימָה
נֶפֶשׁ יְהוּדִי הוֹמִיָּה
וּלְפַאֲתֵי מִזְרָח קָדִימָה
עַיִן לְצִיּוֹן צוֹפִיָּה

As long as in our hearts
There is a Jewish spirit,
And toward the east
Our eyes turn . . . to Zion,

עוֹד לֹא אָבְדָה תִּקְוָתֵנוּ
הַתִּקְוָה בַּת שְׁנוֹת אַלְפַּיִם
לִהְיוֹת עַם חָפְשִׁי בְּאַרְצֵנוּ
בְּאֶרֶץ צִיּוֹן וִירוּשָׁלַיִם

Our hope is not lost,
The hope of two-thousand years,
To be a free nation in our own land,
In the land of Zion, in Jerusalem.

With dignity

N.H. Imber

Kol - od ba-le -vav p' - ni - ma ne-fesh Y'-hu- di ho - mi - ya ul'-

fa - a - te_ miz - rach ka - di - ma a - yin l' - Tsi-yon tso - fi - a

od lo av - da tik-va-te - nu ha - tik - va bat shnot al - pa - yim

li - yot am chof - shi b' - ar - tse - nu e -rets Tsi-yon Y'- ru-sha- la - yim

li - yot am chof - shi b' - ar - tse - nu e -rets Tsi-yon Y'- ru-sha- la - yim

Anu Banu Artza

Folktune

The ḥalutzim (pioneers) of the early 1900s sang this song, puffing and panting as they stamped around in a hora.

אָנוּ בָּאנוּ אַרְצָה   We came to the land
לִבְנוֹת וּלְהִבָּנוֹת בָּה   To build and to be built by it.

This song of the 1930s happily proclaims that Jewish youth will dance and work together to build their homeland.

Kuma Echa

S. Postolsky, Y. Shenhar

קוּמָה אֶחָא סוֹבָה סוֹב,
אַל תָּנוּחָה שׁוּבָה שׁוֹב,
אֵין כָּאן רֹאשׁ וְאֵין כָּאן סוֹף,
יָד אֶל יָד אַל תַּעֲזוֹב.

Get up brothers [*and sisters*], circle around,
Don't stop to rest, come back.
There's no beginning here and no end,
Hand in hand, don't drop out.

יוֹם שָׁקַע וְיוֹם יִזְרַח,
אָנוּ נֵפֶן אָח אֶל אָח,
מִן הַכְּפָר וּמִן הַכְּרָךְ
בַּחֶרְמֵשׁ וּבָאֲנָךְ.

A day has ended, a new day begins.
We turn to each other, brother to brother,
From the village and from the city,
With our scythes and our plumb lines.

Joyously

S.Postolsky, Y.Shenhar

Ku - ma e - cha so - ba sov al ___ ta - nu - cha
shu - va shov en ___ kan rosh v' - en ___ kan sof
yad ___ el yad ___ al ta - a - zov yom ___ sha - ka v' -
yom _____ yiz - rach a - nu ne - fen ach ___ el ach min ha - kfar u -
min _____ ha - krach ba - cher - mesh u - va - a - nach

Finjan

Folktune. Lyrics: C. Hefer

Copyright by the author

A brass coffeepot—a finjan—bubbles over a campfire. Soldiers huddle close and sing to keep warm during the 1948 War of Liberation.

א. הָרוּחַ נוֹשֶׁבֶת קְרִירָה
נוֹסִיפָה קִיסָם לַמְּדוּרָה
וְכָךְ בִּזְרוֹעוֹת אַרְגָּמָן
בָּאֵשׁ יַעֲלֶה כְּקׇרְבָּן
הָאֵשׁ מְהַבְהֶבֶת שִׁירָה מְלַבְלֶבֶת
סוֹבֵב לוֹ סוֹבֵב הַפִנְגָּ'ן.
לללללללל . . .

A cold wind blows,
We'll add a twig to the fire,
And so, in the purple arms
Of flame, it will rise like a sacrifice.
The fire warms us, singing breaks out
As the coffeepot passes around.
La-la-la . . .

ב. הָאֵשׁ לַקִּיסָם תְּלַחֵשׁ
אָדְמוּ כֹּה פָּנֵינוּ בָּאֵשׁ
אִם לָנוּ תִּגְבֹּרֶת תּוּנַן
מִכָּל בַּדַל עָנָף שֶׁבַּגָּן
כָּל עֵץ וְכָל קֶרֶשׁ
יָשִׁיר אָזַי חֶרֶשׁ
סוֹבֵב לוֹ סוֹבֵב הַפִנְגָּ'ן
לללללללללל . . .

The fire will whisper to the twig,
"Our faces get red in the fire.
If we had help [*reinforcements*]
From every branch in the garden,
Each tree and each board
Would sing softly
As the coffeepot passes around."
La-la-la . . .

Folktune
Lyrics: C. Hefer

A whirling hora from the busy 1950s, when the new state was growing fast.

Hey, Harmonica

Folksong

הֵי, הַרְמוֹנִיקָה, נַגְּנִי לִי,
שֶׁיִּרְעַד כָּל צְלִיל,
אֶת הַהוֹרָה שֶׁרָקַדְנוּ
יַחַד בַּגָּלִיל . . .

Hey, harmonica, play for me,
Make each note tremble.
Play the hora that we danced
Together in Galilee.

הוֹרָה הוֹרָה
שֶׁרָקַדְנוּ יַחַד בַּגָּלִיל!

Hora, hora
That we danced together in Galilee.

עוֹד נִזְכֹּרָה
אֶת הַהוֹרָה
שֶׁרָקַדְנוּ יַחַד בַּגָּלִיל.

We still remember
That hora
That we danced together in Galilee.

Chai, Chai, Chai

Ehud Manor, Avi Toledano
Copyright by the authors

Despite Israel's many problems in the 1980s, this song cries proudly "The nation of Israel lives!"

שִׁמְעוּ אַחַי
אֲנִי עוֹד חַי
וּשְׁתֵּי עֵינַי עוֹד נְשׂוּאוֹת לָאוֹר
רַבִּים חוֹכַי אַךְ, גַּם פְּרָחַי
וּלְפָנַי שָׁנִים רַבּוֹת מִסְפוֹר
אֲנִי שׁוֹאֵל וּמִתְפַּלֵּל
טוֹב שֶׁלֹּא אָבְדָה עוֹד הַתִּקְוָה

Listen, my brothers [*and sisters*],
I am still alive,
And my eyes are still raised to the light.
I have many thorns, but also many flowers.
And there are countless years yet before me.
I ask and I pray,
It's good that my hope is not yet lost.

עוֹבֵר מִזְמוֹר מִדּוֹר לְדוֹר
כְּמַעְיָן מֵאָז וְעַד עוֹלָם
אֲנִי שׁוֹאֵל וּמִתְפַּלֵּל
טוֹב שֶׁלֹּא אָבְדָה עוֹד הַתִּקְוָה

A song passes from generation to generation
Like an ancient well that lasts forever.
I ask and I pray,
It's good that my hope is not yet lost.

פִּזְמוֹן :
חַי חַי חַי
כֵּן אֲנִי עוֹד חַי.
זֶה הַשִּׁיר שֶׁסַּבָּא שָׁר אֶתְמוֹל לְאַבָּא
וְהַיּוֹם אֲנִי . . .
אֲנִי עוֹד חַי חַי חַי
עַם יִשְׂרָאֵל חַי
זֶה הַשִּׁיר שֶׁסַּבָּא שָׁר אֶתְמוֹל לְאַבָּא
וְהַיּוֹם אֲנִי . . .

Refrain:
I live, live, live,
Yes, I still live.
This is the song that my grandfather once sang
     to my father,
And today I . . .
I still live, live, live,
The nation of Israel lives.
This is the song that my grandfather once sang
     to my father,
And today I . . .

Ehud Manor, Avi Toledano

You can buy sheet music, records, and tapes of Israeli songs at your local Judaica shop, or you can order them from Tara Publications, 29 Derby Avenue, Cedarhurst, New York 11516.

Ha-Naavah Ba-Banot

Israelis dance a slow, twisting circle dance as they sing this love song of the 1960s. It was borrowed from King Solomon's Song of Songs.

הַנָּאוָה בַּבָּנוֹת
אָנָא הָאִירִי פָּנַיִךְ אֵלַי
בּוֹא דוֹדִי כִּי יָפִיתָ
אַף נָעַמְתָּ לִי מְאֹד
שְׁלַח יָדְךָ וְחַבְּקֵנִי
אַמְּצֵנִי עוֹד וָעוֹד

Loveliest of girls,
Please let your face shine upon me.
Come, my beloved, for you are handsome
And you make me very happy,
Reach out and embrace me.
Hug me again and again.

This stamping, whirling dance started out as a Romanian circle dance called "hora." Early Zionist settlers brought the hora to Palestine and turned it into a Jewish national dance.

The hora has six basic steps that are repeated over and over. The instructions show a dancer with a white leg and a shaded leg. The dancer's *weight* is on the *shaded* leg. "Anu Banu Artza" is a good hora song (the words can be found on page 170). Dancers form a circle and put their hands on each other's shoulders or hold hands.

DANCE THE HORA

1 STEP RIGHT WITH RIGHT FOOT

2 PLACE LEFT FOOT BEHIND RIGHT FOOT

3 STEP RIGHT WITH RIGHT FOOT

4 HOP ON RIGHT FOOT

5 STEP LEFT WITH LEFT FOOT

6 HOP ON LEFT FOOT

11 Talking Israeli

Don't think you're an ignoramus if you can't speak Israeli. Hebrew is the major language of Israel, but Arabic and English are also official languages of the country. Many street signs and all stamps and money are printed in the three languages.

Although Arabic, Hebrew, and English are taught in the schools, most Israeli citizens can't speak all of them. Arab Israelis usually speak Arabic. Jewish Israelis usually speak Hebrew. Jewish Israelis from Arab lands speak both. And everybody speaks some English.

There's one phrase that everybody in Israel can understand. It is "Shalom aleihem" in Hebrew and "As-salamu alaykum" in Arabic. They both mean "hello" and "peace be with you." The words are similar because Hebrew and Arabic both grew up in the same neighborhood—in the Middle East—and belong to the same language family—the Semitic family.

English comes from a different language family. It was brought to the Middle East by the British who ruled Palestine for twenty-eight years. Although it comes from far away, English has become a very important language in Israel. Students in the universities study from books written in English. Israeli kids sing the words of American rock music. And everybody goes to English-language movies and watches American and British TV programs.

In this chapter you will find out how modern Hebrew blossomed out of the ancient Hebrew of the Bible. Under "Borrowing and Lending" you'll discover how Hebrew, Arabic, and English got mixed up together. You'll also discover some peculiar things about the Hebrew language. "Naming News" may tempt you to trade your old-fashioned name for a snappy new one. And you can finish up with "The Perils of Toby the Tayar (Tourist)."

KING SOLOMON'S HEBREW MEETS THE SPACE AGE

If King Solomon dropped into a Tel Aviv café for a cup of coffee, he'd be in big trouble. He wouldn't know how to use the forks and teaspoons, and he'd be amazed by the sunglasses and tight blue jeans of the other customers. But worst of all he wouldn't understand what people were saying. Well—at first he wouldn't understand. After a second cup of coffee King Solomon, the wisest of all people, would surely begin to catch on to modern Hebrew.

You may be wondering why Solomon, a great Hebrew poet and writer of the Biblical Song of Songs, should have trouble understanding Hebrew. The answer is that modern Hebrew is very different from Biblical Hebrew. An important reason for the difference is the work of one man—Eliezer Ben-Yehudah. Ben-Yehudah moved to Palestine from Russia in 1881 and began, almost single-handedly, to pull the ancient Hebrew language into the modern world. To explain how it all happened, let's go back to King Solomon.

When King Solomon wrote his poetry 2,400 years ago, there were about 7,500 words in the Hebrew language. They were quite enough for him to whisper sweet compliments to the queen of Sheba. They were even enough for his people to run their farms, worship at the Temple, and buy and sell in the marketplaces.

As years passed, the people of Israel began to use another Middle Eastern language—Aramaic—for their daily business. Part of the Talmud, a later holy book, was written in Aramaic. But the Bible, the Torah, continued to be written in the original Hebrew. When the Jews left Israel, they carried Hebrew with them, written on the long scrolls of their Torahs. Wherever they lived, they continued to study and pray in Hebrew. But they cooked, argued, joked, bought, and sold in the languages of the lands in which they lived.

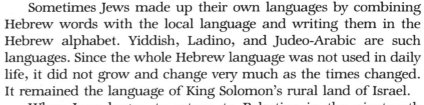

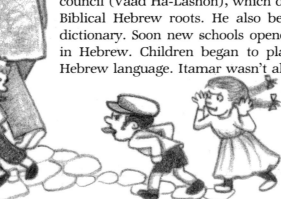

Sometimes Jews made up their own languages by combining Hebrew words with the local language and writing them in the Hebrew alphabet. Yiddish, Ladino, and Judeo-Arabic are such languages. Since the whole Hebrew language was not used in daily life, it did not grow and change very much as the times changed. It remained the language of King Solomon's rural land of Israel.

When Jews began to return to Palestine in the nineteenth century, they wanted to be free, proud citizens of a Jewish land. But how could they build a homeland together when they spoke many different languages? Here's where Eliezer Ben-Yehudah came in.

Ben-Yehudah settled in Jerusalem in 1881 with his wife and little son. He was determined to turn the ancient Hebrew language into the daily language of all the people of the new Jewish homeland.

"How can I go shopping for a kerosene heater or a bicycle or even a newspaper?" protested Mrs. Ben-Yehudah. "There are no Hebrew words for such things."

"Don't worry," said Ben-Yehudah. "We'll make up words. And we'll publish a Hebrew newspaper to teach everybody the new words. You and I will show the way. In our home only Hebrew will be spoken. Our son Itamar will be the first Hebrew-speaking child in seventeen hundred years!"

Poor Itamar. He was a lonely little boy. The kids in the neighborhood spoke only Yiddish, and they laughed at him and mimicked his Hebrew. The neighbors scolded the Ben-Yehudahs for using the holy language of the Bible for everyday needs. They even yelled "heretic" and threw stones at the Ben-Yehudahs.

But the idea of a modern Hebrew language began to spread. In 1890 Ben-Yehudah gathered a group of scholars into a language council (Vaad Ha-Lashon), which developed modern words out of Biblical Hebrew roots. He also began work on a huge Hebrew dictionary. Soon new schools opened where subjects were taught in Hebrew. Children began to play and study and sing in the Hebrew language. Itamar wasn't alone any more.

Today the Vaad Ha-Lashon has become the Academy of the Hebrew Language. Its members search the Bible and other Hebrew writings for words they can reshape to modern meanings. They have drawn the word for computer—*maḥshav*—from the Hebrew word for "think." Atomic power—*koaḥ garini*—came from the Hebrew word for "seed" or "nucleus." And "baby-sitter," a word nobody needed in King Solomon's time, is *shmartaf*. It comes from the words for "guard" and "little child."

The English language has been growing and changing for 1,000 years. It has 500,000 words. Each year, old, unused words are dropped and about 1,000 new words are picked up. But modern Hebrew has only 80,000 words. The Academy of the Hebrew Language must keep hunting through its books and running hard in the race to bring the language of King Solomon into the world of space exploration and computers.

Eliezer Ben-Yehudah used to stand at a tall desk all day working on his books and papers. On the wall opposite him hung a sign that read "The time is short, and the task is great." Despite all the council meetings and research in the sixty-odd years since his death, the task of developing modern Hebrew is as great as ever, and the time is still short.

BORROWING AND LENDING

"Neither a borrower nor a lender be," advises Shakespeare. If languages followed that advice, we would still be squeaking and grunting instead of using words. Languages borrow words from each other all the time. And with each borrowing they become richer and better.

In a high-traffic area like the Middle East, where soldiers and merchants and herdsmen are always moving through, many words are borrowed and carried off to the ends of the earth. Here are some examples:

- Abraham and the early Hebrews came to Canaan and borrowed the twenty-two–letter alphabet of the Phoenicians or Canaanites.

- The Greeks adopted the Phoenician alphabet, too. The Etruscans and Romans picked it up from the Greeks and made some changes.

- The Jews later switched to the clearer Aramaic alphabet, which, slightly changed, is still used in modern Hebrew.

- The Christians borrowed Hebrew words from the Bible and carried them into European languages.

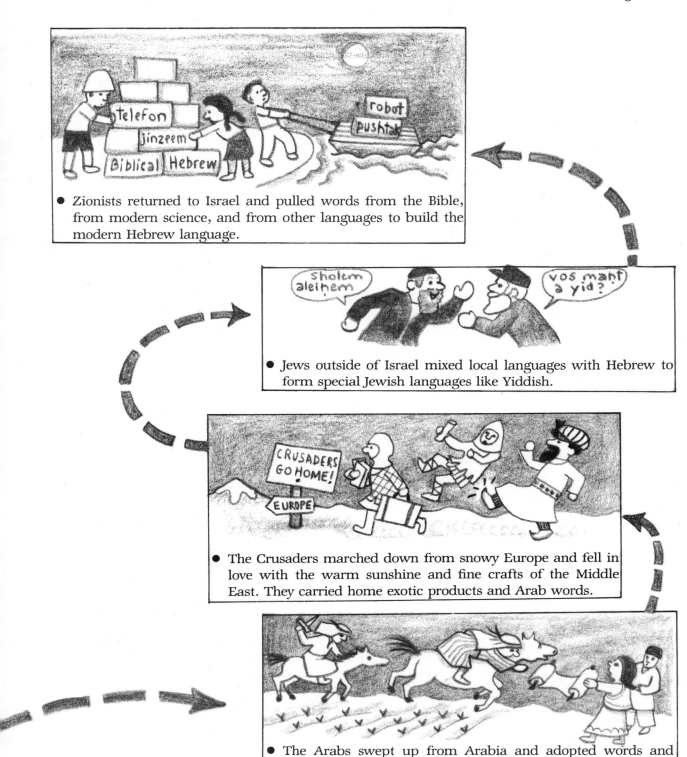

- Zionists returned to Israel and pulled words from the Bible, from modern science, and from other languages to build the modern Hebrew language.

- Jews outside of Israel mixed local languages with Hebrew to form special Jewish languages like Yiddish.

- The Crusaders marched down from snowy Europe and fell in love with the warm sunshine and fine crafts of the Middle East. They carried home exotic products and Arab words.

- The Arabs swept up from Arabia and adopted words and stories from the Jews, the Persians, and many of the other peoples they conquered.

Let's trace some borrowed words back to their first owners:

English words borrowed from Arabic:

algebra   from *ar-al jabr* ("to reduce")
zero   from *zero*
chess   from *shah* ("king")
almanac   from *al manakh* ("calendar")
giraffe   from *zirafah* ("giraffe")
mattress   from *matras* ("to throw")
sugar   from *sukkar* ("gravel")
orange   from *naranj* ("fragrant")
cotton   from *qutun* ("hair plant")
crimson   from *qirmiz* ("bright red")

English words and English slang words borrowed from Hebrew:

amen   from *amen* ("truly," "so be it")
babble   from *Bavel* (the site of the tower of Babel)
camel   from *gamal* ("camel")
cinnamon   from *kinnamon* (a spice)
cumin   from *kamon* (a spice)
Eden   from *eden* ("a place of pleasure")
gauze   from *Gaza* (a town in Israel)
hallelujah   from *hallelujah* ("praise God")
ḥutzpah   from *ḥutzpah* ("impudence")
kosher   from *kasher* ("suitable," "permissible")
lemon   from *limon* ("lemon")
meshuggah   from *meshuggah* ("crazy")
paradise   from *pardes* ("orchard"; originally a Persian word)
sack   from *sok* ("bag" or "sack")
sapphire   from *sapir* ("a precious stone")
Satan   from *Satan* ("Satan" or "archenemy")

These words are
Hebrew, Arabic, and English

scallion from *Ashkelon* (a town in Israel)
shamas from *shamash* ("attendant" or "janitor")
sofa from *sapa* ("couch")
tunic from *kutonet* ("shirt")

Hebrew words borrowed from Arabic, English, and Yiddish:

balagan "a mess" (from a Yiddish-Russian combination)
boobelleh "cute girl," "doll" (from a Yiddish-Hebrew combination)
chik-chok "hurry up" (from English)
la-asot daweenim "to bluff" or "to fool around" (from Arabic)
goy "a non-Jew" (from the Yiddish meaning given to a Hebrew word for "nation")
inshallah "may God be willing" (from Arabic)
jinzeem "blue jeans" (from English)
klavteh "a tough woman" (from a Yiddish-Hebrew combination for "bitch")
kum-zitz "a social gathering" (from the Yiddish for "come and sit")
l'fassfess "to miss out on something" (from Arabic)
l'fasteir "to pasteurize" (from English)
l'talfen "to telephone" (from English)
ma'alesh "who cares?" (from Arabic)
mabsoot "satisfied" (from Arabic)
okay "okay" (from English)
poncher "a mishap" (from the English for "puncture")
protektzia "influence" (from Yiddish)
pushtakim "tough, ignorant people" (from the Russian for "hollow nuts")
robot "robot" (from English)
sababa "great," "a good time" (from Arabic)
televiziah "television" (from English)
tremp "hitchhike" (from the English for "tramp")
zeh lo fer "that's not fair!" (from a Hebrew-English combination)

SAY IT OR SWEAR IT

The Arabic language is full of pithy proverbs. It also has picturesque curses that come in handy for loud arguments. Hebrew-speaking Israelis borrow both whenever necessary.

- The enemy of my enemy is my friend.
- His brains hang at the top of his fez.
- Only an empty walnut rattles.
- The tar of my own country is better than the honey of others'.
- An old monkey won't learn to dance.
- Trust in God, but tie your camel.
- What is brought by the wind will be carried away by the wind.
- He who has money can eat ice cream in hell.
- May your luck fall into a manure pile.
- May the sweat of a thousand camels infest your armpits.
- The camel doesn't see his own hump, only that of his father's sister.
- Man begins, and God completes.

Two "made in Israel" curses:

- May your telephone go out of order (a very nasty curse because phone repairs in Israel move more slowly than turtles in the Negev).
- May you win the lottery and have all your relatives come and live with you.

WERBEH SI TNEREFFID
(Hebrew is different)

- Hebrew has a twenty-two–letter alphabet that looks very different from the English alphabet.
- Hebrew has no capital letters and is printed without vowels—except in texts for students and children.
- Hebrew is written from right to left.

You can see from the heading at the top of this section that "right to left" can be confusing for a beginner. Reading without vowels is confusing, too. See if you can read this almost vowelless sentence:

A PRSN MST BE A GNIS TO RD THS SNTNC WTHT VWLS.
Did you figure it out? You're a genius!

Hebrew vowel signs are a "new" addition to the language. They were worked out 1,100 years ago in Tiberias, several thousand years after the Jews began to speak, write, and read Hebrew. The signs are dots and dashes that are placed above, below, or inside the letters, like this:

אֵיפֹה הַבֶּבָה

Vowels are not written on scrolls of the Torah, and they are usually not used in Israeli newspapers and books. So Israelis have to guess at the vowels as they read. Two words with letters that are exactly alike may have very different meanings when their vowel sounds are added. For instance דוד (*DVD*) can mean either "uncle" (*DOD:* דוֹד) or "David" (*DAVID:* דָוִד).

Chanting from the scrolls of the Torah. The tiny marks above the letters aren't vowels. They are like musical notes, telling the reader when to sing higher or lower.

Ed Toben

Hebrew words usually grow out of a few root letters. As one word grows from another, the meaning can change until it is very far from the original root. It's like playing "Telephone," where a word is whispered from person to person in a circle. As the word is passed along, it changes. When the last person says the word aloud, the first person may not recognize it.

Let's plant the three root letters ‏ספר‏ (*S, F, R*) and see what a varied word-tree grows out of them.

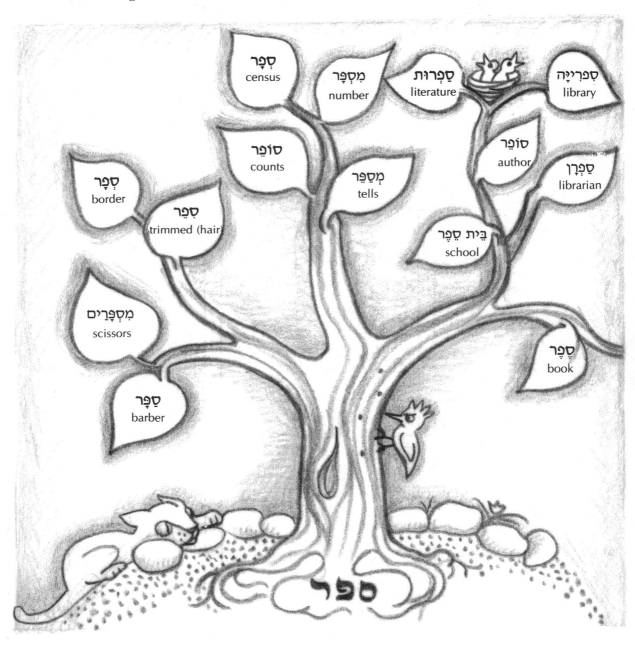

‏סְפָר‏ census

‏מִסְפָּר‏ number

‏סַפְרוּת‏ literature

‏סִפְרִיָּה‏ library

‏סוֹפֵר‏ counts

‏סוֹפֵר‏ author

‏סַפְרָן‏ librarian

‏סְפָר‏ border

‏סִפֵּר‏ trimmed (hair)

‏מְסַפֵּר‏ tells

‏בֵּית סֵפֶר‏ school

‏מִסְפָּרַיִם‏ scissors

‏סֵפֶר‏ book

‏סַפָּר‏ barber

‏ספר‏

A Hebrew-English Mishmash
What is ma.
And me is who.
And who is he.
And he is she.
So what is what?
What is ma.

Sarah, David, Esther, Joseph, and other names of Bible people used to be favorites in Israel and among all Jews. Today the Bible names are still popular but many new names are growing out of the Hebrew language. Here are some of them:

NAMING NEWS

Girls' names and their meanings

אַיָּלָה	**Ayala**	deer
אֲמִירָה	**Amira**	princess or queen
אַרְאֵלָה	**Arella**	angel
דַּפְנָה	**Dafna**	laurel
דִּיקְלָה	**Dikla**	date palm
לִיאַת	**Liat**	you are mine
נִיצָה	**Nitza**	blossom
נוֹעַ	**Noa**	movement, activity
נוֹגָה	**Noga**	brightness
נוּרִית	**Nurit**	a light
עוֹפְרָה	**Ofra**	young deer
אוֹרְלִי	**Orli**	my light
רִינָה	**Rina**	song, rejoicing
שִׁירָה	**Shira**	song
סְגָל	**Sigal**	violet (flower)
סִימוֹנָה	**Simona**	pleasant sounds
טַלִי	**Tali**	young lamb
תָּמָר	**Tamar**	palm tree
וַרְדָה	**Varda**	rose
יָעֵל	**Yael (Yoli)**	mountain goat
יַרְדֵּנָה	**Yardena**	Jordan (river)
יְפְעַת	**Yifat**	beauty, splendor

Boys' names and their meanings

עֲמִי	**Ami**	my people
אַמִיר	**Amir**	top branches of a tree, prince
אֲרִי	**Ari**	lion
דָּן	**Dan**	judge
דּוֹרוֹן	**Doron**	gift
אֵהוּד	**Ehud**	compassion or sympathy
אֵיתָן	**Eitan**	strong, firm
אֱיָל	**Eyal**	strength, power
גָּד	**Gad**	fortune
גִּיל	**Gil**	joy
גּוּר	**Gur**	lion cub
אִילָן	**Ilan**	tree
נִיר	**Nir**	a plowed field
אוֹפֶר	**Ofer**	meadow
רָמִי	**Rami**	my high point
שַׂגִּיא	**Sagi**	lofty, great
טַל	**Tal**	dew
אוּרִי	**Uri**	my light
יָאִיר	**Yair**	he will shine
יָרוֹן	**Yaron**	he will sing
צַחִי	**Zaḥi**	pure, clear

"Israel is a country where mothers learn the mother tongue from their children."
—Ephraim Kishon

Many Jewish immigrants to Israel were so eager to feel part of their homeland that they changed their surnames (last names). Instead of keeping names that came from the German, Russian, or English, they chose new Hebrew names.

Some translated their old names into Hebrew:

Applebaum ("apple tree") became **Peri.**
Berg ("mountain") became **Harari.**
Feld ("field") became **Sadeh.**
Fliegel ("bird's wing") became **Zippori.**
Gold became **Zahavi.**
Lehrer ("teacher") became **Mori.**
Schneider ("tailor") became **Ḥayati.**
Schuster ("shoemaker") became **Sandlar.**
Schwartz ("black") became **Sheḥori.**
Waldman ("woodsman") became **Yaari.**
Wein ("wine") became **Gafni.**
Weiss ("white") became **Livni.**

Some expressed their love of the land by choosing names of regions of Israel:

Galili   **Tavori**
Giladi   **Yerushalmi**
Negbi

Some chose names with new, hopeful meanings: David Green became David Ben-Gurion ("son of a lion cub"), Israel's first prime minister; Moshe Shertok became Moshe Sharett ("one who serves"), Israel's first foreign minister. Other popular names are Ben-Ami ("son of my people"); Boneh or Banai ("builder"); Marom ("high in the sky")—a favorite of air-force officers; Tzur ("rock" or "fortress"); Shamir ("thorn" or "cutting tool"); Tamir ("tall" or "erect").

And some named themselves after their parents or children:

Ben-Yehudah ("son of Judah")
Ben-Ezra ("son of Ezra")
Ben-Shaul ("son of Saul")
Avigad ("father of Gad")
Amihud ("mother of Ehud")

But most new Israelis refused to change their names at all. Stubbornly and proudly they remain Goldbergs, Horowitzes, and Greenspans, just like their parents. Immigrants from North Africa and the East usually had no surname problem. Their names had always remained Hebrew or Arabic, so they felt right at home.

THE PERILS OF TOBY THE TAYAR ("TOURIST")

tourist
תַּיָּר
tayar

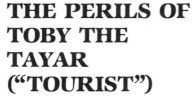

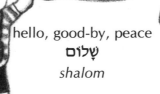

hello, good-by, peace
שָׁלוֹם
shalom

car
מְכוֹנִית
m'honit

traffic light
רַמְזוֹר
ramzor

plane
מָטוֹס
matos

city
עִיר
eer

house
בַּיִת
bayit

ice-cream
גְּלִידָה
glidah

restaurant
מִסְעָדָה
misadah

table
שֻׁלְחָן
shulḥan

girl
יַלְדָּה
yaldah

sol
ל
ḥa

sun
שֶׁמֶשׁ
shemesh

thank you
תּוֹדָה
todah

you're welcome, please
בְּבַקָשָׁה
b'vakashah

snow
שֶׁלֶג
sheleg

mountain
הַר
har

forest
יַעַר
ya-ar

Yikes!
yikes!
אוֹי וַאֲבוֹי
oy v'avoy

cactus, sabra
צַבָּר
tzavar

camel
גָּמָל
gamal

Help!
help!
עֶזְרָה
ezrah

dog
כֶּלֶב
kelev

fish
דָּג
dag

sea
יָם
yam

walk, outing
טִיּוּל
tiyul

boat
סִירָה
sirah

12 Digging into history

Why is an archaeologist like a curious garbage collector? Because they both like to check out other people's rubbish.

Of course, archaeologists don't go digging through broken TV sets and rusty bed springs in a modern garbage dump. They're only curious about ancient garbage—the tools and dishes and buildings that people discarded a long time ago. Archaeologists examine such old things to learn about the ways people once lived. Israel is a treasure trove of ancient things. It has kept teams of Western archaeologists digging for 150 years. But all this digging has hardly scratched the surface. New ancient sites turn up each year. This chapter describes some of the interesting and dramatic finds that were made under Israel's cities and hills. You'll also find ideas for do-it-yourself archaeology.

TELLS, TABLETS, AND CAVES

What's exciting for archaeologists in Israel is only frustrating for builders. When foundations are dug for a house or when ground is leveled to build a road, ancient objects are often uncovered. All work stops while somebody runs to call the Department of Antiquities. If the department's expert decides that the site is important, the builders must twiddle their thumbs while the archaeologists check it out.

Why did ancient people bother to bury their pots, their clay tablets, and even their houses and places of worship? To make life interesting for archaeologists? No. Actually, except for a few hoards of coins or jewelry, most things weren't buried at all. They were just dumped. When a cook dropped a pottery jug and broke it, she threw it out the back door. When a house caught fire and burned to the ground, the family left the heap of blackened bricks and stones and built another house nearby. And when an enemy attacked a town, its people grabbed as much as they could carry and ran away, leaving pots, furniture, and children's toys behind.

Over the years blowing earth covered the broken and leftover things. Grass and bushes grew in the cracks of buildings. The walls crumbled. At last, all that could be seen of the old town was a mound of earth and rocks. New people came and built houses on the old site. They, too, broke jugs, had fires, and were driven out by enemies. And their leftovers were also slowly covered by earth and bushes. The mound grew taller.

An archaeologist begins to tingle when he or she sees a smoothly rounded mound or hill rising out of a flat plain. It is likely to be made of layers of ancient towns built on top of each other. This kind of hill is called a tell (*tel* in Hebrew), and Israel is dotted with them. Tel Ḥatzor in northern Israel has twenty-one layers of towns and fortresses that have been built one on top of the other over a period of 4,000 years. The tell beside the town of Jericho on the Jordan river is even older. Its bottom layer is made of houses that were built when lions, bears, and leopards hunted in the jungles of the Jordan valley.

The grassy tell that covers ancient Yokneam stands at the edge of the Valley of Jezreel. Modern Yokneam's factories and red-roofed houses crowd around it.

Why are there so many tells and so many more ancient buried things in Israel than, for example, in New Jersey? One of the reasons is that Israel is part of a land bridge between Asia and Africa. Many more soldiers and merchants and herdsmen have traveled through or settled down in Israel over the centuries than in New Jersey. And each group of people has left a layer of things behind.

With such treasures underfoot and tucked into odd corners, any Israeli might be lucky enough to make a fantastic discovery. For example, early one morning in Jerusalem a man followed his sniffing dog through a crack in a stony hillside. He found himself inside a huge, echoing, chilly cave, a cave he had never known about. He snatched up the dog and rushed home to get a torch and a ball of string. Then he tied one end of the string to a rock near the entrance and slowly unraveled it as he explored a chain of great, dark caves. The dog walker had accidentally discovered King Solomon's quarries. They are a group of giant caves under the city from which King Solomon's builders had cut stone blocks to build Jerusalem.

Digging Generals

Moshe Dayan, Israel's former defense minister, always lived dangerously. He lost an eye fighting in World War II, and he led Israeli troops into battle in three other wars. But he came closest to violent death when the earth caved in on him at an archaeological dig.

Yigael Yadin, another famous Israeli general, was an archaeologist and led the work at the top of Masada. Like many Israelis, Yadin changed his last name from a European to a Hebrew name. His father was Eliezer Sukenik, the scholar who risked death by crossing into East Jerusalem to buy the Dead Sea Scrolls while war was raging between the eastern and western parts of the city.

A lost goat led a Bedouin shepherd boy to the greatest Bible discovery of the century. When the goat wandered away from the herd down near the Dead Sea, the boy climbed the nearby cliffs to look for it. He squirmed along a ledge and found a narrow cave opening. Aha, thought the boy, I got him. And he threw a rock into the cave. But instead of a frightened bleating, he heard the sound of breaking pottery.

Pots? In an empty cave? The boy was so frightened that he almost fell off the ledge in his hurry to get down. But he soon came back with another boy, and they crawled inside. At the back of the cave they found several tall covered jugs. Each jug held a tightly wrapped package covered with black pitch. The boys dragged some of them down to their camp. Somebody might want to pay a few pounds for them, they thought.

A sharp-eyed dealer in Bethlehem was happy to buy a few of the scrolls. He showed them to Eliezer Sukenik, an archaeologist from Jerusalem's Hebrew University. Sukenik could not believe his eyes when he unrolled the scrolls. They were written in ancient Hebrew script, perhaps 2,000 years old. The words of one scroll were from the Biblical book of Isaiah. Sukenik's hands trembled as he realized that he was holding the oldest Hebrew Bible scroll ever discovered! Two thousand years before, when Jews were battling the mighty Roman Empire, the owners had hidden their beloved scrolls in the cave near the Dead Sea. They never came back for them, and the scrolls have been waiting ever since.

Central Zionist Archives

Bar Kokhba led the Jews in a revolt against the Romans in 132 C.E. For four years his soldiers fought from hard-to-reach caves and mountaintops. Archaeologists had to lower themselves by ropes to reach this cliffside cave in the Judean desert. Inside they found letters that Bar Kokhba had sent to his fighters more than 1800 years ago.

If I forget you, oh Jerusalem, let my right hand forget its cunning. Let my tongue stick to the roof of my mouth if I do not remember you, if I do not set Jerusalem above my greatest joy.
(The cry of Jews being driven into exile twenty-six centuries ago)
Psalms 137:5—6

In Jerusalem you can walk along a street that people used 1,800 years ago. You can even go shopping in the same stores in which they shopped. The street is called the Cardo. Built by the Romans, it was a wide street that went from one side of Jerusalem to the other. Only a short part has been dug up. The rest is buried under the buildings of the city. Little shops with thick stone walls sell posters, paintings, and crafts along the sides of the Cardo. Eighteen centuries ago these shops sold olives, spices, and grains. A roof held up by Roman columns makes it a cool, shady shopping mall.

The ever-curious archaeologists dug below the Cardo and found two stone city walls that had been built long before the Romans came. King Hezekiah built one of them about 750 B.C.E., and the Hasmonean kings, Judah Maccabee's relatives, built the other. There's a lot of history in and under that shopping mall.

On top of a steep, lonely hill near the Dead Sea stands the ruined fortress of Masada. It wasn't accidentally discovered. People always knew about Masada because its tragic story was told by the historian Josephus many years ago. But it's a grim, hot, forbidding place, and nobody explored it carefully until in 1963 a team of young Israelis climbed up the hill.

The bloodthirsty King Herod built Masada as a hideout from his enemies. Two hundred years later, in 70 C.E., Jewish men, women, and children escaped from the burning city of Jerusalem. They climbed the steep, rocky hill and fought for freedom against the Roman army for two years. When the enemy finally broke through the defense wall, they found all the Jews dead. The Jews had chosen to kill themselves rather than become Roman slaves.

Israeli archaeologists found scrolls of law, synagogues, ritual baths, storehouses for grain, and giant cisterns for water at Masada. They also found many small clay tablets with one letter written on each. And they wondered: Could the tablets have been used to draw lots on that last terrible night, when the Romans were breaking through the wall, to choose those who would put their friends and families to death before killing themselves?

Today a cable car carries tourists to the top of Masada. But new soldiers in the Israeli army, Zahal, climb up the hard way— along a steep, winding "snake" path. At the top they vow to defend Israel with their lives. "Masada will not fall again," they promise.

A Jewish legend tells that the gold and jeweled treasures of the Temple were smuggled out of Jerusalem under the noses of the Roman attackers and buried in the Bet Shean valley in northern Israel. Hopeful treasure hunters have been digging there ever since.

What makes Israelis archaeology nuts? Why do they care about ancient cisterns and jugs and gravestones when there are exciting new things to play with like video games and computers? Well, they enjoy the new things, too, but, as a sunburned volunteer at a dig explained, archaeology is special. "I like to dig," she said, "because it shows me how deep are my roots in this place. My grandfather came from Boston and my great grandmother from Russia. But my ancestors were here. See?" And she pointed to the stone she was carefully cleaning. Hebrew letters were carved deep into the gray surface. "It's my language. It proves to me that my people were here many centuries ago and wrote these words."

This chapter only begins to describe Israel's archaeological wonders. There are hundreds of other places to explore. Look for books on archaeology in Chapter 14. They'll take you to an echoing, underground city in Acre ('Akko), a looming Crusader fortress in the Galilee, a gigantic tomb built by a genius-madman-king at Herodian, and even farther. Or, better yet, don't read another word—fly to Israel, and join a dig.

GOD'S HOUSE

The Holy Temple

Long, Sad Memories

The Ninth of Av (Tishah Be'av) is a day in midsummer when Jews remember the destruction of the Temple by fasting and reading the sad words of the prophet Jeremiah.

A small section of wall is often left unfinished in a new house or synagogue, and the words "Zechor l'churban" ("Remember the destruction") are inscribed on the surface.

Even at happy times, Jews refuse to forget their loss. At a wedding the bridegroom smashes a glass to remind himself and everybody else of the destruction of the Temple.

King Solomon built a house for God, a temple, on top of Mt. Moriah in Jerusalem. It was made of giant cedars from Lebanon and polished granite. The walls were carved and decorated with gold leaf and precious stones. Deep within the Temple was the Holy of Holies, a room that only the high priest could enter, where the ark of the covenant was kept. The people of Israel had carried the ark through the Sinai desert, through the land of Israel, and now at last it was at home.

Three times each year, at the Passover, Shavuoth, and Sukkoth holidays, Jews came to the Temple bringing gifts from their harvests. The priests tended to the sacrifices, and the Levites stood on the broad marble steps and sang and played music in honor of God. In the sunny Temple courtyards the worshipers sang along and feasted and celebrated. They were proud of their beautiful Temple and felt safe and happy in God's care.

All this was destroyed in 586 B.C.E. by Babylonian invaders. The Temple was looted and the people driven out. When the enemy broke into the Holy of Holies, they found it empty. The ark was gone.

Years later, the Jews returned and built a second Temple. King

Herod added more columns, made the building taller, and built a great flat courtyard around it by filling in the mountaintop with earth. The earth was held in place with thick stone retaining walls.

It was a glorious sight. Pilgrims coming up the mountain roads danced with pride and joy when they saw the Temple gleaming high on its mount. The Talmud sages wrote, "Whoever didn't see the Temple of Herod missed seeing the most beautiful building in the world."

But in 70 C.E. the Temple was destroyed again, burned to the ground by the Romans, and the Jewish people were again driven out of their land.

Nothing could keep them away. Through the centuries Jews returned to pray at the last wall, the Western Wall of Herod's Temple mount. They remembered their beautiful Temple even as the Romans built a temple to their god Jupiter on the burned stones. And they continued to pray when a Christian emperor replaced Jupiter's temple with a church. Later, when the Moslems built a great domed mosque on the mount, the Jews still prayed below at the Western Wall.

Today archaeologists have dug 25 feet into the earth (about two stories) around Herod's wall. They've uncovered the ancient gates and stairs that led up to the Temple mount. Nearby they dug up ritual baths and other buildings where the worshipers had prepared themselves to go up to the Temple. When you go to Israel, you can stop to pray at the Western Wall and look out across the hills of Judaea, just as the Jewish pilgrims did when they came to the Temple with their harvest gifts 2,000 years ago.

If your last name is Cohen, Kahn, Cahan, or Katz (from the Hebrew Kohen tzedek, meaning "priest of righteousness"), your ancestors may have been priests in the Temple in Jerusalem 2,000 years ago.

If your last name is Levy, Levi, Levine, or Segal (from the Hebrew segan Levi, meaning "head of the tribe of Levi"), your ancestors may have played music and sung songs to God during services at the Temple.

Herod's Temple was described by the historian Josephus and by the writers of the Talmud. It probably looked very much like this picture. You can build a model of the Temple for yourself by using the pictures on the next seven pages.

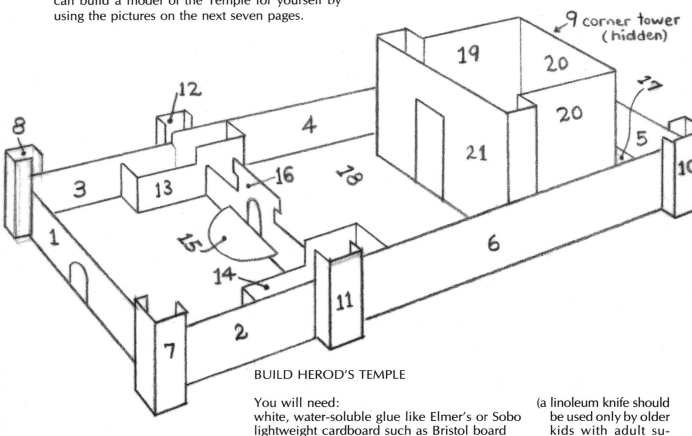

9 corner tower (hidden)

BUILD HEROD'S TEMPLE

You will need:
white, water-soluble glue like Elmer's or Sobo
lightweight cardboard such as Bristol board
scissors and/or a linoleum knife

(a linoleum knife should be used only by older kids with adult supervision)
stapler

1. Make photocopies of pages 201–207 (many libraries and post offices have copying machines). Glue the copies to the cardboard.
2. Cut out along the heavy black outline. Cut all the slots marked "Cut."
3. Find parts 1, 2, 3, 4, 5, 6 (the outer wall). Bend flaps on dashed lines. Apply glue and join pieces. Hold flaps together until the glue dries.

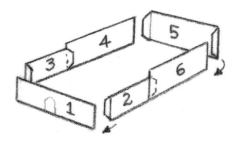

4. Find parts 7, 8, 9, 10. Bend on dashed lines. Fit tabs A, B, C, D into slots marked A, B, C, D on the four corners of the outer wall.

5. Find parts 11 and 12. Bend on dashed lines. Fit tabs E, F, G, H into slots marked E, F, G, H in long side walls.

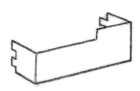

6. Bend parts 13 and 14 (storage rooms) on dashed lines. Fit tabs I, J, K, L into slots I, J, K, L from the inside of the long side walls.
7. Fit tabs of part 15 (steps) into slots of part 16 (gate).
8. Fit tabs M, N, O, P of part 16 into slots M, N, O, P of parts 13 and 14.

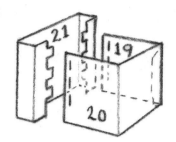

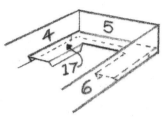

9. Bend flaps of part 17 (rear platform). Glue or staple the outside flaps to lower edges of 4, 5, and 6.

12. Bend part 21 (sanctuary front) on dashed lines.

13. Bend part 20 (sanctuary side and rear wall) on dashed line. Bend flap of part 19 (sanctuary side wall), apply glue, and join parts 19 and 20.

14. Fit the six tabs of part 21 into the slots of parts 19 and 20 to form the sanctuary. Place the sanctuary in the opening of the platform.

15. Glue or staple the inside flaps of part 17 to the lower edge of the sanctuary wall.

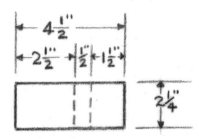

17. To make storage room roofs, cut this shape, bend on the dotted lines, bend the flaps, and glue them to the walls.

18. Place the completed Temple on a large board. Color the board's surface tan or gray to represent the paving stones of the Temple Mount.

NOTE:

Make all bends *away* from the illustrated surface.

Flaps for glue are marked xxxxxxxxx.

Dashed lines are bend lines.

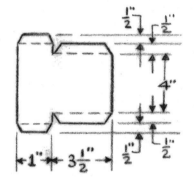

10. Bend flaps of part 18 (front platform). Do not bend the two short flaps that have no dashed line. Glue bent flaps to lower edges of 4, 6, 13, and 14.

11. Glue the two short flaps to part 17 (rear platform).

16. To make a sanctuary roof, cut this shape out of cardboard, bend the flaps, and glue them to the sanctuary walls.

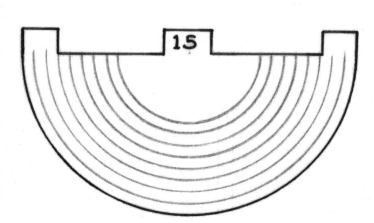

this symbol → " means 'inches'

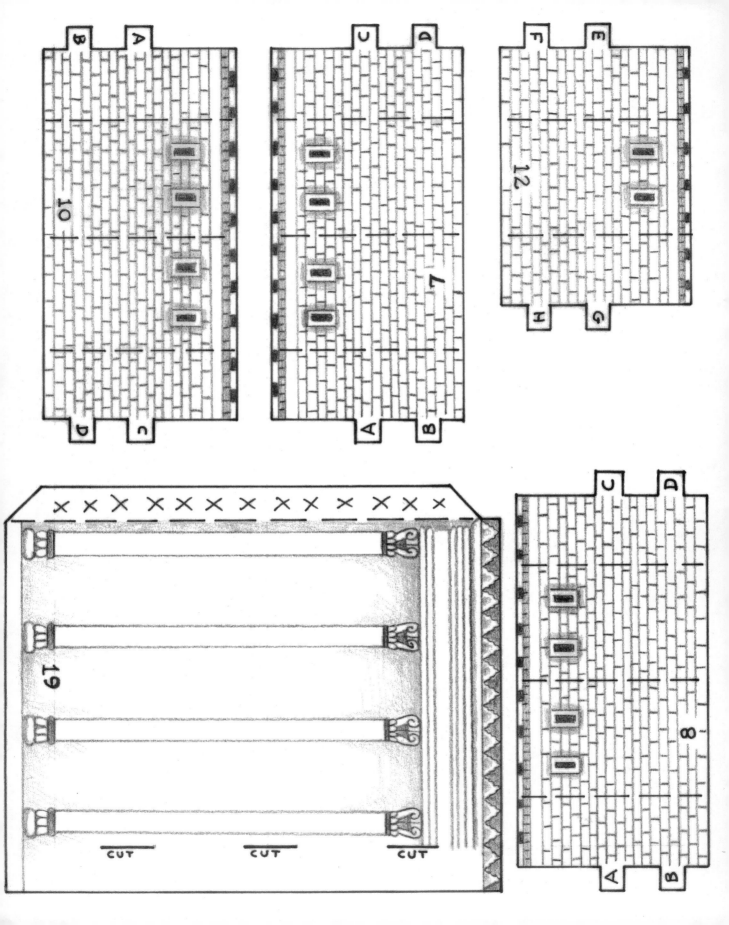

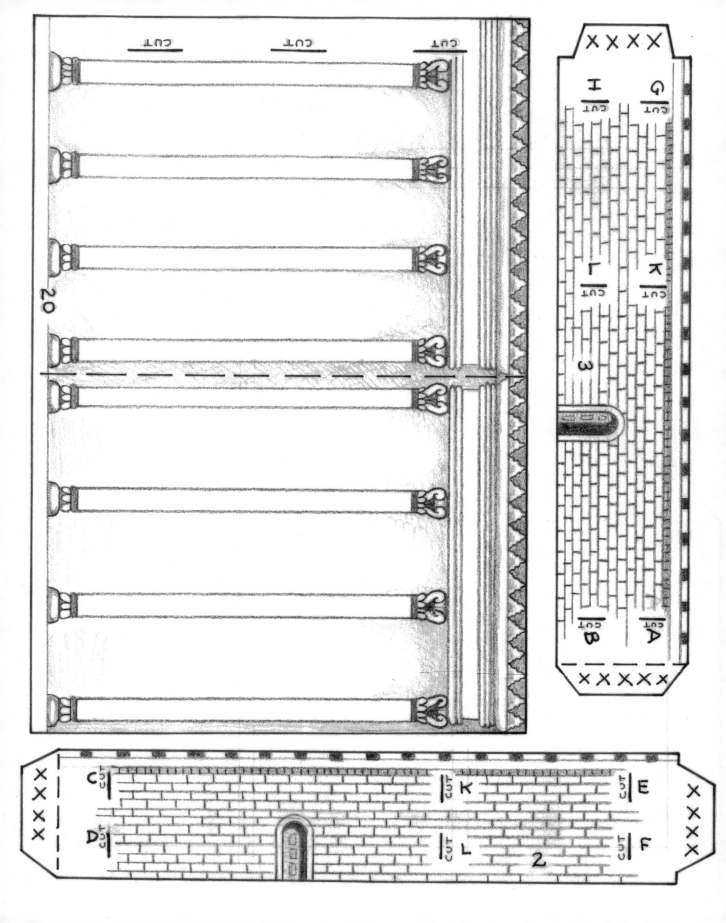

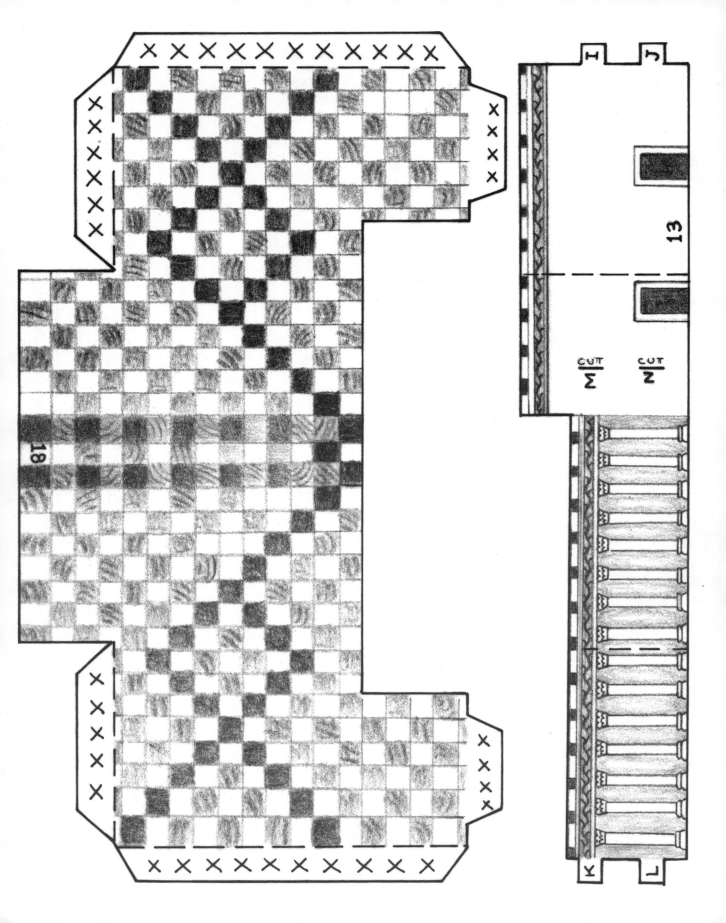

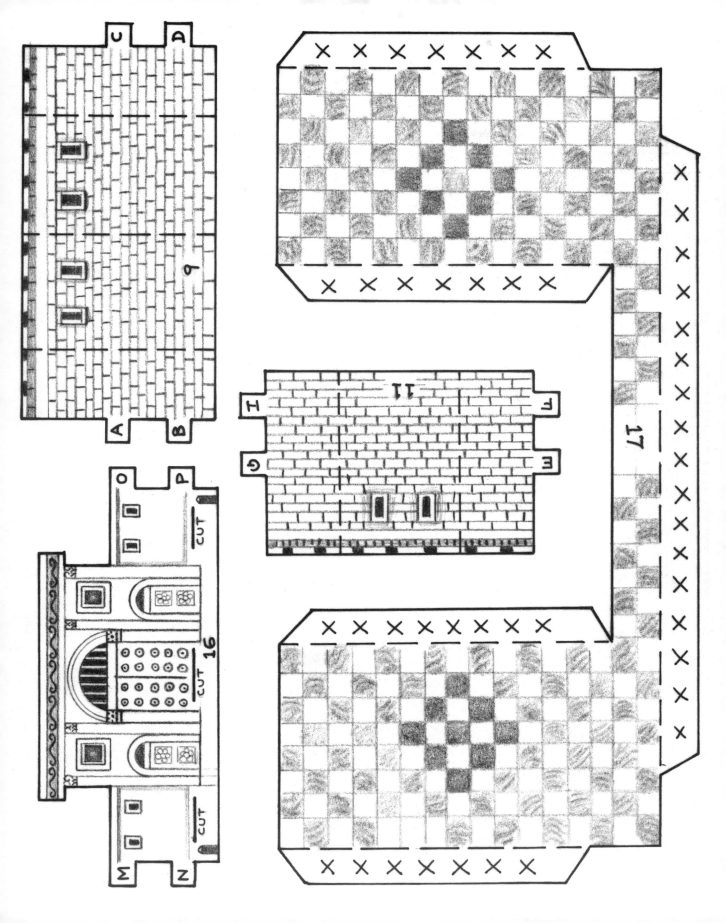

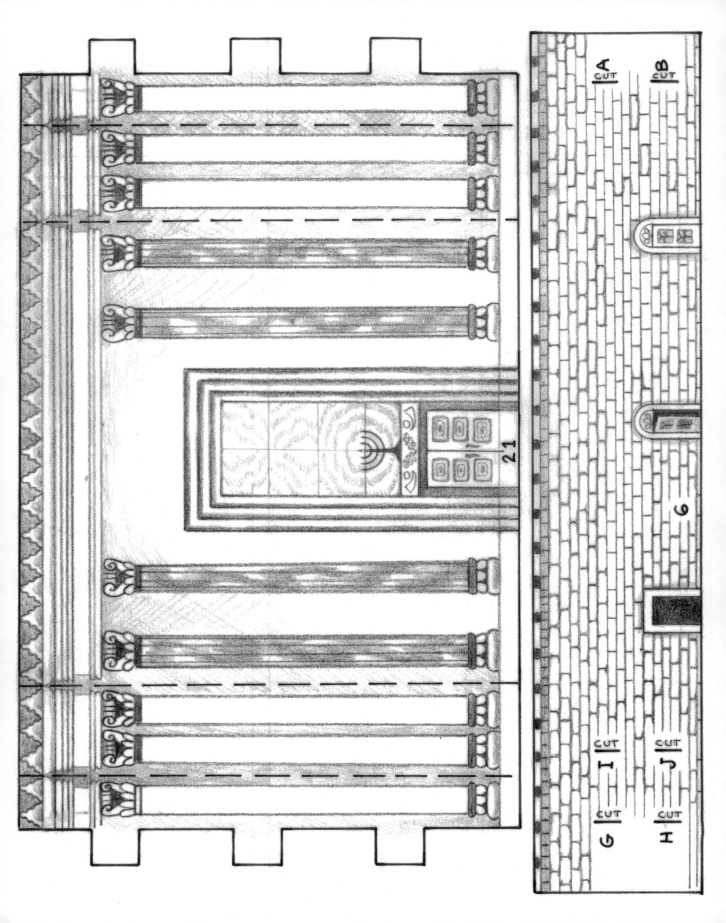

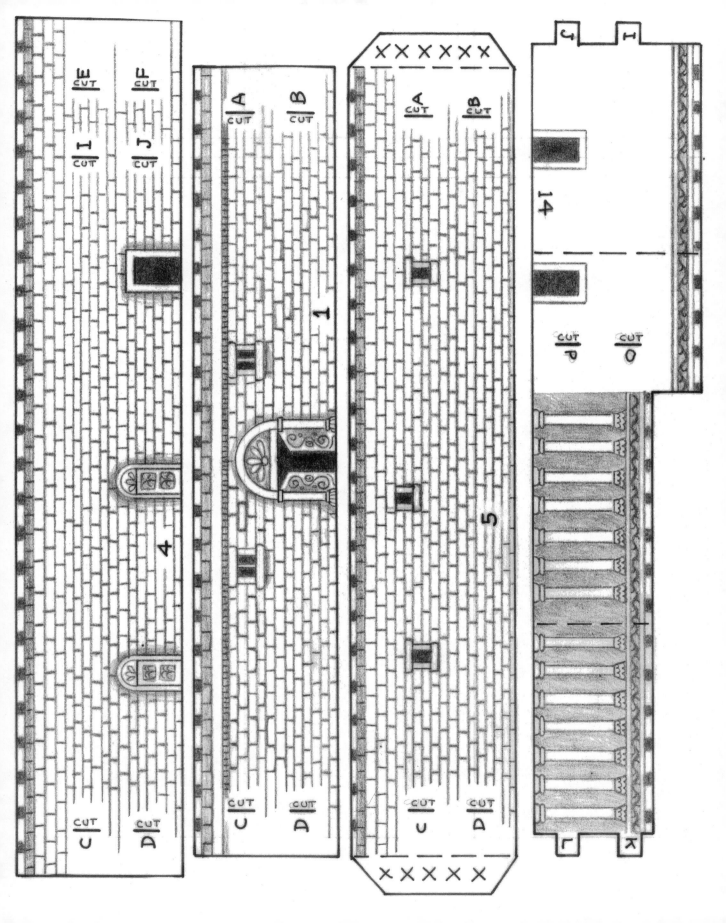

TWO THOUSAND YEARS AGO—AND TODAY

These objects have been found at digs all over Israel. Can you guess what they are? Which modern objects on the opposite page serve the same purpose? Check your answers at the bottom of the page.

Canaanite Goddess 1700 B.C.E.

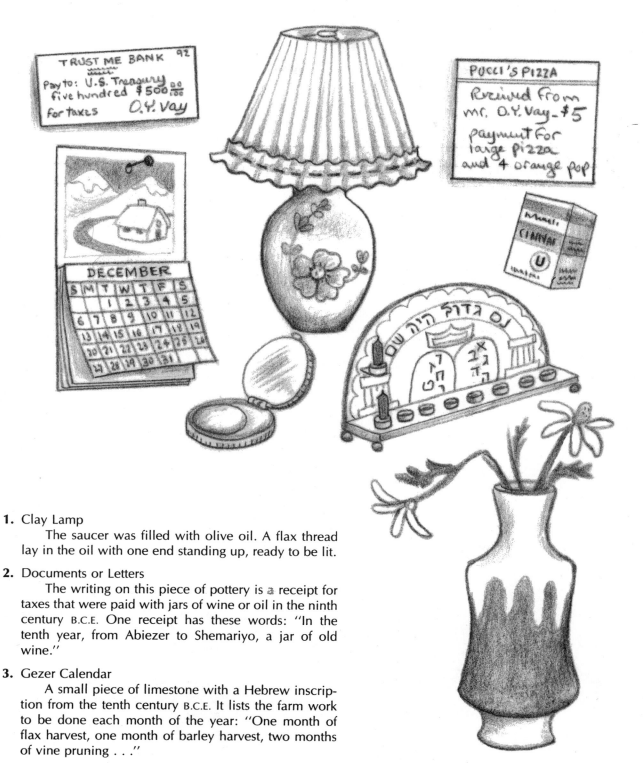

1. Clay Lamp

The saucer was filled with olive oil. A flax thread lay in the oil with one end standing up, ready to be lit.

2. Documents or Letters

The writing on this piece of pottery is a receipt for taxes that were paid with jars of wine or oil in the ninth century B.C.E. One receipt has these words: "In the tenth year, from Abiezer to Shemariyo, a jar of old wine."

3. Gezer Calendar

A small piece of limestone with a Hebrew inscription from the tenth century B.C.E. It lists the farm work to be done each month of the year: "One month of flax harvest, one month of barley harvest, two months of vine pruning . . ."

4. Ḥanukkah Menorah

Archaeologists guess (they're not sure) that this clay lamp from the first century C.E. is the earliest Ḥanukkah lamp. Like a ḥanukkiya, it has eight wick holes. But there is no writing or pattern to identify it for certain.

5. Shekel from the city of Tyre

    Jews sent tax money from all over the world to support their Temple in Jerusalem. In the first century C.E. the priests would accept only the Tyrian shekel as payment because only that coin had a reliable amount of silver.

6. Make-up Dish

    A lady powdered her face from this alabaster stone bowl twenty centuries ago.

7. Vase

    "Jericho John" is the name archaeologists gave this big-nosed vase dug up in Jericho. The potter who made it almost 4,000 years ago had a great sense of humor.

8. Stamp of Kashrut

    This bronze stamp of the fifth century C.E. was pressed into fresh bread to show that the bread was ritually pure or kosher.

Ghosts of long-gone Israelite housewives flit around this kitchen that was found buried under modern Jerusalem. It has deep burn scars on its rocky walls. Archaeologists think it was burned and buried during the Judean rebellion in 70 C.E., when the Romans destroyed Jerusalem.

Ed Toben

What do you get at a dig? A sunburn, and sometimes nothing more. Archaeologists must dig through tons of earth using only hand tools. Larger tools might accidentally smash important finds. It's hard, patient work. But each year many Americans come to work at digs in Israel.

A WASTEPAPER-BASKET DIG

Suppose this is the year 3000. Now suppose that you're an archaeologist studying ancient American culture of the twentieth century. But the only twentieth-century object you can find is one wastepaper basket full of garbage. (Quick. Get permission to borrow your sister's or brother's or friend's full wastepaper basket. Dump it out on some newspapers.) What can this ancient basket and its contents tell you about the life and culture of its owner?

Apple cores and banana peels or soft-drink cans and candy wrappers would be a clue to the person's eating habits. Stubs of pencils and crumpled notes, doodles, or computer printouts, comic books, sports or movie fan magazines would tell you something about his or her interests. The amount of plastic or other garbage—broken pens, toys, gadgets—could give you an idea of the person's world. Is it a rich world with lots of products and much waste, or is it a world of scarcity? How advanced is its technology? Are there any clues to the person's nationality or religion?

Ask yourself questions about every object you find, and soon you'll be thinking like an archaeologist. Maybe you'll also get to know your sister, brother, or friend a little better.

13

Centuries of stories

Stories about Smurfs and Sesame Street people, bejeweled princes, bewitched talking animals, and just plain Israeli kids crowd the children's section of an Israeli bookstore. It's usually the busiest part of the store because Israelis buy lots of children's books. Pretend you're browsing in a bookstore on Ben Yehuda Street as you look through this chapter.

The first five stories will start you off in the folk-tale section. Many of Israel's folk tales were brought from such faraway places as Iran, Turkey, and India. They had been told and retold for centuries at weddings, funerals, and holiday celebrations.

Today, people gather in front of their television sets rather than around the town storyteller. But the old stories are not lost. Nearly 6,500 stories were collected from storytellers of many lands and are kept in the Folklore Archives at Haifa University in Israel.

The next few stories are in the adventure-and-war section. They tell about Israeli boys and girls who helped to defend their country, about Arab and Jewish children who became friends even while their parents were fighting, about a smart carrier pigeon, and more.

Then move on to a section that's quieter. Just like kids in the United States, kids in Israel have problems with their parents and friends, with school and with moving to new neighborhoods and new countries. The last few stories are chapters taken from books that tell about such experiences.

If you were really in a bookstore on Ben Yehuda Street, you would also find comic books about the Wild West, space adventures, and sports magazines—all in Hebrew. Check them out when you go to Israel.

The Crowning Flower

adapted from Legends of Galilee, Jordan and Sinai *by Zev Vilnay*

SOLOMON walked up and down the lanes of the royal gardens searching for a perfect blossom. He was to be crowned king of Israel, and he wanted a crown that would be shaped like the most beautiful flower in the land. But the bold, flashy flowers on each side bored him—they were so ordinary. Then he saw a small flower peeping up from between two rocks. Its graceful petals reached up in the shape of a delicate crown. "Perfect!" cried Solomon. He called his craftsmen to copy this most beautiful flower, the rakefet or cyclamen, to fashion his crown.

For many years the rakefet bloomed proudly on Israel's rocky hillsides. And the kings and queens of Israel proudly wore their rakefet-shaped crowns. But when enemies marched into the land and destroyed Jerusalem and the Temple, the flowers began to droop. When the royal crowns and other treasures were carried out of Israel, all the rakafot dropped their heads in sorrow. To this day the rakefet grows with its face to the ground.

The Al-T'nai Synagogue

a legend

BY the ninth day of Av in the year 70 C.E. the battle for Jerusalem had been lost. Thundering battering rams of the Roman enemy crushed the walls of the Holy Temple. Fire roared through the marble courtyards. The remaining defenders fought on grimly and hopelessly.

Suddenly white wings sliced through the clouds of smoke. Angels swooped into the fire, snatched up blackened Temple stones, and carried them high into the air.

They flew far away, over the entire world, scattering the stones as they went. Wherever a stone fell Jews built a new synagogue.

In Prague, Czechoslovakia, where many stones fell, the Jews built a great synagogue. They named it Al-T'nai. In Hebrew those words mean "on condition." The builders promised that they would use the stones "on condition" that when the Holy Temple was rebuilt in Jerusalem the stones would be returned to their place in the Temple wall.

The Al-T'nai synagogue still stands in Prague. But over the years its name has changed to Alt-Neu.

The Girl, the Donkey, and the Dog

an Arab folk tale adapted from Adventures in the Galilee *by Yehoash Biber*

THE first man to live in the Galilee was an old man with three sons. He had a donkey, a dog, and a young serving girl. The old man's eldest son was a shepherd, the middle one a farmer, and the third a hunter.

One day, as the old man sat at the entrance to his tent, his eldest son, the shepherd, came to him bringing a big cheese and a pitcher of fresh milk.

"Peace be with you, Father."

"And peace be with you, my son. How are your sheep?"

"They are all healthy and fat, thanks be to God. Their milk is plentiful and their wool excellent. Yet, despite these blessings, I am lonely. Please, Father, give me your servant girl for a wife. She can milk the sheep, make the cheese, and churn the butter. She can weave cloth from the wool and be the mother of my children."

The father replied, "I'll think about it. Come back in a week's time, and I shall give you my answer."

Just as the eldest son had gone, the second son, the farmer, came to the old man. He kissed his father and presented him with a basketful of fresh vegetables.

"How are you, my son?"

"Thanks be to God, I am well and healthy. I till the soil and bring forth bread from the earth. I have only one request to make. Give me the girl for a wife. She can help me work the land. She can cook my meals, dry vegetables for the winter, and be the mother of my children. A man without a wife is like a plow without soil."

"I shall think about it, my son," replied the old man. "Come back in a week's time, and I shall give you my answer."

The farmer had only just left when the third son, the hunter, came to the tent carrying a fresh chunk of meat from an animal he had killed. The hunter gave the meat to the girl to cook. Then he sat down by his father and laid his huge bow at his feet. "How are you, Father?"

"Thanks be to God, I am very well—healthy and happy. How does the hunting go, my son?"

"There is much game. The fields contain many wild animals. I lack nothing but a wife. Father, give me the girl for a wife. She can tan the hides and make garments and blankets from them. She can roast and boil the meat so that we can eat our fill, and we can raise children."

His father replied, "Come back in a week's time, my son, and I shall give you my answer."

The third son bade his father farewell, and the old man sat in thought. To which of his sons should he give his servant girl for a wife? How could he give her to one and thus discriminate against the other two?

While he sat deep in thought, an angel appeared before him. "Why are you sad? Do you lack for anything?" asked the angel.

The old man poured out his troubles to the angel. The angel said, "Do not worry, O beloved of God. I shall turn the dog and the donkey into girls so that you can give each son a wife."

The angel turned the dog and the donkey into girls and fashioned them in the likeness of the first girl. The three resembled each other so closely you could not tell them apart.

A week later the three sons returned. Their father gave them each a girl for a wife. Each son took his wife away and went home full of joy and contentment. So when you walk in the Galilee, if you meet a man who is intelligent, wise, and good-natured, he is surely a descendant of the first girl, the daughter of man. If he is stupid and stubborn, then he must be descended from the offspring of the donkey. And if he shouts and weeps and wails and bemoans his fate for no reason at all, then he must be one of the descendants of the children of the dog.

The Two Brothers

a legend

MANY years ago, on a beautiful hill in the land of Canaan, there lived two brothers. Both were farmers; both tilled the soil. One lived with his wife and children on one side of the hill; the other lived alone in a little hut on the other side of the hill.

One summer God showered His goodness upon that land and upon that hill. When the brothers had sown their seeds, God sent rain to make the seeds sprout. The warm sun looked down and made them grow. When the time for the gathering of the harvest came, the reapers found a bountiful crop. The sheaves were piled high in the fields on both sides of the hill.

Both brothers came to the fields in the evening to thank God for His mercy.

On the east side of the hill stood the married brother, looking at his sheaves. "How good is God," thought he. "Why does He bless me with as much as my brother has? I have a wife already and children, but my brother has neither wife nor children. How many years will he have to toil before he can live as I do, with a loving family? I do not need all these crops. He needs all he can get. When my brother is asleep tonight, I shall carry some of my sheaves to his fields. He will never notice what I have done."

While the married brother thought thus to himself on the east side of the hill, the unmarried brother stood musing in his fields on the west side of the hill.

He said to himself, "God be praised for His kindness! But I wish He had done less for me and more for my brother. I have need of little, but my brother has a wife and many children to share his goods with him. At midnight, when all are asleep, I shall place some of my sheaves on my brother's fields. He will never know that he has more or that I have less."

Thus both brothers waited, each happy in the thoughts that had come to him. Toward midnight each loaded his shoulders high with sheaves and turned toward the top of the hill. The married brother went west, the other one east. And it was midnight when on the summit the brothers met and embraced.

When God saw the meeting of the brothers and the love each had for the other, He chose that place to be the site of the Holy Temple.

IN the woods near the village of Shebreshin there once lived a poor, pious Jew, his wife, and their two she-goats. Each day the wife would tether the goats in a field, and each evening she would bring them home. She and her husband earned a meager living from the small amount of milk, butter, and cheese they obtained from the goats.

One day the woman went to milk the goats but could not find them. She had forgotten to tether them that morning. She searched in vain and then began to cry and shout. But her husband stopped her. With a smile he said, "Don't be upset. Everything is from heaven."

To the woman's surprise the goats came home at sunset. And that evening they gave more milk than ever before. They have been blessed, thought the wife. On the next day again she did not tether them and they returned in the evening heavy with milk. And such milk! Sick people in the village became well after drinking it.

The Two She-Goats from Shebreshin

told by an elderly Jew from Poland

Six days passed in this manner. On the seventh morning the Jew followed the goats from the field to see where they might go. They went deep into the woods and entered a dark opening in the ground. The Jew followed and found himself in a cave. A beam of light shone far ahead. The goats went toward the light with the Jew following close behind.

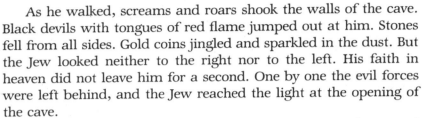

As he walked, screams and roars shook the walls of the cave. Black devils with tongues of red flame jumped out at him. Stones fell from all sides. Gold coins jingled and sparkled in the dust. But the Jew looked neither to the right nor to the left. His faith in heaven did not leave him for a second. One by one the evil forces were left behind, and the Jew reached the light at the opening of the cave.

He climbed out into a green, sunny field where a boy stood piping a tune for his two she-goats. "*Shalom aleichem*," said the boy. "Are you new in our land?" The Jew began to tremble with joy. He realized that he was standing on the holy soil of the land of Israel.

"*Aleichem shalom*," he answered and threw himself on the ground, kissed the soil, and gave thanks to the Lord. Then he sat down and wrote a letter to the Jews of Shebreshin and to all the Jews in exile. He called upon them to come and not to be frightened by the devils in the cave. He wrapped the letter in a fig leaf, addressed it to the rabbi of Shebreshin, and tied it to the neck of one of the goats.

That evening the goats returned home heavy with milk. The wife was worried that her husband did not return with them. She was so worried that she did not notice the fig leaf tied around the goat's neck. The next morning she tethered the goats for fear that they would get lost like her husband. She waited one day, two days, three days. At last the wife decided sadly that robbers had killed her husband in the forest. She could not continue to live alone in the woods. It would be better to move to the village of Shebreshin.

So she said, and so she did. And what did she need goats for in the village? It would be better to have them slaughtered and sell the meat. So she said, and so she did. Only then, after the goats were slaughtered, did the butcher find the letter in the fig leaf and run with it to the rabbi.

When the rabbi read the letter, he began to weep. "What can be done now? The goats cannot be returned to life, and only they know the way to the Holy Land. Now we must continue to wait in exile for the day of redemption."

The rabbi of Shebreshin kept the letter for many years in the synagogue. When the great fire came and most of Shebreshin went up in flame, the letter from the Holy Land was lost, too.

EVERY Thursday, Amos waited impatiently for the evening. Then he would take his flashlight, go up to the roof of his house in the Rehavia neighborhood of Jerusalem and start flashing a message to Pearl, his contact in the Geula neighborhood. He had never met Pearl. But once, on a dark night, her clear voice sounded over the rooftops, "Hello Star—here is Pearl. Come in."

Though it was dangerous Amos answered, "Hello Pearl—here is Star. Come in."

Ruth, in Geula, also waited impatiently for Thursday nights when she could go up to her roof to "speak" to the boy she had never met.

It all happened before Israel became independent. The British were in charge of the country, and bitter fighting was taking place between Arab bands and Jews. Those were days of worry and nights of black-out and curfew when nobody was allowed out on the streets. People shut themselves up in their houses, and heavy silence and darkness fell on the town.

But not everything was sunk in darkness. Boys and girls like Ruth and Amos, members of the youth movements and the Haganah, the underground Jewish army, were the invisible guardians of the town. They saw and heard everything. When evening fell, those boys and girls climbed to the roofs of their houses and sent messages between the city's neighborhoods by Morse code, a language in which letters are translated into dots and dashes. Messages were spelled out with a short flash of light for a dot and a long one for a dash.

At daybreak the boys and girls took their schoolbags and ran off to school. And sometimes their eyes would close while they sat at their desks. Amos learned to keep one eye open so as not to be

Pearl to Star . . .

by Sara Eshel

caught by the teacher. But one day both of his eyes closed. The teacher's voice rang out, "Amos, are you dreaming?"

He awoke immediately. "What did I do, teacher?" he asked in an innocent voice.

"*You* are asking?" That's what *I* am asking *you*. What do you do all night—that you come to school and fall asleep during the first period?"

"There was a curfew last night," Amos answered. "What could I do?"

Nobody suspected that Amos had spent the night on the roof, awake and alert until morning, talking to Pearl in the language of dots and dashes.

One evening in the spring some important information passed from Amos to Ruth and vice versa. Then Ruth added a question that didn't belong with the message. She asked, "When all this is over and we have our own country, do you think we could meet just like ordinary people on the streets of Jerusalem?"

Amos was embarrassed. He didn't expect such a personal question. "Of course we'll meet," he answered.

"How?" asked Ruth with dots and dashes. "How shall I know you? Give me some clues."

But Amos knew he was not supposed to do that. In the underground they had to be secretive so that if they were arrested no one could identify them. "I don't know how, but I promise you that we'll find each other on the day of our independence," he replied.

Days passed, and then weeks, and then months. Boys and girls continued to climb to the roofs and pass on messages. Pearl and Star continued to signal to each other, but there was no more talk about meeting after the war.

At last, after a time that seemed like forever, the State of Israel was proclaimed. Everyone rushed to Jerusalem's main square to dance and sing and celebrate.

Ruth was in the middle of the dancing crowd. Suddenly a strong voice was heard all through the square: "HELLO, PEARL. STAR SPEAKING. COME IN."

Shocked and surprised, Ruth separated herself from the crowd, and called in a strong voice: "HELLO STAR. HERE IS PEARL. COME IN."

Amos and Ruth had met at last.

Pigeon to the Rescue

by Shulamith Singer

adapted from the World Over Story Book

NIZAH lived with her father and mother in a little house in a tiny village in Israel. The house had green shutters, a flower garden in front, and a vegetable patch in the back. Before the war Nizah thought her house was the best in all Israel. But now that her father was a soldier in the army of Israel, serving at the front, her home seemed empty.

One day an army truck drew up in front of the house. Two soldiers jumped down to help a third soldier off the truck. Nizah would have paid no attention, except that her dog Cushy suddenly started to bark and jump all over the third soldier. It was her father! His leg was in a cast, his arm in a sling, his head bandaged. For a moment everyone stood still. Then Nizah's father yelled cheerfully, "Are you all struck dumb? I'm home and all in one piece! I've got both legs, both arms, both ears, both eyes, and my heart is where it always was!"

It was almost a half hour before everyone could stop talking long enough to sit down to eat. Father was still finishing the story of his adventures, when suddenly there was a little noise. Peck, peck, peck, peck, it went. . . . Nizah ran to open the door, but no one was there. As she turned around, one of the soldiers opened the window. In flew a white pigeon. It circled the room and landed on her father's shoulder.

"Hello, there!" shouted Father. "This is my pal," he explained. "The bomb that wounded me also hit the tree on which she was sitting. The explosion knocked her off, right into my hands. She was shivering and frightened and . . ."

"And when we found them, they were both unconscious," put in one of the soldiers.

"Oh, yes," said Father. "And since that time we have always been together."

Three wonderful weeks passed. The house was full of Father's voice and the smell of his cigarettes. Father was well now, the cast had been removed, and he was going back to the front.

Again the house was empty. Mother did her work in silence. Even Cushy seemed unhappy, walking around and around aimlessly. And the pigeon fluttered all over the house, never standing still for more than five seconds at a time.

More weeks passed. "Mother," Nizah said one day, "how do you write the word *lonesome?*"

Her mother looked at her daughter. "Why do you want to know?"

"Oh, no reason at all," said Nizah.

Mother wrote the word, and Nizah carefully copied it onto a note she was writing. When Nizah finished, she rolled the note up. With a thin piece of thread she tied it carefully to the pigeon's leg. Then Nizah whispered to the bird, opened the window, and let it fly. In a moment the pigeon had disappeared.

Far away in an Israeli outpost, Nizah's father and six other soldiers were counting the minutes. They were stretched out in a trench, Sten guns in hand, watching for the enemy. Behind them a shack with a gaping hole in one of its walls and broken pieces of a radio strewn on the floor told their story. The only means which the little outpost had of communicating with headquarters and calling for help had been destroyed.

And now seven Jewish soldiers were waiting for the final Arab attack.

Something stirred behind the shack, and a sharp rat-tat-tat was heard. It couldn't be a machine gun—the sound was too soft. Nizah's father turned to the man next to him: "Dan," he said, "crawl around and see what's happening back there."

Slowly Dan wriggled away. He returned in a few minutes. "It's your pigeon," he said to Nizah's father. "She must have come back here to spend your last day with you."

Nizah's father hurried to the back of the shack. In a moment he returned, pigeon in hand. He lay down, fumbled with the thread around the bird's leg, and unrolled Nizah's note. "At least we still get postal service around here," remarked Dan, at his elbow.

"Sure," said another man, "but try sending a letter where it would do some good. Too bad this pigeon doesn't know the way to headquarters."

"Headquarters," repeated Nizah's father thoughtfully. "Why not? Who says she has to fly to headquarters? All she has to do is fly!"

His companions looked at him as if he had gone suddenly mad.

"Of course," Nizah's father shouted and sat up. "It will work. It must work. Listen! We know that the pigeon will fly only to my house. But the Arabs don't know it. The Arabs will assume that this is a trained war pigeon, carrying a message to headquarters. It's our only chance. I'm going to release the pigeon. The Arabs will shoot at her. If they don't hit her, we may be safe. If they think reinforcements are coming, they may retreat."

With trembling fingers Nizah's father tied a piece of paper, on which he had scribbled one line, to the bird's leg and sent her aloft. A volley of rifle fire broke the desert silence. Smoke filled the sky, but as the Jewish soldiers watched, the white pigeon flew higher and higher until she was out of range. . . .

It was Friday night two weeks later. Nizah and her mother were sitting in their tiny house with the green shutters. On the table the Sabbath candles were burning brightly.

Suddenly there was a sharp rap at the window. Nizah ran to open it, and in flew the white pigeon. It took only a second for Nizah to untie the tightly rolled note around the bird's leg. "I am coming home. Father," said the note.

As she looked up, there was her father, standing in the room. Nizah threw herself at him. "The pigeon brought you. I knew she would."

"Yes, daughter," he said. "The pigeon brought me."

It took a long time for father to explain how the pigeon had saved his life and how the Arabs retreated when they thought that a message had gone through to Israeli headquarters. By that time, Nizah was half asleep. But there was one thing she understood clearly. The pigeon brought her father back.

Ahmed

by D'vorah Omer

adapted from The Dog That Flew

"HEY, Uzi! Come here, fellows. Here's Uzi!"

The boys ran toward Uzi. He was sitting on the lawn by the dining hall. They encircled him, pleading, "Come on, Uzi, tell us how you captured the bandits."

Uzi sat quietly among the young children, his head and shoulders higher than the tops of their heads.

Uzi had driven off a group of bandits who had sneaked into the kibbutz cowshed the night before. But he tried to shrug the whole thing off.

"What is there to tell?" he asked. "I simply fired a few shots, and they ran. That's all."

The children did not give up so easily.

"Come on, Uzi! Please, tell us. . . ."

When he realized that he really had no choice in the matter, Uzi reluctantly agreed, and told them what had happened:

"At about one o'clock in the morning we caught a bandit who had entered the kibbutz through our barbed-wire fence. He was a young Arab, about my own age. He wore rubber-soled shoes and held a machine gun.

"The Arab gave himself up by walking toward our watchmen with his hands over his head. We took his weapons and locked him up in the guard room, the one with the barred window. When I started to leave the room, he called out, 'Havajah'!" (Mister!)

"I turned back toward him, and to my amazement he began to speak in perfect Hebrew: '*Havajah!* There is something important I must tell you.'

"The whole thing seemed very strange to me. I looked at him and replied, 'Fine—go ahead.'

" 'Later tonight bandits from Jordan plan to steal your herd,' he said.

" 'Who are you? Why are you telling me this?' I asked in surprise.

" 'I am one of the gang, and I have come to warn you.'

" 'Oh! Now I understand. You want money,' I said. He seemed offended.

" 'I don't want a thing from you,' he said roughly.

" 'In that case, what is it you're after?' I asked.

" '*Havajah!* Once, when I was a child, the members of this kibbutz saved my life. I feel that I must . . .'

"The moment the Arab uttered these words something flashed through my mind. Where on earth had I seen this Arab before?

" 'What's your name?' I asked.

" 'Ahmed. Ahmed Ben Yousouf.'

" 'Ahmed!' I shouted. 'Ahmed! It's me, Uzi! Don't you remember me?'

"Indeed, children, it was Ahmed. You youngsters don't know who Ahmed is, but the fellows of my age group remember him well. We met him long ago when we were youngsters in the last grade of school. At that time we often roamed through the hills around the kibbutz. During one of our hikes we discovered a wounded Arab boy lying in a ditch by the road, moaning and bleeding.

"The first thing we did was to run frantically in the direction of the farm, but we stopped even before we reached the gate. We realized we were acting like foolish children. The Arab boy was lying wounded, and it was our duty to help him. We went back, and, with the little Arabic we knew, we tried to talk to him. He looked at us with the eyes of a wounded animal and did not reply, so we decided simply to take him back with us.

" 'Come on' we told him. 'You'll sleep with us tonight.'

"We tried to help him to his feet, but he drew away from us. He stood, frightened and shaking, and then started to run. He took a few steps and fell. We picked him up and carried him between us. He was so weak that he could not resist.

"We took him to the store by the swimming pool, fetched him some food and a blanket, and fixed up a place for him to sleep on the floor. We emptied our first-aid box and carefully cleaned and dressed his wounds.

"We spent the whole first evening with him. From his broken

sentences, we made out that his name was Ahmed and that he was a child-slave, the property of Sheik Hussein, who was camping in the black tents beyond our fields. He was miserable and unhappy, so he had decided to run away and return to his family, who lived across the Jordan river. But the sheik's servants caught him, beat him mercilessly, and returned him to camp. On the day we found him he had tried to run away again, only to be overcome by his wounds.

"Ahmed ended his grim story with the words. 'I can't understand why you are so kind to me.'

"We had no reply for him. That was the way we felt, and we had to act upon it. That evening we were all glad that we had.

"Days went by. We spent many hours with Ahmed. We brought him food, changed the dressings on his wounds, and looked after him devotedly. But his condition seemed to grow worse; daily he was weaker and more feverish. Finally we took him to the sick bay of the kibbutz. He stayed there for a long time, and we visited him whenever we had an hour to spare.

"When Ahmed was finally well again, he came to live with us. He was given new clothes, he learned Hebrew, and soon he became one of our gang.

"About three months later we went up the hill to pick flowers. We stood at the very top and could see all the bends of the Jordan river unfolding before us. Ahmed looked at the scene for a long time. He was very quiet.

" 'Uzi,' he turned to me suddenly, 'I am going home!'

"We begged him to stay, but his mind was made up. 'I want to go home!' he repeated.

" 'Where is your home?' we asked.

" 'Over there,' he said, pointing to a hidden spot on the slopes of the Gilead range.

"Ahmed bade us farewell and began walking slowly downhill.

" 'Wait, Ahmed,' cried Yael, running after him. She took the gold chain off her neck and gave it to him. 'Take it, Ahmed. Don't forget us.'

" 'I won't ever forget you. Not ever,' said Ahmed softly, and we watched him quickly walk off until he disappeared in the dark.

"We have never seen him since, until I met him in the guardroom.

"Ahmed did not forget us. He returned to warn us of the

planned robbery. Do you understand what he did, children? Ahmed crossed the Jordan river, entered through mined fences surrounding the kibbutz, risked his life. He faced many grave dangers, but they did not deter him.

" 'I felt I had to repay you,' he told me.

"In his hand he held a gold chain with a miniature heart. This was the chain Yael had given him! It was his charm and token of our affection. He told me that he was sure the charm would protect him from the dangers facing him upon his return.

"This is the whole story, children. Later on at night, we laid ambush to the bandits at the time and place he told us, and drove them off."

"What about Ahmed?" asked Nurit.

"Ahmed? He went back to Jordan. We parted friends, shaking hands. When he left, I watched him disappear in the dark just as I had many years before."

The Brothers

by Shalom Hektin

adapted from the World Over Story Book

THE large ship was alive with the hum of excited voices. It overflowed with children who sang, laughed, and raced the length of the deck.

But one small boy leaned against the rail and gazed out over the ocean, indifferent to the happy scene.

"Yosele, Yosele," a child's voice called to him. The boy did not answer. Two girls running past stopped as they reached him. One of them tugged at his sleeve and spoke to him gently.

"Come, Yosele, come and join us. Don't be so grouchy. Come!"

Yosele turned angrily away from her and again stared far into the distance.

It was March 1943. Warm spring air enveloped the Red Sea. The passengers of this ship were eight hundred Jewish children who had been rescued from the Nazis. Besides the children, there were a few hundred adults who had also escaped. For more than a year they had wandered on dangerous waters, until at long last the joyful news arrived that they would be welcomed to their own permanent home—to Eretz Yisrael.

The children had already begun to forget their weary wanderings, anger, and disappointment when countries refused to let them land on their shores and forced them to toss about on the seven seas in all sorts of weather. Now they were happy. They were on the Red Sea, and in a day or two they would be in Eretz Yisrael, in their new home.

Yosele was the only one on the ship who was not happy. He was the smallest of the children, only seven years old. He was always alone—dreamy and sad.

Yosele was not the only orphan among the children on the ship. Very few of the children had both—or even one—of their parents. They had all suffered. But little Yosele seemed to suffer more than the others. He had been only four years old when his parents were murdered. Yosele couldn't even remember whether he had a brother or a sister anywhere. He did remember, though, how his mother had played with him and how she used to hold him in her arms and kiss him. How his mother looked—he couldn't remember. No matter how much he tried, he couldn't recall her face. Neither was his father's face clear, but at least he could remember him. At times it seemed to little Yosele as though his father's tall figure was standing beside him.

Yosele seldom laughed. But often, when he fell asleep, he would dream of his father. Then he would laugh and whisper, "Father, Father."

Night covered the countryside, and the people of the kvutzah at Naan were asleep. Only the watchman Dov was awake. He was a young man of twenty-three who had left Poland five years before to come to Palestine as a ḥalutz. As he stood leaning lightly on his rifle in the dark, his thoughts went back to the little Polish village that had been his home for eighteen years. He recalled his mother and father and his little two-year-old brother.

When Dov had first come to Palestine, he had planned to bring his whole family from Poland. But the war had shattered his careful plans. Now Dov didn't even know where his family was. It was a long time since he had heard from them. Perhaps they were no longer alive.

Dov thought of the hundreds of newly arrived children who were to pass through the Reḥovot station near Naan the next day. He was glad that so many children were rescued from death, and he was happy to welcome them. But what of his own family? His little brother? Was the child still alive? Would he ever find him?

Suddenly, Dov heard a faint rustling nearby. He peered into the darkness and recognized Yigal and Amos, two of the kibbutz children.

"Who goes there?" he shouted with fake sternness. "Don't you know I have a full right to shoot at you?"

Nine-year-old Amos hung his head in shame, but Yigal put up a brave front. "Well, go ahead, shoot," he teasingly called and like a flash he vanished in the darkness. With catlike stealthiness he crept behind Dov, jumped on his back, and again teased: "Come on, shoot me. Come on, shoot."

After a few moments of silent wrestling, Dov sat on a rock with the children at his feet. "Tell me, what brings you out so late?" he asked.

"We couldn't sleep," Yigal said. "Even though we have to be up extra early tomorrow."

"Why?" asked Dov, as though he didn't know.

The children looked at him in amazement. "Don't you know?" Yigal said. "Tomorrow morning we are going to march to the station in Reḥovot to meet the children from the ship. People are coming from all the nearby towns. Maybe we'll be able to bring some of the new children home to Naan to live with us."

"You should come to the station with us, too," Amos added.

Dov's face clouded. Maybe my brother will be among the children, he thought. But even if his little brother were there, would they be able to recognize each other?

The children went home to sleep, but Dov remained lost in thought. He began to think of his own childhood, of his father and mother. He remembered that when he was still a child, people always said that he resembled his father. "Just like his father," they used to say, looking from father to son.

"Just like his father," Dov suddenly said aloud, and the echo returned from the dark depths—"his father."

He wrinkled his forehead in amazement and shrugged his shoulders, wondering why he had spoken aloud. The next moment another thought came to him. He would go to greet the children who were passing through the station at Reḥovot.

A large crowd of men, women, and children from all the kvutzot in the vicinity gathered at the Reḥovot station the next morning. The children carried white-and-blue banners. Many of them had boxes filled with oranges and other good things to eat.

The sun shone brightly in a cloudless sky, and the perfume of fresh oranges filled the air.

A long train thundered into the station. The windows were filled with the happy, laughing faces of children. The crowd on the platform roared its welcome.

No sooner did the train halt than the children tumbled out like a gushing sea. Nothing could have stopped these children. They knew they had finally come home. Strangers kissed strangers. They began to cry and to laugh, and they were no longer strangers— just one half of a large family welcoming the other half.

The train had emptied, but one lonely child remained. Yosele was still inside. His pale face peeped forlornly out of the window. Suddenly he stiffened. He looked in bewilderment at one of the men. Then his thin, joyful voice cut through the crowd like a razor: "Father, Father!"

A shiver went through the crowd. Among the first who ran to the coach was Dov, the watchman from Naan. Dov looked deeply into Yosele's lonely, childish face. Yosele looked at Dov, whose face had made him cry out "Father!" Dov caught the boy up in his arms, and suddenly it occurred to him. This was Yosele, his own little brother for whom he had yearned all these years.

Dov followed the procession of children returning to Naan. In his strong, young arms he carried his little brother. Yosele rested his head confidently on his brother's chest. Every now and then he would look at his brother with a joyful smile.

"What is your name?" Yosele asked his brother.

"My name is Dov or Berl, whichever you want to call me," answered Dov.

"Dov, Berl—not Father," Yosele said to himself, and his face again became troubled.

Dov felt the little boy's sorrow and pressed him closer. Yosele lay against his brother, deep in thought. Then he shook himself as if awakening from a dream. He looked around at the green fields and at the sunny road stretching ahead. He filled his lungs with the clean fresh air. For the first time Yosele noticed the happy children marching and singing together.

He began to laugh. Then he slid out of Dov's protecting arms and ran to join the marching children.

It is difficult to explain why, but Yosele ran directly to the place where the two young friends, Amos and Yigal, were marching side by side. The two boys grasped his hands and held them tight, and they marched together.

THRILLING news swept through the Yemenite town where twelve-year-old Shalom lived. The Jews in the marketplace whispered excitedly to each other, "Israel has arisen again after 2,000 years. A new David rules in Jerusalem!" As the news spread throughout Yemen the Jews gathered their household goods and children and began a long trek through the desert toward Aden. From British-controlled Aden they would somehow find a way to reach the Promised Land. God would provide a miracle.

On Eagles' Wings

by Laszlo Hamori

from Flight to the Promised Land

One scorchingly hot morning a glistening silver airplane appeared over the El Hasched settlement in Aden. Flying low, it circled the tent city twice.

The people rushed out of their tents, turned their faces upward and stared at the circling plane.

A shrill voice shouted, "The Lord God has sent us a silver bird."

And as if on command, four thousand Yemenite Jews—men, women and children—bowed to the ground and, with their arms lifted up, recited the creed of their faith:

"Hear O Israel! The Lord our God; the Lord is one."

A few days later Shalom and his fellow-villagers climbed calmly aboard the huge plane. The only sign of emotion they showed was that the men covered their heads with their shawls and prayed aloud during the entire trip. Shalom spent every minute looking out of the round window of the plane. He could see the Red Sea below and the reddish-gold coast lines of Arabia and Africa.

When they were about three hours out of Aden the little children began to complain that they were hungry. The mothers, who were dressed in their best clothing festooned with silver jewelry, tried to calm their youngsters, but not even a nasty look from the head of the family helped. The women decided to take things into their own hands.

At that point the stewardess was sitting in the pilot's cabin writing a report for the airport officials in Israel. Suddenly the captain sniffed the air.

"Harry, Leah," he said to the others. "Don't you smell smoke?"

"By golly, you're right," the copilot agreed. He quickly checked his instruments and found everything normal. The noise of the engines was even and quiet. Nothing seemed to be wrong.

A sudden hunch made Leah jump up from her seat. As she opened the door leading to the passenger cabin, smoke began to pour through. The stewardess and copilot rushed out. In the aisle between the seats they discovered a small burning pile of newspapers and little pieces of wood. One of the women squatted beside it holding a kettle of food over the fire.

The copilot did a wild war dance with his size thirteen shoes and managed to stamp out the fire. The woman with the kettle screamed wildly and tried to shove aside the gangly American.

"Idiotic woman! You'll set the whole plane on fire. I've seen some stupid things in my life, but never anything to equal this!" shouted the copilot.

Leah quickly poured water on the dying embers. Then she explained to the woman that it was dangerous to build a fire on an airplane. Finally she pushed the angry copilot back into his own cabin and began to pass out sandwiches, hard-boiled eggs and tea to the passengers.

Having eaten, Shalom made his way up to the door between the passenger cabin and the cockpit. Each time anyone opened the door he stared longingly at the pilots, the strange steering mechanisms, and all the buttons surrounding the pilots' seat. Yitzḥak, an Israeli truck driver he had met in Yemen, had told him about motors and airplanes. He would give anything in the world to be able to watch the pilots fly the plane. But he didn't dare ask.

So much had changed in a short time, thought Shalom. At one time back home he had dreamed of the day when he would be a teacher and would interpret Jewish law for his congregation. But Yitzḥak had told him there were many rabbis in Israel. Now Shalom began to dream of a different future. One day he would be a pilot whose plane would bring Jews to Israel from all over the world.

Azit in the Judaean Desert

by Motta Gur

RUTHIE and Ḥayyim knew all about the flowers and animals and bugs in their neighborhood. They wanted to find exciting new species, like the strange plants and animals that live in the hot, dry Judaean desert.

Ḥayyim borrowed a canteen and a map of the desert from his brother Rami, a paratrooper. Ruthie borrowed a first-aid kit from her uncle, a medic with the tank corps. And they pooled their savings and bought a guide book of desert plants and animals.

Early one spring day they took a bus down to Arad, a town on the edge of the desert, and began to hike along a path that led deep into rocky wilderness. All morning they wandered up and down the hills. They found strange striped lizards, clumps of tiny flowers, and scurrying insects. Ruthie raced from plant to plant and stopped to look up each "find" in the book. Ḥayyim filled his notebook with notes.

When the sun was high they spread out the map and located the nearest water well. They soon reached the mound of rocks topped by a concrete platform with a round opening. A cool clump of trees grew in a hollow beside the well. Ḥayyim climbed to the top of the mound, lowered a can on a string through the opening, and brought up cold, delicious water. When they had enough to drink they scrambled down into the hollow to rest.

Suddenly, Ḥayyim saw a movement out of the corner of his eye. Two desert antelopes were coming toward the well.

The children held their breath as the antelopes jumped lightly up to the well platform and began to drink from the half-empty can.

"There's not enough water in there," Ḥayyim whispered. "I'll get some more." He started to tiptoe up the rocks.

The antelopes raised their heads in alarm, sniffed, turned, and seemed to float from the platform.

"Stop!" yelled Ḥayyim. "Don't run away. We want to help you." He scrambled higher.

"Wait, you'll fall," Ruthie cried.

Just then, just as he almost reached the fleeing antelopes, Ḥayyim's leg twisted, and he tumbled over and over down the mound. A shower of stones came rattling down with him.

Ruthie grabbed the first-aid kit and slid down to him. Ḥayyim lay silent, biting his lips to keep from crying. Ruthie quickly bandaged his leg.

"Swallow this pill," she said. "It'll stop the pain." Then she tucked the knapsack under his head.

"I can't walk," said Ḥayyim after a few minutes. Ruthie's eyes grew wide and anxious. "Don't worry," he said. "My brother will call home and find that we're missing. Then he and his buddies will come and find us."

"But our parents will be frightened," Ruthie said.

"We can't help them," said Ḥayyim sadly.

"No," said Ruthie. "We'd better help ourselves. I'll collect twigs to make a fire, then we'll have some tea. It'll be a cold night."

At dusk Rami called home to ask how the trip had been.

"Ḥayyim and Ruthie aren't back," his mother told him anxiously.

"Don't worry." said Rami. He rushed to tell his commanding officer.

Within half an hour the unit was on the road to Arad. Two hours later they were searching the dark desert, flashing their lights under every tree and behind every boulder. At dawn a scout plane was sent up to search from above. But Ḥayyim and Ruthie were tucked deep in the hollow under the trees. The pilot saw nothing.

Suddenly Rami had an idea, "We forgot about Azit. Let's call her in."

"Azit?" asked a new paratrooper. "Who's she? Your girlfriend?" The men burst out laughing.

"Azit is a special rescue dog. She has saved many of our boys," Rami told him. "If anybody can find Ḥayyim and Ruthie, Azit can."

A short while later Azit's master, Dr. Ḥaruvi, received an SOS call from paratroop headquarters.

"We have a job to do, Azit," said Dr. Ḥaruvi to his big German shepherd dog. Azit's ears perked up, and her tail wagged. They hurried to the airport, where a paratroop carrier waited. Rami had put some of Ḥayyim's and Ruthie's clothing aboard the carrier for Azit to sniff.

Dr. Ḥaruvi put a special parachute on Azit. Then she trotted eagerly up the ramp into the plane and settled down between two rows of seats. Dr. Ḥaruvi fastened her safety belt and attached an intercom set to her collar through which he would speak to her after she jumped.

The plane soon reached the search area and began to circle. The paratroopers could be seen on the ground below.

"Arik speaking," the pilot spoke into the intercom. "Azit is here. Do you have a jump area? Over."

"Rami speaking," came the answer from below. "We found tracks. The drop path should be west to east. We'll put down a red smoke marker. Over."

"Good," the pilot replied. "We'll make the drop in five minutes. Over and out."

The jump-officer released Azit's safety belt. He attached the parachute's strap to the bar which ran the length of the plane. Azit understood that it was time to jump. Her body tensed, her legs braced, and she yawned a deep, long yawn.

Dr. Ḥaruvi kissed Azit on the nose. "Azit, you're a good dog," he whispered in her ear and hugged her.

A red light blinked over the door.

"Get ready!" called the jump-officer. He moved Azit to the doorway. Above the door the light suddenly turned green. "Jump!" roared the jump-officer and tried to push Azit out. But Azit was already gone. She had leaped far out into the open air.

A strong wind hit Azit and rocked her from side to side. The parachute cords tightened, and the parachute opened wide. Azit wiggled her legs until the parachute steadied itself. Then she began to float slowly down. Her legs soon touched the ground. The parachute was automatically released, and Azit was ready for action.

"Azit," called Dr. Ḥaruvi through the intercom, "go and search."

She began to run in great circles sniffing the ground and seeking the smell she knew from Ḥayyim's and Ruthie's clothing.

The paratroopers watched Azit eagerly. The circles grew, but Azit had not yet found the trail.

Suddenly she stopped and began to sniff around one place. She moved away and then came back. Then, with small steps, Azit began to move along the path that Ḥayyim and Ruthie had taken.

In less than an hour Azit reached the well. She jumped onto the well platform, ran across it, and found Ḥayyim and Ruthie lying in the hollow on the other side.

Azit barked loudly. But the children seemed to be asleep.

Dr. Ḥaruvi heard Azit barking through the intercom. "She found them," he cried. "I'm sure of it. Go find them, Azit," he called to her. "Good dog!"

Azit licked Ḥayyim's face and eyes. Ḥayyim opened his eyes and cried out in terror, "What's this?"

"It's an animal!" Ruthie cried, sitting up. Azit didn't move. She kept licking and making friendly little growling noises.

Suddenly Ḥayyim saw the name "Azit, paratroop dog" on the bag that hung from her neck.

"This is our Azit," he cried happily. "Azit the paratrooper."

And immediately the voice of Dr. Ḥaruvi crackled out of the intercom, "Ḥayyim and Ruthie, *shalom*! In the package you'll find medicine and water. Do you hear?"

"Yes, we hear. We're okay. Only Ḥayyim's leg is broken," Ruthie called.

Rami and the other paratroopers will reach you in a little while," Dr. Ḥaruvi told them.

"Thank you," Ruthie and Ḥayyim cried happily.

"Say thank you to Azit," laughed Dr. Ḥaruvi. "She's the one who found you. We'll drop you some food. Be sure to give her some of it. She's entitled."

Little Guy Falls into the Hole

by Poochoo

from Methuselah's Gang

WITH a hard whack the kids on Pastry Street could get four or five candies out of the candy machine in front of Mrs. Goodfat's bakery. But one day an old man with a gray beard and a red satchel sat himself down in the sun beside the machine . . . and that was the end of the free candy. The children dubbed the old man Methuselah, after the 900-year-old Bible patriarch. When they made friends with him they discovered two strange things. One—Methuselah's gray beard was yards and yards long, all neatly folded into his red satchel. Two—he would not cut his beard until he had solved a sad and ancient mystery.

The neighborhood children were playing jump rope. Uri and Roy turned the rope and Edna, Miri and Naomi jumped. The game would have ended in the usual fight between the boys and the girls, had it not been for little Guy. He kept getting in the girls' way.

"It's bad enough you don't want to turn the rope, you don't have to pester us too," yelled Edna.

"I don't want to turn," the five-year-old yelled back. "I want to jump."

"But you don't know how!"

"Oh yes I do. Watch!" He grabbed the rope and took off across the street.

"What a pain in the neck," Miri complained.

"Hey look, he's running to the lot with the holes," Edna yelled.

Two years before someone had begun to build an apartment house on the lot. Holes had been dug for foundations but for some reason, the building was never put up. The holes were now covered and warning signs had been put up. But what did signs matter to a five-year old? Guy ran through the middle of the dangerous lot. Suddenly he tumbled through a half-covered opening and down into a pit. When he looked up he burst into loud sobs.

The children ran to him screaming in panic.

"Are you still alive, Guy?" Naomi called down.

Guy cried louder.

"We have to get him out of there. Where can we get strong rope?" asked Uri.

"At Zeraḥ's store," said Edna. "Miri, you stay here. We'll get the rope."

Huffing and puffing, Edna and Uri arrived at Zeraḥ's store, only to realize that, like all other stores, it was closed between one and four in the afternoon. Desperately, they started back. It was then that they noticed Methuselah sound asleep on his rickety chair.

"METHUSELAH!" they both shouted. In two seconds they had shaken him awake.

"You've got to come with us," Edna pleaded.

"Where?" asked Methuselah.

"To save a little boy. Come on," said Uri, pulling Methusaleh's hand.

"Wait a second," said Methuselah, "I've got to get my satchel."

Of course! What good is Methuselah without his beard and red satchel?

When they arrived at the hole Methuselah got right to work. "Uri," he said, "take the bag and run ahead so that my whole beard is laid out flat on the ground." Then he began to lower his beard into the hole.

"We're sending a rope down," Edna called to Guy. "Hold on real tight and we'll pull you up."

"I'm slipping," whined Guy. The children could feel the beard slackening in their hands.

Methuselah thought quickly. "We'll lower my satchel. Guy will get into it and then we'll pull him up."

He divided his beard into two long strips and tied each to a handle. Then the satchel was slowly lowered.

"Get into the satchel," Edna called to Guy.

After a long, tense minute he yelled, "I'm in."

Then the children formed a line and, following Methuselah's instructions, they held onto the beard and slowly pulled Guy up.

"Now me! Now I want a ride," yelled Roy, the other five-year-old.

"Stop yelling," said Miri. "Methuselah didn't grow a beard just to give you a ride."

"Well then, why do you have such a long beard?" asked Roy.

The old man didn't answer at first. The children helped him fold his beard neatly into the satchel, picking thorns out of it as they went. Then Methuselah said, "I vowed not to cut my beard until I solved an ancient mystery. Maybe you can help me."

(To find out what happens next, look for "Methuselah's Gang" in the "Good Books" chapter, and ask for it at your library.)

14 Good books about Israel

Here's a list of storybooks (fiction) and books of factual information (nonfiction) about Israel. Some of them are out of print, but you may find them at your library. If not, your librarian might be able to borrow them from another library. Those that are in print can be ordered through your local bookstore or Judaica shop.

FICTION AND NONFICTION FOR YOUNGER READERS

Clear, brief text and photographs of the land and the people.

Adler, David A. *A Picture Book of Israel*. New York: Holiday House, 1984. 40 pp.

A stubborn Bedouin girl gets her way.

Alexander, Sue. *Nadia the Willful*, illustrated by Lloyd Bloom. New York: Pantheon, 1983. Unpaged.

Frankel, Max, and Judy Hoffman. *I Live in Israel*. New York: Behrman House, 1979. Unpaged.

Children on a kibbutz.

Goldman, Louis, and Seymour Reit. *A Week in Hagars's World*, photos by Louis Goldman. New York: Macmillan, 1969. Unpaged.

Meet Israeli children of all types, sizes, and colors.

Grand, Samuel, and Tamar Grand. *The Children of Israel*, illustrated by Alona Frankel. New York: Union of American Hebrew Congregations, 1972.

Kibbutz kids solve a mystery.

Hillel, O. *A Kibbutz Adventure*. New York: Frederick Warne, 1963. Unpaged.

A picture book of Israelis and their customs.

Rutland, Jonathan. *Take a Trip to Israel*, photos by the author. New York: Franklin Watts, 1981. 32 pp.

Comical, colorful picture-book view of Israel.

Sasek, Miroslav. *This Is Israel*. New York: Macmillan, 1962. 60 pp.

Weingrad, Bracha. *Dani on the Kibbutz*, illustrated by Sabbatai. Reseda, Calif.: Ridgefield, 1982. 24 pp.

FICTION FOR OLDER READERS

Banks, Lynn Reid. *One More River*. New York: Simon and Schuster, 1973. 228 pp.
Lesley takes a giant step from Canada to the Jordan valley.

Barash, Asher. *Jewish Folktales—Arabic Folktales*, illustrated by Dudu Geva and Davis Grebu. Israel: Massada, 64 pp.

Biber, Yehoash. *Adventures in the Galilee*, translated by Josephine Bacon, illustrated by Assaf Berg. Philadelphia: Jewish Publication Society, 1973. 149 pp.
Sheep-rustling and other daring deeds in Israel's mountains.

Forman, James. *My Enemy, My Brother*. Des Moines: Meredith (hard), Scholastic (paper), 1968. 125 pp.
Friendships and problems shared by an Arab boy and a Jewish boy.

Goldreich, Gloria. *Lori*. New York: Holt, Rinehart and Winston, 1979. 181 pp.
An American high-school drop-out changes in Israel.

Gutman, Nahum. *Path of the Orange Peels*. New York: Dodd Mead, 1979. 140 pp.
Tricking the Turks in old Tel Aviv.

Hamori, Laszlo. *Flight to the Promised Land*. New York: Harcourt Brace Jovanovich, 1961. 190 pp.
A Yemenite boy reaches Israel.

Hoban, Lillian. *I Met a Traveler*. New York: Harper & Row, 1977. 192 pp.
Fun and trouble at an Israeli immigrant center.

Nurenberg, Thelma. *The Time of Anger*. New York: Harper & Row, 1975. 208 pp.
Friendships between Arab and Jewish youngsters are torn by war.

Ofek, Uriel. *Smoke over Golan: A Novel of the 1973 Yom Kippur War*, translated by Israel I. Taslitt, illustrated by Lloyd Bloom. New York: Harper & Row, 1979. 192 pp.
A boy faces war alone.

Ofek, Uriel, ed. *The Dog That Flew and Other Favorite Stories from Israel*. New York: Funk & Wagnalls, Sabra Books, 1969. 154 pp.

Omer, D'vorah. *Path beneath the Sea*, translated by Israel I. Taslitt. New York: Funk & Wagnall's, 1969. 192 pp.
Adventures of underwater demolition teams.

Orgad, Dorit. *An Adventure in the Kingdom of the Crusaders*. Israel: Massada, 64 pp.

Oz, Amos. *Soumchi*, illustrated by Pappas, translated by the author and Penelope Farmer. New York: Harper & Row, 1981. 90 pp.
An Israeli boy's first love.

Poochoo. *Methuselah's Gang*, translated by Nelly Segal, illustrated by Hank Blaustein. New York: Dodd Mead, 1980. 192 pp.
Israeli kids befriend the man with the longest beard in the world.

An American boy is caught up in archaeology and terrorism.

Richard, Adrienne. *The Accomplice*. Boston: Little Brown, 1973. 173 pp.

Six wise, magical stories from pre-war Palestine.

Soyer, Abraham. *The Adventures of Yemina*, translated by Rebecca Beagle and Rebecca Soyer, illustrated by Raphael Soyer. New York: Viking, 1979. 70 pp.

An Israeli soldier and an Arab boy struggle to become friends.

Trigoboff, Joseph. *Abu*. New York: Lothrop, Lee & Shepard, 1975. 120 pp.

Delightful stories about a thumb-sized Jewish boy.

Weilerstein, Sadie Rose. *The Best of K'tonton*, illustrated by Marilyn Hirsh. Philadelphia: Jewish Publication Society of America, 1980. 94 pp.

Weilerstein, Sadie Rose. *K'tonton in Israel*, illustrated by Elizabeth Safian. New York: National Women's League of the United Synagogue of America, 1965. 178 pp.

Two boys travel between Israel and the United States to solve a mystery.

Zakon, Miriam S. *The Egyptian Star*, illustrated by Nina Gaelon. New York: Judaica Press, 1983. 114 pp.

NONFICTION FOR OLDER READERS

Ashabranner, Brent. *Gavriel and Jemal: Two Boys of Jerusalem*. New York: Dodd Mead, 1984. 91 pp.

Dramatic stories of how Jews returned to Zion from all over the world.

Eisenberg, Azriel, and Leah Globe, eds. *Home at Last*. New York: Bloch, 1976. 324 pp.

Detailed picture of Israel's history, geography, and problems.

Fine, Helen. *Behold, the Land*, illustrated by Rose Zamonski and Yuri Salzman. New York: Union of American Hebrew Congregations, 1977.

How the Jews forged a nation.

Goldstone, Robert. *Next Year in Jerusalem: A Short History of Zionism*. Boston: Little Brown, 1978. 242 pp.

Many colorful, imaginative views of the city of peace.

Gordon, Ayala, ed. *Children of the World Paint Jerusalem*. New York: Bantam, 1978.

Refugees struggle to escape Europe and reach Palestine.

Kluger, Ruth, and Peggy Mann. *The Secret Ship*. New York: Doubleday, 1978. 136 pp.

Facts about the history, geography, and government of Israel.

Kubie, Nora B. *Israel*. New York: Franklin Watts, 1978. 66 pp.

Meir, Mira. *Alina: A Russian Girl Comes to Israel*, translated by Zeva Shapiro, photographs by Yael Rozen. Philadelphia: Jewish Publication Society of America, 1982. 48 pp.

Fitting into a new land is hard work.

Rachleff, Owen S. *Young Israel: A History of the Modern Nation, the First Twenty Years*. New York: Lion Books, 1981.

Silberman, Mark, ed. *Jews of Israel: History and Sources*. New York: Behrman House, 1975. 128 pp.

Spector, Shoshanah. *The Miraculous Rescue: Entebbe*. New York: Shengold, 1978. 48 pp.

A witness recalls the scene.

Williams, Lorna, and Denise Bergman. *Through the Year in Israel*. Batsford, Eng.: David & Charles, 1983. 72 pp.

Worth, Richard. *Israel and the Arab States*. New York: Franklin Watts, 1983. 90 pp.

Origins of the wars in the Middle East.

Yadin, Yigael. *The Story of Masada*, retold by Gerald Gottlieb. New York: Random House, 1969.

The history of Masada and the story of its archaeological exploration.

Zim, Jacob, ed. *My Shalom, My Peace*, selection of poems by Uriel Ofek, translation by Dov Vardi. New York: McGraw-Hill, 1975. 96 pp.

Paintings and poems by Jewish and Arab children.

BIOGRAPHIES

Adler, David A. *Our Golda, the Story of Golda Meir*. New York: Viking, 1984. 64 pp.

Follows Golda from her Russian childhood to the leadership of Israel.

Berkman, Ted. *Cast a Giant Shadow*. Philadelphia: Jewish Publication Society of America, 1967. 200 pp.

Mickey Marcus, the West Pointer who fought for Israel.

Cowen, Ida, and Irene Gunther. *A Spy for Freedom: The Story of Sarah Aaronsohn*. New York: Dutton, 1984.

Sarah and her friends risk their lives for the Jews of Palestine.

Davidson, Margaret. *The Golda Meir Story*, rev. ed. New York: Scribner's, 1981. 228 pp.

Compelling, detailed biography.

Hastings, Max. *Yoni, Hero of Entebbe*. New York: Dial Press, 1979. 248 pp.

A soldier with high ideals and great courage.

Keller, Mollie. *Golda Meir*. New York: Franklin Watts, 1983. 128 pp.

The life of Israel's first woman prime minister.

Twenty-eight Israelis tell about their lives.

Levine, Gemma. *We Live in Israel*. New York: Bookwright Press, 1983. 64 pp.

Miller, Shane. *Desert Fighter: The Story of General Yigael Yadin and the Dead Sea Scrolls*. New York: Hawthorn, 1967. 178 pp.

Leaders of Israel, from Moses to Yonatan.

Reichwald, Faye. *Eighteen Lives*, illustrated by Daniela Rosenhaus Bar-Zion. New York: Board of Jewish Education, 1981. 245 pp.

St. John, Robert. *They Came from Everywhere: Twelve Who Helped Mold Modern Israel*. New York: Coward, McCann, 1962. 256 pp.

REFERENCE

All in one volume.

Alcalay, Reuben. *The Massada English-Hebrew Student Dictionary*. Englewood Cliffs, N.J.: SBS, 1980. 734 pp.

Well-written, well-illustrated books about archaeology and its finds.

Avi-Yonah, Michael, ed. Lerner Archeology Series. 6 vols. Minneapolis: Lerner, 1974–1975. 88–96 pp. each.

Horas, debkas, and more—with clear directions.

Berk, Fred. *Ha-rikud: The Jewish Dance*. New York: Union of American Hebrew Congregations, 1972. 102 pp.

Maps and illustrations of Biblical sites, archaeology, and artifacts.

Frank, Harry Thomas, ed. *Atlas of Bible Lands*. Rev. ed. Maplewood, N.J.: Hammond, 1979. 48 pp.

A kids-centered tour of Israel.

Kretzmer, Marcia. *Adventure in the Holyland*. Israel: Massada, 1982. 80 pp.

Music of Israel from prestate days until 1976, as well as Hassidic and liturgical music.

Pasternak, Velvel, and Richard Neumann, eds. *Great Songs of Israel*. Cedarhurst: Tara, 1976. 107 pp.

Pasternak, Velvel, and Richard Neumann, eds. *Israel in Song*. Cedarhurst: Tara, 1974. 107 pp.

Covers all aspects of life in ancient and modern Israel.

Sirof, Harriett. *The Junior Encyclopedia of Israel*. New York: Jonathan David, 1980. 470 pp.

NOT JUST BOOKS

There are games, filmstrips, records, tapes, video tapes, and activity books about Israel. Find out what's available at your local bookstore, Judaica shop, or synagogue gift shop. Here are some examples:

- *A Tree Grows in Israel*. A filmstrip of Israeli schoolchildren planting trees on a barren hillside. Produced by Union of American Hebrew Congregations in New York City.

- *Scrabble*. A Hebrew edition of a good game. Available in bookstores or from Selchow & Righter Company, Bay Shore, New York.

- Going Up: The Israel Game. Play and learn about Israel. Distributed by Alternatives in Religious Education of Denver, Colorado.

- *What's an Israel* by Chaya Burstein. An activity-storybook about seven-year-old Benjy's adventures in Israel. Published by Kar-Ben Copies of Rockville, Maryland.

- *If I Forget Thee O'Jerusalem*. A tape that traces Jerusalem's dramatic history from Abraham until today. By Alternatives in Religious Education of Denver, Colorado.

At the beginning of each school term kids set up shop in the town squares and sell last year's textbooks at bargain prices.

15

A kid's tour of Israel

Being a tourist is like window-shopping in a big toy store. You want to see one of these and one of those and a little of something else, but there's no way you can see everything. It's even harder to be a tourist in Israel than in other countries. It is a land where you can walk in the footsteps of your Biblical ancestors. You can sit on a rock in Judaea or beside the Kotel in Jerusalem and think deeply about God and history and yourself—as they did. But it's also a place to snorkel, ride a camel, take hundreds of photos, and eat new foods.

If you want to explore all of Israel and enjoy it, you'll have to come back again and again. Even Israeli kids never stop exploring their land. Wherever you go, you'll bump into classes and groups of Israeli youngsters hiking and picnicking.

This chapter will take you to some odd, out-of-the way places. Locate each place described in the chapter by matching the numbers on the map with the number next to the description. Other important and interesting places like the Kotel and Masada are described in Chapters 1 and 12.

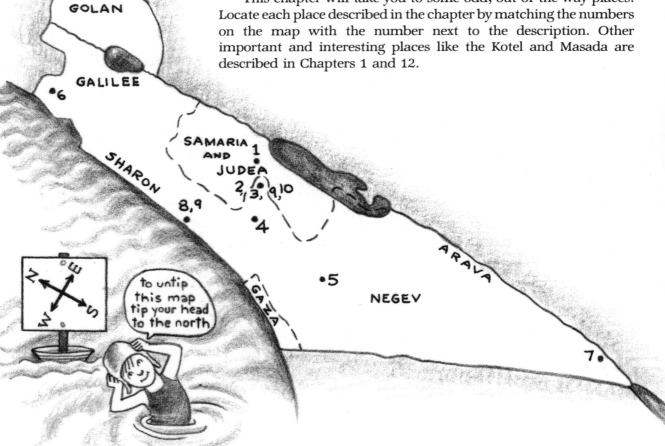

The Society for the Protection of Nature in Israel (SPNI) plans hikes, guided tours, and even trips on camelback and horseback. Visit their office in Tel Aviv or Jerusalem.

UNFORGETTABLE WADI KELT IN THE JUDAEAN DESERT (1)

Let's go on a hike down Wadi Kelt in the Judaean desert.

"It's a very interesting walk," says the guide, a young female soldier. "Terrorists used to come up this narrow valley to attack Jerusalem."

"T-t-terrorists?" you stutter, as you scramble after her down into the green, flower-filled wadi. It is very peaceful. A little brook gurgles beside the trail. You forget to be scared and take off your shoes to wade in the cool, sparkling water.

Suddenly the brook vanishes into a dark opening in a hill. The hike leader strides in and disappears. You follow. It gets darker and darker. The water gets deeper, and soon you and your lunch bag are swimming.

Hurray—there's sunlight ahead. The tunnel ends. You climb out, squeeze the water out of your sandwich and sneakers, and hurry to catch up. The trail is rising higher and higher into the hills, following a narrow aqueduct (water carrier). The trail ends abruptly, and the aqueduct turns and heads out into empty space across a deep valley. There are miles of sky above you, more miles below, and only a narrow concrete top to walk along.

The leader trots ahead, sure-footed as a mountain goat. You inch along, wishing you had a parachute, wishing you had overslept that morning, wishing your knees would stop shaking.

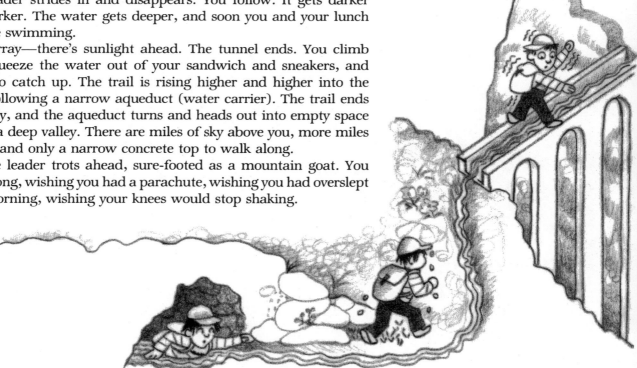

Aah—you reach solid ground. The trail and the aqueduct continue along the side of the mountain and climb to the gate of a monastery. The monastery hangs from the mountainside like a wasp's nest. The leader marches in, and you follow. It is dark, musty, and dusty inside. Gold crosses and gilded paintings gleam in the shadows. Pale monks tiptoe about and bring cold water for the hikers to drink.

Back in the bright sunlight there's only a short stretch of trail to go. You wave good-bye to the aqueduct, which continues down toward Jericho. The bus is waiting on the road. There's a blister on your heel, and you've found a new set of aching muscles.

"What a great hike," you tell the leader. "I'll never, ever forget Wadi Kelt!"

Saint George's monastery in Wadi Kelt is filled with treasure—ancient gold and silver religious objects. But it's a lonely place that echoes with the steps of the few loyal, remaining monks.

Teak Silberman

THE SHILOAH TUNNEL UNDER JERUSALEM (2)

"The other events of Hezekiah's reign, and all his exploits, and how he made the pool and the conduit and brought the water into the city, are recorded in the Annals of the Kings of Judah."
—Kings 20:20

If you didn't get wet enough at Wadi Kelt, go to the Shiloah tunnel in Jerusalem. You'll need a flashlight and a bathing suit. Climb down the steps, and splash onto the rough stone floor of the water tunnel. As you slosh along, your flashlight beam will pick a path between jagged walls. The tunnel was cut through the rock more than 2,500 years ago to bring water into Jerusalem from a spring outside the city walls.

Enemies surrounded the city in the days of Hezekiah, king of Judah, and cut off the supply of food and water. They wanted to starve the people and make them surrender. But the water from the Shiloah tunnel helped the Jerusalemites to hold out.

If you're tall, you may have to duck as you walk under Jerusalem through King Hezekiah's tunnel. Here and there the roof is low. If you're small, you may have to get up on tiptoe where the water is deep. It's not easy to follow in the footsteps of the ancient builders.

If you should ask why the chosen people ended up in a small land without oil, coal, minerals, or water resources, the Israelis give this answer:

When Moses led his people out of Egypt, God decided to help them reach their new home.

"Moses," He asked, "where would you like to go?"

Moses wanted a large land rich in natural resources, so he started to say "Canada." But since he was a stutterer, all he could squeeze out was "Ca-ca-ca-ca."

"As you wish," God replied, and led the Jewish people straight to tiny Canaan.

THE SHUK (MARKET) IN JERUSALEM'S OLD CITY (3)

Cool off in the shuk on a hot summer day. The twisting, narrow stone streets are always damp, and the arched roofs keep out the sun. Some of the smooth pavement stones were laid down 2,000 years ago. You are walking in the footsteps of ancient Romans, Jews, and Christians. One street in the Old City is called Via Dolorosa. The Christian Bible tells that Jesus carried a wooden cross along this street as he went to his crucifixion.

"Oops, watch out," you yell as a boy leading a loaded donkey bumps you against a booth of glittering jewelry.

"Look here, look here. Beautiful silver necklace!" The stallkeeper jingles a handful of chains at you, and his black mustache curves up in a wide smile.

The walls of the shuk are hung with sheepskin jackets, embroidered black Arab dresses, blouses from India, and woven rugs. Smells of strange herbs and spices tickle your nose. Wailing Arab music floats from the radios of the tiny shops. And tourists speaking every language on earth jostle and push around you.

At a sweets stand your mouth waters while you choose between almond halvah, honey pastry, pistachio squares, nougat, or sesame bars—or maybe one of each. Then you go blinking out into the sunshine to sit on the steps beside one of the city gates, share your "nosh" with the pigeons, and watch priests, tourists, school kids, soldiers, Bedouins, goats, and donkeys stroll past.

If you can't get to the Museum of the Diaspora, it may come to you. Exhibits from the museum travel all over the world.

An exhibit at the Diaspora Museum describes Jewish wandering with these words: "A people embarked on a long journey with only a book as a guide."

MUSEUMS (4)

Give your brain a break at two bustling museums. The Museum of the Diaspora in Tel Aviv will lead you along the trails that the Jewish people took after they left the land of Israel. You won't need hiking boots. You can explore the past by sitting at a computer terminal, punching in the name of your great-grandparents' home-town, and getting a printout on its people, industries, and history. You can watch animated films that show the adventures of medieval Jewish wanderers. All around you Israeli kids will be running from exhibit to exhibit, taking notes, and punching buttons—just like you—because this is the most popular museum in Israel.

The Israel Museum in Jerusalem keeps kids hopping, too. In the children's wing there's a dark tunnel with objects along its side walls. You feel the objects to identify them (some feel yucky). Or you can go on a treasure hunt through the museum to find something special—for instance, an Israeli elephant's tooth that's 4,000 years old. In the Shrine of the Book you'll find something very special—a scroll of the Biblical Book of Isaiah written by a careful scribe nearly 2,000 years ago. If you can read Hebrew, you'll be able to read some of his words. Then relax with a puppet show or arts and crafts in the museum workroom.

Some museums are out-of-doors. A Maccabee village was reconstructed near the ruins of Judah Maccabee's hometown—Modin. Kids come here to make clay pots, draw water from a well, and bake pita in an ancient cone-shaped oven.

Donkeys for sale in Beersheba. On market day Bedouins come in from their villages or tent camps to buy and sell camels, donkeys, goats, and fine embroidery.

Ed Toben

THE PALMAH MEMORIAL AND THE CAMEL MARKET IN BEERSHEBA (5)

Giant white sculptures cover the top of a windy hill in the Negev in southern Israel. There's a great tower with a ladder, a long tunnel, and a maze of low walls. It's fun to race and climb and slide around. But stop to read the words carved into the concrete. This huge sculpture is a memorial to Israeli soldiers and settlers in the lonely kibbutzim of the Negev. They fought off Egyptian tanks and artillery in 1948 and saved southern Israel.

Come down from the hill with its sad, brave memories. You are near the tell of ancient Beersheba. Abraham, Sarah, and their tribe lived here many years ago. They dug a well and made an agreement with their neighbors. *Beer-Sheba* means "well of the vow."

Tribes of Bedouin Arabs come to modern Beersheba, just down the road. At dawn each Thursday the Bedouins come out of the desert leading their camels, which are loaded with bales of wool, hides, blankets, and jewelry. They spread their wares on the sand and wait for customers. You can buy a bag of fresh almonds or a chain of tinkling brass bells for your doorway. The Arab women flash their gold teeth as they bargain for live chickens or lambs and proudly show off their embroidery. Maybe you want to buy a camel? No? Then for a small fee you can take a high, rocking ride around the market on a camel, the "ship of the desert."

"Hence that place was called Beer-Sheba, for there the two of them swore an oath. . . . [Abraham] planted a tamarisk at Beer-Sheba, and invoked there the name of the Lord."
—*Genesis 21:31, 33*

Montfort—a ruined mountain stronghold.

MONTFORT NEAR NAHARIYYA (6)

A strange, fierce army swept into Palestine many years ago. They were Christian Crusaders from faraway Europe who came to snatch the land from its Muslim rulers. Since Palestine was the birthplace of Christianity, the Crusaders believed that it must be ruled by Christians.

High on a mountaintop in the Galilee, the Crusaders built Montfort ("strong mountain"), one of their many fortresses. It had 2-foot-thick stone walls, tall stone lookout towers, and a wide moat to keep enemies out. The Crusaders feasted, hunted boar, had great parties, and were lords and tax collectors of fifty peasant villages.

But one day the Muslim armies returned. After a long battle the Muslims overran the moat and killed the defenders. The walls were burned and smashed, the towers crumbled. From that time seven hundred years ago until today only lizards and jackals have lived on the mighty mound of Montfort.

Climb the hill, jump over the moat, and explore the great walls. You might find a stash of jewels hidden by a knight just before the enemy broke in. Go up the steps of the tower that pokes high out of the ruin. From the top you can see the mountains of Lebanon. But don't fall into "the Crusader's revenge," a deep pit beside the tower steps.

When you're done exploring, scramble down the hill to the nearby brook, Naḥal Kaziv, for a picnic. The Crusaders once drank its clear water, just as you are doing.

The Bible says
> *about the ostrich: God hath deprived her of wisdom.*
> *about the onager: She is used to the wilderness and snuffles up the wind in her pleasure.*
> *about rabbits: They are weak—yet they make their houses in the rocks.*

253

A kid's tour of Israel

AT HOME IN HAI BAR NEAR ELATH (7)

You have to jump fast at the Ḥai Bar Biblical Nature Reserve, a wildlife park in the Negev, otherwise a lumbering ostrich will run you down. And if you're in a car, the nosy bird will peck at your window. When there are no ostriches in sight, relax, sit quietly, and watch a herd of shy addax or onagri (wild asses) graze peacefully nearby.

There's an ingathering of gazelles, ostriches, antelopes, and other animals and birds at Ḥai Bar. They had been driven away or hunted down in past centuries. After Israel was established in 1948 experts were sent to search the world for the species of lost animals and birds that had once lived in the area.

Most of these animals are home again at Ḥai Bar. And they're ready for company.

This oryx (a type of gazelle) found something delicious to eat in the dry sand of Ḥai Bar.

Nat Schwartz

THE SHALOM TOWER, TEL AVIV (8)

Israelis are proud of their little land. After a walk along glittering Broadway in New York City an Israeli visitor said, "This is just like Dizengoff, Tel Aviv's main street."

If Dizengoff is just like Broadway, then Tel Aviv's Shalom Tower is just like the Empire State Building. It is the tallest building in Israel, and it looms up out of Tel Aviv's busy banking and shopping district. From its top-floor observatory you can look far out over the Mediterranean and down on the beaches, the crowded city streets, and the nearby arches and domes of the old city of Jaffa.

Tel Aviv, with its proud skyscraper, is just a baby as cities go— only seventy-five years old. It has been built up from the sand dunes. Today you'll find fancy stores for shopping and a wax museum for fun in the Shalom Tower.

THE SOREK CAVE NEAR BET SHEMESH (9)

It's pitch black and quiet as a tomb. You're afraid to move. Suddenly the guide pushes a light switch, and a huge, eerie, shadowy cavern looms around you. Towers of stalagmites rise to the ceiling. Dripping daggers of stalagtites hang over your head. You're standing deep inside the rocky Judaean hills in the Sorek cave.

For hundreds of centuries water dripped through the mountain, carrying the rock away, grain by grain, to make this cave. When the Biblical hero Samson was picnicking with Delilah in the woods above, the stalagmites of the Sorek cave were 38 feet long. Today they're 40 feet long. The waters of the Sorek aren't in a hurry.

The cave was discovered when rock was being quarried from the mountain for building material. Israelis rushed to explore it. A few got lost and had to be rescued. It's safe now, but strange shapes seem to flit through the darkness. Is that Samson's ghost drifting past that stalagmite? *Turn the lights on!*

A hill called Mt. Moriah in Old Jerusalem carries a heavy weight of history. On a great stone at the top Abraham prepared to sacrifice his son Isaac. Later it became the Temple Mount—the site of King Solomon's temple. Long after the First and Second Temples were destroyed, the Muslim prophet Mohammed dreamed that he stepped up to paradise from Abraham's stone. Mohammed's followers built a mosque with a golden dome above the holy stone.

Today many Jews will not walk on the Temple Mount for fear that they might unknowingly walk where the Holy of Holies once stood. This was the inner part of the Temple where the ark of the law had been kept and which only the high priest might enter.

Atop the Temple Mount is the gleaming Dome of the Rock mosque. It is decorated with bold designs and graceful Arabic letters formed of ceramic tile. Worshipers leave their shoes at the doorway and step into a cool, carpeted space, where they pray on their knees, bowing and touching the ground with their foreheads.

Near one of the entrances a bare rock juts up out of the floor. Muslims believe that this is the same stone that Abraham used as a sacrificial altar many centuries ago when the Temple Mount was a bare, wind-swept hill.

THE TEMPLE MOUNT IN JERUSALEM (10)

The Temple Mount in the center of old Jerusalem is a holy place for Jews, Muslims, and Christians. Muslims worship at the centuries-old mosques that were built on the Mount—Al Aksa and the Dome of the Rock. Jews worship below at the Kotel, the Western Wall of the Temple Mount.

Nat Schwartz

A bar mitzvah at the Kotel. The family stands close beside the bar mitzvah boy and listens proudly. All around him other people are praying, studying, and writing messages that they will place between the stones. Judaism's holiest site carries a heavy weight of hopes and prayers.

Nat Schwartz

Prayer at the Kotel.

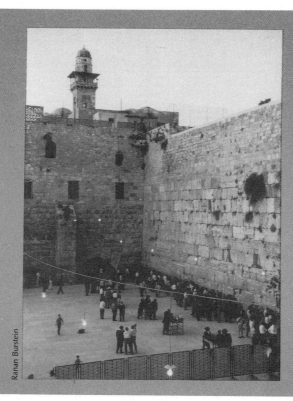

Ranan Burstein

Do you want to stay awhile—to do things as well as to look at things? You can go to tennis camp at Ramat Ha-Sharon, learn to scuba dive in Elath, study the Bible at a yeshiva (religious school), dig for archaeological treasures, milk cows, go spelunking (exploring caves), and more.

For information write the American Zionist Youth Foundation (AZYF) at 515 Park Avenue, New York, New York 10022.

QUICKIES

Go to a movie. Take plenty of peanuts and sunflower seeds. When the soundtrack is English, the audience gets so noisy that you can't hear a word. Don't get upset. They're not listening—they're reading the Hebrew captions.

Go to a soccer game, but wear a football helmet for safety. The fans get very excited, and there's no telling what may happen if they disagree with the umpire.

Go swimming in the creamy-thick, stinging water of the Dead Sea, in the toasty-warm Gulf of Elath, in the rushing Mediterranean Sea, in peaceful Lake Kinneret. Too peaceful? Try the Kinneret amusement park, where you can ride a typhoon, a Kamikaze slide, or a parachute.

Sit at an outdoor café. Order Israeli iced coffee—it's like an ice-cream sundae with coffee flavoring—and play a game of chess or checkers while you watch people go by.

Take a train ride on Israel's poky little railroad. It meanders through dark, rocky mountains and fertile fields, past villages and kibbutzim through Jerusalem, Tel Aviv, and Haifa. Pack a lunch. Maybe a supper and breakfast, too.

Go to the zoo, especially the Biblical Zoo in Jerusalem, where you'll find every living creature that is mentioned in the Bible.

Go to a rock concert. Rock across the centuries at the Roman amphitheater in Caesarea or at the ancient Sultan's Pool in Jerusalem.

16 Israel is the only country

Israel is the only country that has a majority of Jews in its population.

Israel is the only country that is no bigger than Massachusetts but often gets bigger newspaper headlines than the world's largest countries.

Israel is the only country that uses the Hebrew and the Arabic words for peace—*Shalom* and *Salamu-alaykum*—as a daily greeting, even though the country has been at war for much of its short life.

Israel is the only country that has a national flag patterned after a prayer shawl. The two blue stripes of the Israeli flag were taken from the stripes of the tallith (prayer shawl). The six-pointed star in the center of the flag was a popular design in synagogue decorations.

Israel is the only country that is very old and very young. The old land of Israel was conquered and destroyed 2,000 years ago. The new, young Israel is being rebuilt by the descendants of the ancient Israelites—the Jews.

Israel is the only country that prints more than one book each year for each 1,000 people in the population. Nearly 4,500 books were published in 1983. That's the largest number of books per person in the world. According to surveys, Israeli kids read at least a book a month, outside of textbooks.

Israel is the only country that plants millions of trees and hardly ever chops any down. The Jews found no forests, only bare, eroded hillsides, when they returned to Palestine. Since then they've planted more than 150 million trees.

When a tree is cut down, it's for a good reason. For instance, last year evergreens were cut and given to Jerusalem churches for use as Christmas trees.

that . . .

Israel is the only country that sells knickknacks to tourists in a shopping center that is 2,000 years old (the Cardo in Jerusalem) and holds rock concerts in an ancient Roman amphitheater (Caesarea). The earth of Israel is layered with history.

Israel is the only country that contains the major holy places of the Jewish and Christian religions, and the third holiest site of the Muslim religion.

Israel is the only country that packs the variety of a large country into a tiny one. In a comfortable day-and-a-half drive you can get from the southern to the northern tip of Israel. In midwinter you can go sleighriding in the snow on the Galilee mountains after breakfast and then drive down to the Jordan valley in time for a dip in warm Lake Kinneret before lunch. Schoolchildren come up to the Galilee from the sunny valley to have snowball fights and to build snowmen. When the Kinneret is cool, the sparkling Gulf of Aqaba is still as warm as bathwater. If Tel Aviv seems noisy, the solitary desert is only a few miles south. And if the desert is too bare, the orchards and green fields of the coast are a few miles north.

Israel is the only country that had to teach many of its citizens their own national language—Hebrew. And Israeli scholars had to push and pull and stretch the vocabulary of the ancient Hebrew language until it could be used to operate computers and jet planes as well as camels and water wheels.

ISRAEL IS THE ONLY COUNTRY THAT . . . .

Israel is the only country that has a thriving experimental type of community called the *kibbutz* ("collective"). Kids in a kibbutz share their bikes, sandwiches, clothing, and toys. Adults share their wages, tools, and jobs. People had two reasons for forming the first kibbutzim sixty years ago. First, they wanted to build a strong Jewish homeland. And second, they wanted to build a socialist community where each person would work for the benefit of the whole group and would get whatever he or she needed from the group. Children were raised together in children's houses. Meals were cooked and served in the community's kitchen and dining hall. And nobody got a paycheck. The group decided on a small allowance that the members would receive and spend any way they wanted. Kibbutzim were often established in dangerous border areas and on land that was so dry and rocky or so swampy that no private farmer wanted it.

Today some kibbutzim are rich. The members swim in the kibbutz pool after work, and their allowances are big enough that they can travel abroad. The children in many kibbutzim live with their parents instead of in the children's house. So the kibbutz has changed over the years, and it is still changing. But it continues to be a sharing, socialist community.

Even today kibbutzim are tackling tough sites that nobody else wants. In the hot dry Saraba, south of the Dead Sea, young American immigrants have built Kibbutz Yaḥel. They've planted date palms, grape-vines, and vegetables. A big plus—Yahel's kids have plenty of sand for their sandbox.

Ed Toben

THE ONLY COUNTRY THAT

A solar dish reflector collects and concentrates the sun's energy at the Technion, Israel's university of engineering in Haifa. It helps students design new ways to use solar power.

Richard Nowitz; courtesy of American Society for the Technion

Israel is the only country that harnesses the sun to work overtime. More solar energy (the light and heat of the sun) is used per person in Israel than in any other country. That's because the country is mineral-poor, with no oil to pump or coal to mine. Solar collector plates tilt up from half of Israel's rooftops, and a large water drum stands beside them. The plates collect the sun's heat to warm the water in the drum. That hot water is used for washing and sometimes also for heating and air-conditioning.

Another solar system developed in Israel catches and concentrates the sunlight with mirrorlike reflectors. It is being used in California.

Down by the Dead Sea scientists use the sun to make electricity. They dig wide, shallow ponds filled with salt water. The sun heats the water at the bottom of the pond to a temperature that's hot enough to drive a generator. Today a giant solar-pond project using Israeli technology is being built in California.

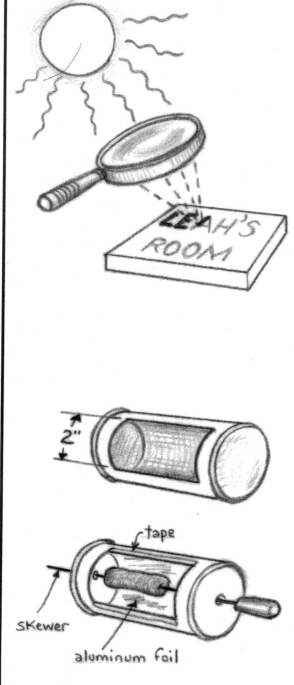

PUT THE SUN TO WORK

Solar energy works well for Israel. Here are two projects you can try to make the sun work for you, too.

Wood-burn a sign for your house or room.
You will need:

Pencil	Magnifying glass with a handle
Wood or plywood	Bright sunshine

Write your first or last name or draw a design in pencil on the wood or plywood. Hold the magnifying glass above the wood, and let the sun's rays focus through the glass onto the name or design. The wood will start to smoke and burn. Move the glass slowly along the wood, above the pencil lines, to complete the design. Protect your eyes with sunglasses while you work, otherwise you'll see spots all day.

Hungry? Let the sun cook your hot dog.
But make sure an adult is nearby to help with cutting and taping the sharp edges.
You will need:

Old scissors or tin shears	Aluminum foil
Aluminum soda-pop can	Skewer or 8-inch piece
Masking tape	of wire clothes hanger
Hammer and nail	Hot dog
	Bright sunshine

Cut out a 2-inch-wide section along the can. Cover the cut edges with masking tape. Use the hammer and nail to make a hole in each end of the can. Line the inside of the can with the aluminum foil. Poke the skewer or wire into one end of the can, through the hot dog, and out the other end of the can. Place the can so that the opening faces the sun.

The curved aluminum foil will collect the light, concentrate it on the hot dog, and produce enough heat to cook it. To speed up the cooking, you can put a small mirror in the can behind the hot dog. Angle the mirror to focus the sun's rays onto the hot dog.

Israel is the only country that has a huge lake where you can float all day even if you can't swim. Don't try it in the Kinneret. The life guards will call you a *tipesh* ("fool") as they haul you out. Do it only in the Dead Sea. The water is so thick with minerals that everything and everyone, even a nonswimmer, float on the surface.

Israel is the only country that learned how to cultivate the desert from teachers who died 1,700 years ago. Some of Israel's farmers water their crops using a method that they learned from the ancient Nabataeans. Those wise desert farmers would slope the land around each plant or tree into a funnel. Every drop of moisture that fell nearby was led down the slope to water the plant. At Avdat, a spooky, deserted, ancient Nabataean town, there's a modern experimental farm that uses the funnel-irrigation method and produces juicy fruits and vegetables in the middle of the thirsty Negev.

The farmers of Kibbutz Kefar Giladi adapted the old method and now raise the highest per-dunam yield of cotton in the world. Each plant is fed as carefully as if it were a baby in a nursery. An underground pipe drips a formula of water and fertilizer into the plant's roots. The amount of drip is decided by a central computer.

Other countries that have little water, like Australia, Abu Dhabi, and Mexico, have borrowed the technique of drip irrigation. And an Israeli drip system was just laid in the desert sand at Gila, Arizona.

Israel is the only country that is a melting pot of immigrants from forty different countries who belong to nearly forty different political parties. Israelis like to air their opinions in loud discussion on the buses, the streets, and the balconies of their houses. Although they talk and talk, they don't seem to agree on very much. There are those who agree with Matti, the eighth-grader from Carmiel, who said, "We live like a family even though we have troubles." And there are those who disagree.

Everybody is entitled to his or her own opinion.

And now that you've read all about Israel, you probably have an opinion, too.

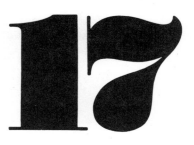

Mini-encyclopedia

A

*Aaronsohn, Aaron (1876–1919) **and Sarah** (1890–1917) Young Palestinian Jews who led a spy ring called Nili, which collected military information for the British during World War I.

Administered areas See *Gaza Strip* and *Judaea and Samaria*.

Aḥad Ha-Am (1856–1927) An influential early Russian Zionist and writer. He believed that Palestine should become a cultural center rather than a national state for the Jews of the world.

*Al-Aqsa Arabic for "the far place." A mosque (Muslim place of worship) built on the Temple Mount in Jerusalem. It is considered to be the third holiest spot in Islamic religion.

Al-Fatah See *Palestine Liberation Organization (PLO)*.

*Aliyah Hebrew for "going up." The honor of being called up to the Torah in the synagogue is an *aliyah*. Immigration to Israel is also called *aliyah*. Zionist history tells of five periods of *aliyah* to Palestine, from 1881 to 1939.

American Zionist organizations Groups of American Jews that help the State of Israel with financial and political support. Groups like Hadassah and Pioneer Women have built and supported hospitals, nurseries, and schools in Israel. Others like B'nai Akivah, Habonim, Ha-Shachar, and Hashomer Hatzair have sent their members to settle in Israel. Some like the Zionist Organization of America, Mizraḥi, and Poalei Zion have spurred investment in Israel and have given political support to the country.

*Arabs A people of the Middle East. Some live in Israel. The majority live in lands bordering on Israel and nearby. Most Arabs are Muslim and speak the Arabic language. According to Jewish and Arabic tradition, the Arabs are descended from Biblical Ishmael, the son of Abraham and Hagar.

Arafat, Yasir (b. 1930) See *Palestine Liberation Organization (PLO)*.

Aramaic A language that was widely used many years ago in the Middle East. Parts of the Talmud and the Siddur (Hebrew prayer book) were written in Aramaic. Some Christian sects in the Middle East still speak Aramaic.

*Army of Israel Most Israeli Jews serve in the country's armed forces for two or three years. Israeli Druse citizens also serve. After finishing their term of service, Israelis are called up for reserve duty for one and sometimes two months each year. Nahal is a branch of the army that sets up farming and military outposts in border areas. Gadna is a youth corps for boys and girls.

Art in Israel Sculptures decorate Israeli parks and plazas. Paintings hang in the public buildings. Even though Israel is a young country, many artists are already working to describe the country and express themselves. Anna Ticho painted the rocks and wild hills around Jerusalem. Shalom of Safed (Zefat) told Bible stories with brightly colored pictures. Yaacov Agam paints and builds vivid patterns of squares and cubes. Eli Ilan sculpted huge bronze figures. And David Palumbo shaped iron bars into great sculptured gateways.

*Ashkenasic Hebrew for "German." A term used in Israel to describe most European Jews from a Yiddish-speaking culture, as well as their descendants.

Assad, Hafez al- (b. 1928) Prime minister of Syria.

B

Baal teshuvah Hebrew for "one who returns." A newly religious Jew, who returns to careful observance and study of the Jewish religion. Many Israelis have become *baalei teshuvah* in recent years.

Baháí A religion that grew out of Islam in the late 1800s. It has adopted some of the beliefs of major religions to create a broadly based faith with members all over the world. Baháí headquarters are in the city of Haifa in Israel.

*Balfour Declaration A document issued by the British government in 1917 supporting the establishment of a Jewish homeland in Palestine.

*Bedouins Nomadic (wandering) tribes of Arab herdsmen who once roamed through the Middle East. Most Bedouins now live in settled towns and villages, but their black tents and flocks of sheep and goats can still be seen in the hills of southern Israel and the Sinai desert.

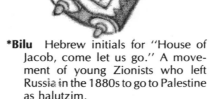

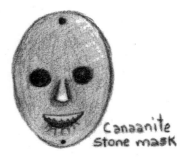
Canaanite stone mask

Begin, Menachem (b. 1913) The sixth prime minister of Israel. Begin was leader of the Irgun underground army in its battle against the British in the years before the State of Israel was established. A high point in Begin's career came in 1979, when, as Israel's prime minister, he signed a peace treaty between Israel and Egypt.

*Ben-Gurion, David (1886–1973) The first prime minister of the State of Israel. He worked as a ḥalutz (pioneer) and helped organize Hashomer, the earliest Jewish self-defense group in Palestine. Ben-Gurion was a leader of Palestine Jewry and urged that the State of Israel be established in 1948 despite warnings that the new state would be smashed.

*Ben-Yehudah, Eliezer (1858–1922) A linguist, writer, and educator who turned Biblical Hebrew into a twentieth-century language. Jewish immigrants from many countries used his fifteen-volume Hebrew dictionary to learn the old-new language of the land of Israel.

*Ben-Zvi, Itzḥak (1884–1963) The second president of Israel. Ben-Zvi worked as a ḥalutz and fought in the Jewish Legion in World War I. He was a leader of the Histadrut labor union and of the Palestine Jewish community. Ben-Zvi also studied and wrote about Middle Eastern Jewish folklore and history.

Bialik, Ḥayyim Naḥman (1873–1934) A Hebrew poet who wrote about love, nature, religion, and even pogroms (attacks on Jewish communities). When he settled in Palestine, he made the Oneg Shabbat a popular custom. On Saturday afternoons, people would come to Ḥayyim's to read aloud, sing, and "nosh."

*Bible The holiest books of the Jewish people. The Bible tells of the origin of the earth and of humankind. It describes the early history of the Jewish people and sets forth many laws and moral principles by which Jews should live. The first five books of the Bible are called the Torah, or Ḥumash.

*Bilu Hebrew initials for "House of Jacob, come let us go." A movement of young Zionists who left Russia in the 1880s to go to Palestine as ḥalutzim.

Binationalism A political program supported by some Zionists in the 1940s that urged that an Arab-Jewish homeland be established in Palestine with equal representation for both peoples. Most Arabs and Jews opposed binationalism.

Borochov, Dov Ber (1881–1917) A writer and leader of Labor Zionism who called on Jews to become workers rather than merchants and to work toward socialism in their Jewish homeland.

Brandeis, Louis Dembitz (1856–1941) Justice of the Supreme Court of the United States and a Zionist leader. Kibbutz Ein Ha-Shofet is named after him.

Buber, Martin (1878–1965) Jewish philosopher, Zionist, and writer who stressed justice and fairness in relations between people. He studied and wrote about Ḥasidism and taught at the Hebrew University in Jerusalem.

C

*Camp David Accords The peace agreement between Israel and Egypt signed at Camp David, Maryland, in 1978. It was a step toward peace between Israel and her neighbors.

Canaan Early Biblical name for the land of Israel, which had been settled by Canaanite tribes before the time of Abraham.

*Christianity A religion founded in the first century C.E. by a small group of Jews who believed that their leader, Jesus, was the Messiah. As other peoples adopted Christianity, they dropped most Jewish customs and added to the Hebrew Bible a new book of religious writings known as the New Testament.

Citizenship Under the Law of Return, all Jews may become citizens as soon as they arrive in Israel. Israelis could not forget that millions of Jews could not escape the Nazis and died in the Holocaust of the 1940s because no country would let them in. Non-Jews must wait to become citizens, as do newcomers to most countries.

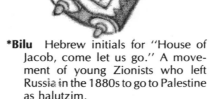

*Congress, Zionist A meeting of representatives from Zionist organizations of many countries that takes place every few years. The first Zionist congress was called by Theodor Herzl in 1897.

D

Dance Halutzim brought the hora and other circle dances from Europe. Jews of the Middle East brought their debkas and belly dances. Slowly, Israeli dancers are combining the movements and working out an Israeli dance style in dance companies like Inbal, Batsheva, and the Kibbutz Dance Company. And just for fun there's always disco dancing.

*Dayan, Moshe (1915–1981) Israeli political leader who served as army chief of staff and as minister of defense. He was known for his black eye patch and his independent ideas.

*Dead Sea Scrolls Biblical manuscripts of the first century C.E. discovered in a cave near the Dead Sea by an Arab shepherd.

Development towns Israeli settlements that were sometimes established far from the center of the country and that have special problems with employment, education, housing, or safety from terrorist attack. Hatzor and Qiryat Shemona in the north and Qiryat Gat in the south are examples of development towns.

Diaspora Greek for "dispersion"; in Hebrew *galut*. The term refers to the whole world except Israel.

*Druse A religious sect that grew out of Islam. Many Druse live in Israel, Syria, and Lebanon. Druse serve as soldiers in Israel's army.

Dunam An Israeli measure of land that is equal to about one quarter of an acre.

E

Eban, Abba (b. 1915) An Israeli political leader and author who was Israel's first ambassador to the United Nations and later became ambassador to the United States.

*Education Education is free and compulsory through high school. Children may attend either religious or nonreligious government schools. In high school, youngsters may choose between academic schools, which prepare them for college, and vocational schools, which combine work skills with academic courses. Half of Israeli students choose vocational schools. College means more choices. There are Bezalel School of Arts and Crafts, Rubin Music Academy, many fine yeshivahs (religious colleges), and universities like Beersheba, Bar-Ilan, Haifa Technion, and Hebrew University.

*Entebbe A daring rescue by the Israeli army of a group of Israeli airline passengers who had been hijacked to Entebbe, Uganda, by terrorists.

Eretz Yisrael See *Israel.*

Eshkol, Levi (1895–1969) Third prime minister of the State of Israel, labor leader, and statesman.

Exodus 1947 A blockade-running ship that carried illegal immigrants, Holocaust survivors, from Europe to Palestine after World War II. The British captured the *Exodus* and forced its passengers to return to Germany, causing world-wide protest.

F

Falashas An Ethiopian word meaning "exiles" or "strangers." Falashas are black Jews who have lived in villages in Ethiopia for many centuries—perhaps since Biblical times. They call themselves Beta Yisrael (House of Israel). Many Beta Yisrael have settled in Israel. Others are waiting to make *aliyah* (emigrate to Israel).

*Flag There was no Jewish flag until 1898, when the Zionist congress chose a flag that had two blue stripes on a white background with a six-pointed star (a popular design in synagogue art) in the center.

*Freier, Reha (1892–1984) German Zionist teacher who, in the early 1930s, gathered Jewish boys and girls and sent them to Palestine to escape Nazi persecution. This program became known as Youth Aliyah.

G

*Gadna See *Army of Israel.*

*Gaza Strip   A small area on the Mediterranean coast administered by Israel and inhabited by native Arabs and by Arabs who formerly lived in Israel.

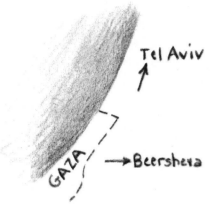

*Government of Israel   The country is run by a democratically elected parliament (Knesset) representing twenty or more political parties and by a cabinet, prime minister, and president. Elections take place every four years or when the ruling parties lose the support of the Knesset. A system of courts topped by a Supreme Court reviews the laws of the Knesset when necessary.

Gush Emunim   Hebrew for "group of believers." Militantly religious Israeli Jews who settle in Judaea and Samaria, the administered areas, because they believe that all of Biblical Israel should be part of the State of Israel.

H

*Haganah   Hebrew for "self-defense." The name of the underground army of the Jews of Palestine before the establishment of the State of Israel. The Palmaḥ was Haganah's elite group (like the marines in the armed forces of the United States) and was largely made up of young kibbutz members.

*Halutzim   Hebrew for "pioneers." Beginning in the late 1800s halutzim went to Palestine and risked disease, hunger, and attack to build a Jewish homeland.

Hamsin   A hot, dry wind that blows out of the desert in the summer and sends Israelis to the showers and the beaches.

*Hashomer   Hebrew for "watchman." An organization of guards who defended early settlements in Palestine against stealing and attack. It was the forerunner of the Haganah.

Ḥasidim   Hebrew for "pious ones." Groups of orthodox Jews, each of which is led by a respected rabbi and forms a close-knit community. The names of some Ḥasidic groups in Israel are the Belzer, the Lubavicher, and the Gerrer.

*"Hatikvah"   Hebrew for "the hope." The song "Hatikvah" is the anthem of the Zionist movement.

*Hebrew   A Semitic language of the same family as Arabic and Aramaic. It was spoken in the days of the Bible, but later it was used mainly for study and prayer. In the twentieth century Hebrew became a spoken language again with the rise of Zionism.

*Herzl, Theodor (1860–1904)   Viennese journalist and founder of modern political Zionism. Herzl reacted to European anti-Semitism by deciding that Jews must leave Europe and build a state of their own. He organized the first Zionist congress in 1897.

Herzog, Chaim (b. 1918)   Fifth president of the State of Israel, former military commander, and ambassador to the United States.

Ḥibat and **Ḥovevei Zion**   Hebrew for "Lovers of Zion." Groups of early eastern European Zionists. The first pioneers to Palestine, the BILU, came from among their members.

*Histadrut Haovdim   The largest labor union in Israel. Most workers and farmers belong to the Histadrut. It has cooperatives that do construction, run buses, market farm products, and more. The Histadrut also has a health-care program and publishes books and newspapers.

*Holocaust   The program of murder carried out against the Jews of Europe during World War II by the Nazi government of Germany under Adolf Hitler. Two-thirds of the Jews of Europe, 6 million people, were killed. A Holocaust memorial called Yad Va-Shem was built in Jerusalem. There the names of the victims and their lost communities are inscribed. The twenty-seventh day of the Hebrew month of Nisan is Yom Ha-Shoah, a memorial day for those who died in the Holocaust.

Hussein ibn Talal (b. 1935)   King of Jordan, Israel's neighbor on the east. Hussein has led his country in two major wars against Israel. The Camp David Accords express hope that he will work with Israel and Arabs of the administered areas to establish a self-governing authority in that region.

I

*Illegal immigration In the 1930s, because of unrest between Jews and Arabs, the British mandatory power began to cut the number of Jews who could enter Palestine. More and more Jews tried to enter as Nazi persecution increased in Germany. But the British turned away the crowded ships of "illegal" refugees. Some, like the *Struma*, sank at sea. Some returned their passengers to Europe to face a slower death at Nazi hands. After the war, illegal ships defied the British blockade again. They faced imprisonment and drowning, but they kept coming until, finally, Palestine's ports were opened with the establishment of the State of Israel.

*Irgun Zvai Leumi Hebrew for "National Military Organization." The name of the army of the rightist Revisionist party before the establishment of the State of Israel. There were bitter clashes between the Irgun and the Haganah, but both became part of the Israeli army in 1948.

*Islam Arabic for "submission." A religion founded in Arabia in 622 C.E. by Mohammed, an Arabian religious leader. Its sacred book is called the Koran. Many sections of the Koran are drawn from the Hebrew and Christian Bibles. The central shrine of Islam is in Mecca, Saudi Arabia. Muslims (believers in Islam) make pilgrimages to Mecca from all over the world.

*Israel, State of Established on May 14, 1948, as the homeland of the Jewish people, in a part of the Biblical land of Israel (*Eretz Yisrael*). The country has a democratic form of government and many political parties. Caring for new immigrants and defending the country have been Israel's biggest challenges.

J

*Jabotinsky, Vladimir (1880–1940) Writer and leader of the Zionist Revisionist party. He pushed for the establishment of a Jewish Legion to fight in World War I and later for the speedy establishment of a Jewish state on both sides of the Jordan river.

*Jerusalem Capital of the State of Israel. In Biblical times the Holy Temple was built in Jerusalem by King Solomon. Jews would come to the Temple to worship and bring sacrifices at holiday time. Throughout the centuries Jews have continued to live in Jerusalem, and Jews in other parts of the world have prayed to return to their holy city. Muslims and Christians also have holy places in Jerusalem.

Jewish Agency An international Jewish organization based in Jerusalem that encourages and assists the immigration and settlement of Jews in Israel.

*Jewish Legion A group of Jewish volunteers recruited in England, Palestine, and the United States during World War I that fought with the British army in the Middle East.

*Jewish National Fund An organization known in Israel as Keren Kayemet Le-Yisrael. In 1901 the Jewish National Fund (NF) began to collect money to buy land in Palestine for the Jewish homeland. Since 1948, when the State of Israel was born, JNF money has been used to build roads, plant trees, and clear land for farms, towns, and recreation areas.

*Judaea and Samaria The hilly central region of the Biblical land of Israel. Today it is also known as the West Bank or the Administered Areas and is largely populated by Arabs. The region was captured by Jordan in 1948 and recaptured by Israel in 1967. Its status is still undecided.

Judaism A religion and way of life that is based on the teachings of the Bible, Talmud, and Commentaries, and on a sense of history and tradition shared with other Jews since the time of Moses.

K

*Kibbutz A farm settlement in Israel where property and work are shared equally by all members. Kibbutzim were the first settlements to appear in the dangerous and infertile regions of the country.

Knesset See *Government of Israel.*

*Kook, Abraham Isaac (1864–1935) Rabbi and religious thinker who became chief rabbi of Palestine and identified with the nonreligious halutzim as well as with his own orthodox followers.

*Koran See *Islam.*

*Kotel Maaravi Hebrew for "Western Wall." The last remaining wall of the Holy Temple in Jerusalem. For centuries Jews came to pray at the Kotel, except when it was under Jordan's control between 1948 and 1967. It became part of Israel when the Old City of Jerusalem was taken in the 1967 Six Day War.

L

Law of Return See *Citizenship*.

*Leḥi Hebrew initials for "Freedom Fighters of Israel," a small, secret group of Jewish fighters who tried to drive the British out of Palestine with acts of violence and terrorism.

Literature Israelis are great readers. They support over eighty publishing companies—more per population size than any other country. Israeli writers include old-timers whose culture was largely Diaspora-based, such as Shmuel Agnon (a Nobel Prize winner) and Ḥayyim Hazaz; writers whose influences were half-Diaspora and half-Israeli, such as Avraham Shlonsky, Leah Goldberg, and Moshe Smilansky; and sabra or almost-sabra writers whose work expresses their lives in Israel as well as outside influences, such as A. B. Yehoshua, Amos Oz, and Yehuda Amiḥai.

M

*Magen David Hebrew for "Shield of David." This six-pointed star is found on the Israeli flag and is often used in decorations for synagogues and on ritual objects. The medieval kabbalists used it as a design on amulets. Other peoples have used it for decorations.

Magen David Adom Hebrew for "Red Shield of David." This is the name given for the Israeli Red Cross, which provides blood banks and ambulance service and meets emergency needs.

*Mandate for Palestine A program set up by the League of Nations (a former world organization) after the First World War that gave Great Britain the responsibility of helping to establish a Jewish national homeland in Palestine.

Marcus, David (Mickey) (1902–1948) A West Point graduate and colonel in the United States Army, Mickey Marcus was one of many American volunteers who helped Israel to fight its war for independence. He was killed while in command of the Jerusalem front.

*Meir, Golda (1898–1978) Zionist leader who became Israel's first ambassador to the Soviet Union and its fourth prime minister.

*Menorah Candle holder or oil lamp with many branches. It is one of the oldest Jewish symbols and can be found on ancient coins and grave markers. The great gold menorah at the Holy Temple in Jerusalem had seven branches. The Ḥanukkah menorah has nine. A menorah is pictured on the seal of the State of Israel.

*Messiah By Jewish tradition the Messiah is God's chosen one, a descendant of the family of King David, who will bring the Jews back to Israel and will bring peace to the world. Some Jews are opposed to the State of Israel because it came about through human effort rather than by God's Messiah.

*Middle East A geographical region that Israel shares with Iraq, Saudi Arabia, Yemen, and other countries. The Middle Eastern countries that border on Israel are Egypt, Jordan, Syria, and Lebanon. The region bubbles with oil and unrest.

Montefiore, Sir Moses (1784–1885) Wealthy British Jew who spent his long life helping his fellow Jews in Palestine, Russia, Syria, and many other countries. In Palestine he bought land for farm settlements and built schools and synagogues. In Syria and Russia he argued, threatened, and pleaded with government officials for fair treatment of persecuted Jews. Montefiore was so well loved that his picture was hung in Jewish homes the world over.

Moshav Farming villages where members live in separate homes and run separate farms but often cooperate in the purchase of supplies, the use of large machinery, and the marketing of produce.

*Museums Musical instruments, tropical fish, Ottoman mosaics—there's a museum to suit every interest in Israel. There are big museums of art, archaeology, and history like the Museum of the Diaspora and the Israel Museum. And there are many smaller, specialized museums.

Music The Israeli Philharmonic Orchestra plays in all the world's concert halls. Classical musicians like violinist Itzhak Perlman and pianist Daniel Barenboim are world citizens. Even Israeli pop and rock groups and stars like Naomi Shemer and Yehoram Gaon go on tour. With all that coming and going there's still enough talent to keep Israeli concert halls and discos vibrating, too.

*Muslim See *Islam*.

N

Navon, Yitzhak (b. 1921) Fourth president of the State of Israel, political leader of the Maarah (labor alliance) political group, and scholar.

*Nazism See *Holocaust*.

*Newspapers, TV, and radio Newspaper stands are crowded with Hebrew, English, Yiddish, Arabic, Russian, and other newspapers. Some, like the daily *HaA'retz*, are set in small, sober type and are packed with information. Some, like the weekly *HaOlam Hazeh*, have screaming headlines and huge pictures. It's a free press. The reader can choose any style and political view. TV, with only one channel, is more limited. The government supports TV but does not control it. A sure sign of television's freedom is the fact that each Israeli government complains that the TV criti-

cizes it unfairly. Radio offers music and drama, but it is most important for its news programs. Bus drivers turn up the radio volume so that passengers can hear the hourly news reports.

*Nili See *Aaronsohn*.

O

Olympics massacre See *Terrorism*.

*Operation Ali Baba and Operation Magic Carpet The airlift that carried most of the Jewish population of Iraq and Yemen to Israel after the establishment of the state.

P

Palestine The Biblical land of Israel. The ancient Greeks and Romans called the area Palestine after the Philistines who lived along the coast. Jews have considered Palestine their homeland since Biblical times. Today, Arabs who live on the west bank of the Jordan river call the area Palestine.

Palestine Liberation Organization (PLO) An umbrella organization of several groups of Arabs led by a chairman—Yasir Arafat. It has used armed attack, terrorism, and diplomatic pressure against Israel in its effort to replace the State of Israel with an Arab-controlled State of Palestine.

Palmah See *Haganah*.

*Parachutists A group of thirty-two Palestinian Jewish men and women volunteers who were dropped into Nazi-occupied Europe during World War II to help organize resistance to the Nazis. They included Hannah Senesh, Enzo Sereni, and Haviva Reich. Seven of the parachutists were captured and executed by the Nazis.

*Peres, Shimon (b. 1923) Eighth prime minister of the State of Israel, former minister of defense, and leader of the Maarah (labor alliance) political group.

Political leaders Shimon Peres, Yitzhak Rabin, and Yitzhak Navon are leaders of the Labor party, the main party in the Maarah coalition. Yitzhak Shamir and Ariel Sharon are leaders of the Herut party, the main party in the Likud coalition. Among other political leaders are Shulamit Aloni, Geula Cohen, David Levi, Victor Shemtov, Aaron Abuhatzeira, and Ezer Weitzman.

Political parties When Israelis vote to elect their Knesset (parliament), they have to choose among twenty to thirty parties, ranging from the communist Rakah to the ultrareligious Agudat Yisrael. The leader of the party that wins the most votes is usually appointed prime minister. To form a government, the prime minister needs the support of a majority of Knesset members. He or she must persuade smaller parties to join a coalition under his or her leadership. The two opposing coalitions in Israel today are a rightist group called Likud and a leftist group called Maarah.

R

*Rabin, Yitzhak (b. 1922) Fifth prime minister of the State of Israel, former military commander, and ambassador to the United States.

Refugees During Israel's war for independence in 1948, about 700,000 Palestinian Arabs fled to neighboring states. Many of them have not been allowed to become citizens of any Arab country. They are still living with their families in refugee camps. In the first three years after 1948 nearly 700,000 Jewish refugees from Arab lands and from Europe arrived in Israel. They also lived in camps at first. Then they were gradually moved to permanent housing. They found jobs and became full partners in Israeli life.

Religion The major religious groups in Israel are Jewish, Muslim, and Christian. In its laws Israel has kept the religious separations that were used by the earlier British and Turkish governments. There are separate schools for children of each religious group. Birth, marriage, divorce, and death are dealt with by the religious community to which the person belongs. And all recognized places of worship are supported by the government.

Rothschild, Baron Edmund de (1845–1934) A member of the wealthy Rothschild banking family. He supported the early farming settlements in Palestine with money and technical advisers. With Rothschild's help, Rishon Le-Zion became an important wine-producing center.

S

Sabra Cactus fruit. Children born in Israel, who are supposed to be prickly and tough on the outside but sweet as sugar on the inside (like the cactus fruit), are known as sabras.

Sadat, Anwar al (1918–1981) Former president of Egypt who led his country into war against Israel on Yom Kippur day in September 1973. Later he became the first Arab head of state to come to Israel on a mission of peace. Sadat and Israeli Prime Minister Begin signed the Camp David agreements in 1978. Sadat was assassinated.

Samaria See *Judaea and Samaria*.

Senesh, Hannah (1921–1944) See *Parachutists*.

*Sephardic Hebrew for "Spanish." Sephardim are Jews whose ancestors came from Spain and Portugal, as well as Jews, like those of Yemen, who have always lived in the Middle East. More than half the population in Israel today is of Sephardic origin.

Shamir, Yitzhak (b. 1916) Seventh prime minister of the State of Israel and leader of the Likud political group.

Sharrett, Moshe (1894–1965) The second prime minister of Israel. Sharrett served in the Turkish army in World War I and learned much about Arab culture and language. He became an important political activist for the Zionist movement, often working in England and the United States. He was foreign minister in Israel's first cabinet.

Shazar, Zalman (1889–1974) Third president of the State of Israel, scholar, writer, and socialist-Zionist leader.

Shekel Measure of money in Biblical times. The Maccabees made a silver coin called a shekel. Modern Israel also uses the shekel.

*Sports Basketball, volleyball, soccer, tennis, and swimming are popular sports. Israeli teams and athletes go abroad for international competitions and for the Olympics. Every few years athletes of other countries come to Israel to compete in Israel's Maccabiya and HaPoel games.

Stern Group See *Lehi*.

*Szold, Henrietta (1860–1945) An American Jewish woman who was editor of the Jewish Publication Society and founder of Hadassah, a women's Zionist organization. She lived in Israel for many years and led the work of Youth Aliyah, which saved thousands of Jewish children from the Nazis.

T

*Temple The First Temple was built in Jerusalem by King Solomon in the tenth century B.C.E. The people went there to worship and celebrate the three pilgrimage holidays each year. It was destroyed by the Babylonians on the ninth day of Av, 586 B.C.E. The Second Temple was built seventy years later and destroyed by the Romans on the ninth of Av, 70 C.E. Today only an outer wall, the Kotel, remains. In later years two mosques were built on the Temple Mount.

*Terrorism Violent acts against civilians (nonsoldiers) happen often in the Middle East and in Israel. Before the state was established, Jews and Arabs battled on streets and roads all over Palestine. Since 1948, Arab terrorists have attacked Israelis within the country and abroad. In one cruel and tragic incident, nine Israeli athletes were held hostage and killed by Arab terrorists at the 1972 Olympics. Some Israeli Jews have broken Israeli law and carried out terrorist acts against Arabs in the administered areas of Judaea and Samaria.

Theater and movies Israel has many theater groups. Some, like the veteran Habimah, are well established. Others are younger and do more controversial plays, and they must struggle to stay alive. Plays of many countries are translated into Hebrew and performed. Most movie houses show American and European films. Israel's film industry is small. But some Israeli films have won international prizes and are shown abroad.

*Trumpeldor, Joseph (1880–1920) A Zionist leader, farmer, and soldier. Trumpeldor lost an arm in the Russian army, but that didn't stop him. He worked as a farmer in Palestine and organized a Jewish army unit in World War I. He was killed defending a Jewish settlement in northern Palestine against Arab attack.

U

Ulpan A speedy language-learning method developed in Israel to teach Hebrew to new immigrants. Schools in other countries have adopted the method. Ulpan also refers to the school that offers the language course.

United Jewish Appeal An American Jewish organization that raises money through contributions and distributes it to member groups such as ORT (Organization for Rehabilitation through Training), JDC (Joint Distribution Committee), JNF (Jewish National Fund), and Keren HaYesod (Foundation Fund) to help meet Jewish needs in the United States, Israel, and other parts of the world.

W

*Weizmann, Chaim (1874–1952) Famous scientist and Zionist leader from the time of the fifth Zionist congress in 1901. In 1948 Chaim Weizmann became the first president of the State of Israel. The Weizmann Institute of Science in Rehovot is named after him.

*Wingate, Orde (1903–1944) A Bible-loving British officer who trained Jewish night-fighting units to combat Arab terrorists and saboteurs in Palestine in the late 1930s. He taught the young Haganah soldiers that the best defense is attack. Although the British recalled Wingate to London after three years, his training had strengthened and inspired the Haganah.

World Zionist Organization Organized in 1897 at the first Zionist congress under the leadership of Theodor Herzl. Since that time, the World Zionist Organization has served as a governing body for Zionist groups throughout the world and has set policies and programs for the Zionist movement at its congresses.

Y

*Youth Aliyah A program that helps immigrant children and needy Israeli children to become educated and adjusted to life in Israel. Youth Aliyah was started in Germany in 1934 to rescue Jewish children from the Nazis.

Z

*Zionism A movement to build a Jewish homeland in Palestine. Its earliest planners and thinkers in the mid 1800s were nationalist Jews and disappointed socialists such as Leo Pinsker and Moses Hess. Many religious leaders were opposed to the Zionist movement, except for a few rabbis like Samuel Mohilever and Isaac Reines. Theodor Herzl turned Zionism from a hope into a vibrant political movement when he called the first Zionist congress in 1897. Halutzim began to go to Palestine and build farms and towns. During and after the First World War, other Zionists like Chaim Weizmann fought for political support in the League of Nations. American Zionist leaders Louis Brandeis, Louis Lipsky, Stephen Wise, and later Abba Hillel Silver urged American support for a Jewish homeland. World Jewry contributed help and money. After another war and the tragic loss of most of European Jewry in the Holocaust, the State of Israel was finally born. May 14, 1948—Israel Independence Day—came just fifty-one years after the first Zionist congress took place.

Index

About the author

Chaya M. Burstein is the author-illustrator of many books on Jewish topics for children including **Rifka Grows Up,** the winner of the 1977 National Jewish Book Award, and **The Jewish Kids Catalog,** published by the Jewish Publication Society and the winner of the 1983 National Jewish Book Award.

Chaya Burstein has a long-standing love of Israel. Soon after the founding of the state, she and her husband, Mordy, moved to Israel to work on a kibbutz that they had helped establish. They moved back to America, where they raised their three children. Now the Bursteins live again in Israel, in the Galil, where they pursue many varied interests.